GO HIRE YOURSELF
AN EMPLOYER

Richard Irish is vice-president and co-founder of TransCentury Corporation, a Washington, D.C., international consulting firm. For ten years, Dick specialized in international executive search and for fifteen years has lectured at over three hundred colleges and universities and conducted workshops for both employers and job searchers on the whole employment process. He is also the author of *How to Live Separately Together (A Guide for Working Couples)* and *If Things Don't Improve Soon, I May Ask You to Fire Me!,* both published by Doubleday/Anchor. Dick and his wife, Sally, live in Marshall, Virginia.

RICHARD K. IRISH

Go Hire Yourself an Employer

A Revised and Expanded
Third Edition

ANCHOR PRESS

Doubleday

NEW YORK   LONDON   TORONTO   SYDNEY   AUCKLAND

Portions of this book appeared in an entirely different form in the Washington *Post*, *Woman's Day*, *Glamour*, *The Graduate*, *Washington Times*, *Association Management* magazines. Some material has been adapted from Mr. Irish's two other books published by Doubleday/Anchor.

An Anchor Book

Published by Doubleday, a division of
Bantam Doubleday Dell Publishing Group, Inc.,
666 Fifth Avenue, New York, New York 10103

Anchor, Doubleday and the portrayal of an
anchor are trademarks of Doubleday, a division of
Bantam Doubleday Dell Publishing Group, Inc.

Library of Congress Cataloging-in-Publication Data
Irish, Richard K.
Go hire yourself an employer.
Includes index.
1. Job hunting. 2. Career changes. I. Title.
HF5382.7.I74 1987 650.1'4 87-6896
ISBN: 0-385-23378-7

2 4 6 8 9 7 5 3

BG

DEDICATION

This book is dedicated to everyone who at one time or another is told, "You're too young, old, qualified, unqualified, experienced, inexperienced, beautiful, plain, expensive, educated, uneducated, or too damn good" for a job . . . and to all who labor in the vineyards of the Lord, whether you press the grapes or work in top management: May your children grow fat in the New Jerusalem.

ACKNOWLEDGMENTS

Now is the time to praise famous men and women.

Credit for the title goes to an old friend and colleague, Fran Buhler, who in his southern drawl said to me, "But, Dick, ol' buddy, seems what, er, you're saying is . . . Go hire yourself an employer." Well, thus are books christened.

I am especially indebted to Warren Wiggins, president of Trans-Century Corporation (where I ply my trade) for his encouragement; Don Cutler, my agent, for placing the book and Loretta Barrett for publishing it. Lila Ballendorf and Rebecca Dembs typed the first and second editions with tender care. Much gratitude and many thanks to my sister, Dot Irish Beall, who made a special big-sister contribution by both typing and editing the third edition. Of course, I'll take the rap for any deficiencies; I'll also welcome any rounds of applause.

The following either made useful editorial suggestions or contributed original material: Bill Josephson, Vic Hirsch, John Evans, David Rice, Judy Nelson, Alfred Kleindienst, Michael L. Metteer, Phil Infelise, Lou Marnao, Ruth Blau, Bob McGlynn, John Coyne, Colin Walters, Bob Gale, Tom Page, Tom Hebert, and Jim McCoy. My thanks to all.

Portions of both the second and third editions were written at Christmas Cove, Maine. I'm especially grateful to Mrs. William Seipp for the use of her summer home and the fine meals and companionship she provided.

It would be impossible to acknowledge the names of all the thousands of job seekers and employers alike, all of whom were grist for my writing mill. Especially all job searchers who shared with me their travail, frustration, and triumph these past twenty years.

The book is divided into three parts: (1) the business of job searchers thinking through next steps in their lives, (2) the job search with its predictable (and unpredictable) elements, and (3) salient issues about employment and being effective on the job, and situational elements of both looking for and working at a job.

As I write, there are certain employment configurations that might or might not be true when you read this book. The first is the incremental and steady decline in the standard of living for many working Americans, the cap on both skilled and white-collar compensation, the increasing containment of fringe benefits, and a general nervousness about our economic future. At the same time, at least on the East and West Coasts, there is a downright labor shortage at the non-skilled, low-skilled end of the employment spectrum, and a positive eruption of new business incorporations—increasing evidence that post–baby boomers are penetrating more easily their chosen lines of work as compared to their older brothers and sisters. It is, as usual, both the best and worst of times.

I'm grateful to the dean of career counseling, Bernard Haldane, for his influence and the writings of Richard Lathrop, et al. Peter Drucker's work has been an especial source of inspiration.

Finally, kudos to my wife, Sally, whose patience, care, and humor were as necessary as pen and paper in writing this book.

October 30, 1986
Marshall, Virginia

CONTENTS

CONTENTS

FOREWORD

From where I sit it's a puppy-kickin' world.

If a doctor is someone who thinks everyone is sick, I'm one who believes everyone is unemployed or soon will be. But as I write, there are more employed people in the United States than ever before, the economy is generating thousands of first-time jobs, and about a third of the work force is looking to find better jobs. So the unemployment scene, depending on your angle, is either a wondrous thing to behold or a tragic scene from *King Lear.*

Every working day as counselor to the jobless (or the unhappily employed), I'm reminded of what it was like either to feel the cold blast of unemployment or go to work every day loathing it. I hated it. And the plain facts are that all of us are repulsed by looking for a job or working at a job we don't love but feel trapped in. It doesn't have to be awful; we are free to quit and find other jobs. Most people, however, would just as soon go three rounds with the heavyweight champ than look for other work. As for the unemployed, well, they have no choice.

For me, my six-month spell of unemployment was easily the most painful period of my life. I blamed my woeful condition on everyone but myself. But, of course, the real blame was my own. Every mistake I excoriate in this book, I committed. Cubed.

Before my first bout with unemployment (hereafter known as my "blue" period), I had the usual stop-loss, squat, or grunt jobs: dishwasher, tour leader, soldier, bartender, camp director—most of which I enjoyed and which satisfied hidden agendas: a college education, my fiancée's wedding ring, a European trip. It was a pleasure to work and have objectives. But, like you, I was learning that these kinds of jobs weren't serious. Parents, peers, and placement counselors stressed careers. Professional employment. Permanent jobs.

I had no "career"; therefore, I was not "serious." It was months before I stopped believing something was wrong with the system and, in bluer moments, with myself—all because of my self-destructive attitude about work and the naïve and clumsy job-finding strategies it implied. My symptoms were obvious to everyone: hostility, self-pity, wanness, and a sense of powerlessness. I developed a lively hostility to employers, sought consolation in Tchaikovsky's Pathetique Symphony (the self-pitying symphony), ate repeated meals of yogurt and garbanzo beans (punishing myself for being useless), frequented libraries and stockbrokerage houses (warm spots for job seekers wishing to come in from the cold), and read deeply in existential philosophy ("forget work; to exist is sufficient").

Finally, I was offered a job I didn't want but for which I "qualified." A small Mom-and-Pop operation known as the Bank of America. Now my troubles began in earnest. This phase (hereafter known as my "chartreuse" period) was characterized by boredom, more self-pity, and pathetic discontent. I was a hopelessly middle-class rebel with seemingly the tritest of complaints: Job Dissatisfaction. And it didn't help that my friends thought I had a great job.

Later, after my blue and chartreuse periods, I became an employer myself. I was suddenly on the other side of the desk, noting in the unemployed all the selfsame mistakes I finally saw in myself. It was what educators call a learning experience. Seeing myself as I had been, I realized that all job seekers acquire a kind of gray incompetence, ineffectuality, and sullenness. So I studied the whole business of finding, keeping, and growing on the job and learning how to find an even better job. Like you, I'm still learning. Especially that all work is fun and that the job search (which is definitely work) can be fun, too.

Having studied successful job seekers who *naturally* "go with the flow," (as they say in California), I've found that some common characteristics are predominant. The foremost is the parenting factor: Some parents, better than "good enough" mothers and fathers, simply impart to their offspring that they are free persons, responsible primarily to themselves. By some alchemy, these fortunate children grow up believing the universe to be neither entirely hostile nor wholly benign. They manage to straddle a mid-course between practical pessimism and realistic optimism.

"It's never too late to have a happy childhood." Especially in looking for work, we can recognize that we are *free:* Nobody forces us to take a job we don't want or, if we accept not to continue the search for work we do so want.

The fortunate few who find fulfilling jobs are additionally blessed: They don't feel bad when they do good. Pleasure, self-fulfillment, and success don't cause—excuse the expression—a loss of identity.

Hardly anyone thinks this is true. Most of us truly think more money, a better job, celebrity, and a corner office with windows will *make us happy.* Alas, the fortunate few who have habituated themselves to success understand that happiness is not in our circumstances but in ourselves. Accordingly, the disappointment often felt by people who suddenly arrive at success results from their belief that something *outside* themselves guarantees their happiness, e.g., a promotion, a new job, celebrity, or more money.

Interviews with younger men and women entering into the world of work reveal an interesting pattern: As they climb the organizational ladder, they often become less happy with their lives. What they thought they wanted isn't what they wanted at all. What they thought they wanted was success when what they really wanted was to feel free. Circumstances change ($65,000 per annum, assistant vice-president, a reserved seat on the company's Learjet, and membership in the racquet club) but the worn-out character stays the same.

This book began as an in-house document to assist unemployed job seekers knocking on our company's door, not all of whom we could employ. Now it's a book for people who want work doing what they *want,* or are thinking about switching jobs and/or changing careers or improving the quality of their jobs. Hiring yourself an employer means your objective is not necessarily to get a job *(any* job), but to *discriminate* among employers. Treating the job search as a lark and choosing among employers won't work if you don't know what kind of work *you want.* This book is about what you *want* (no, not necessarily what your husband, best friend, current employer, or mommy/daddy wants for you). If you think you don't know what you want, not to worry; actually, with some effort, you'll come close to finding out.

Most people want a "judgment" job; academics call these "knowledge" jobs; to business types they are "decision-making" jobs. Judgment jobs are worth defining since all judgment jobs are alike in more ways than they are unalike.

For starters, judgment jobs are never permanent. True, some jobs are more open-ended and longer-term than others. But a major difficulty in thinking through what we want is the perception that any job commitment is seemingly like a life sentence. It's understandable why we can't decide. Death alone terminates the lifelong commitment.

Next, a judgment job is working from desire rather than duty. Work is fun. If we make it an obligation, we destroy the pleasure in it. And since looking for a job is work; the more pleasure we take in it, the better we are at it. Accordingly, job seekers who take the job search altogether too seriously are not nearly as successful as those who treat it as an adventure. If something comes easily to us, we don't associate it with work, which our Calvinist forebears thought must always be difficult. Hey, sports fans, work is a pleasure. Labor, on the other hand, is something that is difficult *all of the time.*

A judgment job improves self-esteem; it makes you *like* yourself. Every day in every way you are becoming more expert at what you do. And what you do—not how much you're paid or where you work or whom you work for—your *function* is central. A judgment job allows the exercise of talent. And while there's difficulty and frustration, it's a price gladly paid to be excellent at what you do.

What you do gives a sense of accomplishment. Sure, other people might think what you do is tedious, frustrating, and monotonous. But surprisingly, that's a common characteristic of a judgment job: You do what you do over and over and over again and you do *not*—repeat, do *not*—*get bored.* Example: A podiatrist treats people's feet all day long, day in day out. If yours is a foot problem, would you want to be treated by someone who was *bored?*

A judgment job addresses real needs in the world at large: Employers hire for what you do because it needs to be done. One trick in thinking through the problem of what job would be right for you, is figuring out how what you do fits other people's needs. It's all very well for me to say, "Do what you want" (how many of your parents have said as much and how many of you parents have said as much to your children?); it doesn't mean other people need it or, even if they need it, they will hire you to do it. It does mean that if you pursue a job search not knowing what you want, you're bound to find jobs you don't want but that employers need done.

Many employers go glassy-eyed listening to the young job seeker's typical refrain: "All I really want to do is help people." It's not a laughing matter. Young people today often feel useless, unneeded. A teenager's self-esteem soars once he lands his first job and feels independent. That's the point in growing up: feeling free. Being needed is a big step for kids. It sure beats being dependent. Being needed is the opposite of being dependent and in need. But grown-ups put childish things away. Being needed is no longer a reason to work. A life in service is a poor philosophy even for a civil servant!

Forget the work ethic. Face it. Most people don't like to work. It's a middle-class idea. Blue-collar types think people who don't have to work haven't missed a thing. Indeed, most people work because they need to. But the point is working at what one wants. That's the Worth Ethic. People work to feel worthy. People without work or people with jobs in which they find little or no worth actually feel *unworthy*.

The Worth Ethic is for people who work for something besides a paycheck. It's a middle-class idea, but it's no myth. Most people work out of need, but the Worth Ethic supports working at what we want. That's the secret of human motivation and as true of an eighth-grade graduate who hates air-conditioning repair (but digs fixing diesel engines) as it is of the business-school grad who hates tax accounting (but loves mapping corporate strategy). Every job has an external and internal side: Outside is how it appears to the boss, the public, and your best friend. Internally is how it feels to you. Accordingly, definitions of success are changing. More and more people define work in terms of its worth to *them* and not necessarily how it is valued by others. The work ethic yields to the Worth Ethic.

Employers increasingly take into account the values of the middle-aging baby boomers now moving into senior management who are often saying no to promotions and relocations and yes to sinking roots in a community, working on a satisfying marriage, and spending time with their children. All of which is called, as if you needed to know, downward mobility.

Downward and lateral mobility are now common features in the professional landscape. The grass, it seems, is no greener on the other side of the fence, and sticking with your craft, trade, or profession—rather than whoring after Success! Power! Status!—is an accepted part of many middle-aging people's psychology. And all of this is happening in a period when the baby-boom generation is increasing while the number of judgment jobs is increasing in much smaller increments. Accordingly, with so many younger people competing for about the same number of upwardly mobile jobs, something was bound to give. What gave was the ethic that said upward is better.

Next, a judgment job causes some manageable anxiety. You don't necessarily know how well you'll do at work that day. There's a chance you'll fail at what you do. This is a longhand way of saying that what we want is challenging work where good judgment is one, maybe the only, job qualification. (Oh, by the way, it's bad form in a job interview to say you want a judgment job that is "challenging.") The job you want is risky. But a job without risk or challenge, that is permanent, where you can't be fired, and for which you are never evaluated, is a non-job. It is a wholly secure position, a sinecure, a fur-lined rut, a life-in-death arrangement, and a grievous blow to self-esteem.

The key to satisfaction in the workplace is neither compensation nor prestige. What everybody wants is a chance to excel; we want to put our mark on what we do; we want to say, "I did that!"

Another little-remarked factor in career preference is *envy,* which might cause some people to back off excellent opportunities: the highly skilled blue-collar machinist who turns down a promotion to shop foreman for fear of what his buddies will think; the woman who fails to leap to management, hating to think what her home-bound friends would feel; the young upward-bound men and women who hesitate to make their mom and dad look bad when they do good.

Any "friend" or relative who begrudges you success is no friend and a pretty poor relative. All your friends are going to be strangers. Taking a step off the deep end where your friends have never ventured, yes, could cause them to envy your daring or good luck. But think twice (three times!), if you find yourself taking into account other people's feelings when you have a shot at the stars.

Finally, a few other aspects of the judgment job: (1) many judgment jobs compensate you on the basis of productivity, not longevity; (2) the job is complete: You think, plan, manage, and are the final judge of your work—even though others might judge it, too; (3) a judgment job generally has a few sensible, elementary, and vital entry qualifications (a poor job is one that has manifold duties and responsibilities but no clearly accountable central *task);* (4) while judgment jobs are often found in competitive environments, self-management and cooperation are fostered and the overall objectives of the organization—no matter how small your role—are supported by what you do; (5) oh, sorry about this, but a judgment job is where you feel free to quit and where, by the way, an employer is free to fire you. Feeling free is basic in the job search and in a judgment job.

Finding that judgment job, which you might create or even sell, is going to take time, money, and *emotion.* Knowing what you want to do and chasing a falling star is romantic. And just because you know what you want *doesn't mean you are going to get it.* It might mean simply taking that first step toward the stars. Knowing what you want and acting on that knowledge, doesn't mean it won't take *time.* Indeed, time, when you think about it, is what's necessary for all things bright and beautiful. Certainly, obtaining that judgment job means saying no to jobs you don't want. Example: If you were looking for a new home and bought the *first* affordable house, chances are you would buy it within a month. But looking for the house of your dreams or a house that could become (with a little work) the house of your dreams is going to take lots of prayer and reflection. It might be something you build yourself (working for yourself is the same thing as hiring yourself an employer). So free up your imagination, your time, and, yes, your money-market account to find a judgment job. Feeling important is important in the job search.

Now, let's review some assumptions about jobs that are true and important, and that you'll hear about again.

(1) Job finding, while fun, is difficult: It always has been and always will be—so long as we have a free labor market. It would be easier if ours were an *un*free society where the government *assigned* us jobs. But, of course, while job finding would be unnecessary, work would be forced labor! And even in the best of times, the

very abundance of jobs, the richness of career options, and the comparative ease of switching jobs or changing careers spoils us. Good times bring out impatient job hoppers, and millions of otherwise satisfied job holders start sniffing about for better opportunities. A kind of inflated job psychology develops and executive turnover, always the enemy of productivity, takes on cyclonic proportions.

Following the crowd is often a bad judgment call. Great spirits feel separated from the crowd. If they follow the crowd, it's because the crowd is going where they want to go. Know thyself: "Am I going back to work to please my neighbor?" asks the traditional housewife. It's not much different from the college senior who asks himself whether he is going to law school so much to please himself as to please his father. Or the wife who wants a child because her mother wants a grandchild. Think twice about what other people are doing. Trend bucking is a sign of great spirit and a tough ego.

The point is, in good times and bad, there are judgment jobs out there. New firms are forming, life is breathed into a thousand old-line endeavors. Necessity makes both institutions and individuals *change.* Like the stock market, the job market goes up and down. And like the stock market again, most stocks might be going down, but some are going up. Even in bad times, jobs open up, although it's harder to find them. New jobs develop every day in response to social forces and economic problems. Think about the number of jobs created by the rise in crime, the debt problem, and our increasingly dynamic information society.

(2) Never has work been more specialized. And all of this is happening at a time of increased organizational tempo, more finite divisions of labor, and souped-up computerized decision-making processes. The nature of work itself is under grave scrutiny.

Hannah Arendt writes profoundly on this problem; other scholars know the nature of modern work to be central to many other problems. The main reason for worker dissatisfaction (whether blue or white collar) is that specialization has ushered in an age when men and women are separated from the fruits of their labor. Our assembly-line culture, our highly specialized and esoteric job functions—no matter how important—leave us alienated from the purposes and the final product of our work.

A special responsibility, therefore, is redefining our jobs in such a way that we reintroduce the human factor into the work equation. Doing something on the job that has seemingly nothing to do with bottom lines often becomes the reason we go to work each day. And, by the way, its *other lines* which have everything to do with the bottom line.

(3) Dream jobs don't exist: The ideal job of all our imaginings is a figment in the minds of thousands of graduate students dumped on the economy each year. But a high percentage of jobs are converted by their holders into dream jobs. The ultimate responsibility for job enrichment lies as much with us as our employers.

Younger people, particularly, are mesmerized by *"glamour"* jobs that exist only in the mind of the beholder, not in reality. But work, remember, is repetitive and for most people boring. The solution is to figure out what bores her and him but not you! Most people would agree that being an actress is a glamour job. But working ten hours straight to film a twenty-second clip is for me and most of you brute labor. For a talented actress, however, satisfaction comes from getting the scene *right* at last.

(4) Many job searchers don't know what they *want;* what is not so well known is that most employers don't know what they *need.* Accordingly, if you can define a job better than the employer, the edge is bound to belong to you. And understanding how "luck", caprice, and whimsy affect the job search is discovering the importance of the well-known second effort. In a word, the human spirit is what animates the effective job search. Arguing that good luck is all that's needed is a sin against the Holy Spirit. The job of the job seeker is to get off his backside and change his circumstances—and *get* lucky!

(5) The central problem in the job search is your *will:* "What do you want to do?" is still the toughest question in a job interview. Don't put yourself down if you don't know, and when you do, assuredly you won't be *absolutely certain.* There is some small voice

of doubt in every major decision. Listen to it. But don't necessarily act on it.

Whether someone stays in his current job or jumps up to another job or down into another career, the change usually causes anxiety. "Am I doing the right thing?" we say to ourselves. Keep in mind, all major decisions cause doubt. In my experience, interviewing thousands of people most of whom succeeded in changing jobs, *none* was absolutely sure it was the *right* move. My message is simple: Don't avoid important decisions until you're absolutely sure, because you'll never make a decision. Instead, spend time getting the information you need to make a decision. Most people, seemingly afraid to make decisions, simply lack the information to make an informed choice. And remember, *no* decision is a decision, too.

Uncommonly effective job-finding methods are necessary in finding what you want. But that's only half the problem. Figuring out what you want is not easy either: It involves finding out who you are, what you've done, then learning how to match your strengths to a job. It makes no sense to learn how to find a job, land one as a drop-forge operator, then realize you hate iron foundries. It's not enough knowing how to find a job, although not many do. That's why you will have an advantage over the competition. But if few people know how to find judgment jobs, even fewer know what they want.

Most effective people reading this book might have four or five careers in their lifetime, even if they work for the same organization. Chances are, at the end of your life, looking backward, you'll perceive a design and a logic in your occupational path that was unrevealed in your youth. That's because an imaginative approach to career development takes into account the marvelous surprises, fascinating culs de sac, unusual convolutions life has in store for everyone. To plan, at age twenty-three, your life from graduate school to cemetery plot is truly irrational, crazy.

One aspect of my job is studying successful people at the end of their careers. Uniformly, successful people say much the same thing: that what they have accomplished seemed "meant to be." It's much easier later in life looking backward to pick out the peaks and valleys of your career topography, much harder at the outset to predict it. Therefore, for those kicking off the second stage in life, keep in mind it's the trip, not the destination, that's important. And very likely, forty years hence, *your* life will have a rhyme and reason that seemed "meant to be."

So a disclaimer.

As you think through next career steps, it's more tentative, hesitating, and irrational than most career counselors would like to believe. The idea that taking this workshop or using that workbook or for that matter reading this book are all that's required to re-order priorities is failing to grasp that the right hemisphere and the unconscious part of the brain need a full workout before making a career breakthrough. And that takes time.

(6) A self-managed job search is above all *rational*. But the job market—sorry to report—is *irrational*. Looking for a job is a crazy experience (ask any job seeker). But that doesn't mean you'll lose your head. And keeping your head means *knowing yourself* while everyone else is researching the job market. Knowing what you want and how to go about it is being rational. Researching the job market and looking for what is *available* is crazy. It sets you up to be hired for your *qualifications* and not your *motivations*.

A self-managed job search puts you first. Most job seekers put organizations first. The difference is attitude: The first are responsible to themselves, the second are responsible to others. Feeling free is central to the self-managed job search; feeling you *must* accept what an organization offers is the traditional wisdom.

A successful job search means a mesh between personal goals and organizational objectives: a definition of job satisfaction. But there's a price. It takes time, money, and imagination. And caring about yourself—no surprise—sometimes causes guilt.

(7) For liberal-arts majors, barefoot boys and girls with cheek, expect seven to nine months after graduation to land that entrance-level judgment job. For mid-careerists switching jobs (but not changing careers—there's a big difference), reckon on one month of job search for each $10,000 you want in salary and cash fringes. For men and women changing careers, homemakers returning to the labor force, those making radical geographical relocations, and people wanting to change jobs while working, count on nine months to a year. Rule #1 is don't quit your job while looking for a job. You've got to eat, feed your kids, and make the mortgage

payments. Who said you have nothing to live for? Of course, every rule is worth breaking. Sometimes circumstances require leaving a hopeless situation to find a judgment job.

(8) Education? It can help, hinder, or not make the slightest difference in your job search. It helps most, obviously, when looking for *jobs* in *education.* It helps least in mid-career, where experience, intuition, business savvy (the good-judgment factors) are most emphasized. It matters not at all for people well along in their careers where job experience and ability can be proven (and checked out). Generally, in order of importance, education comes last after motivation, ability, and experience.

(9) Employers, properly, want to know how you can help them, not how they can help you (that doesn't mean they won't help). The point is to define your abilities so as to *prove* your *effectiveness.* Showing that you really *want* the job is central. Not knowing what you want and faking it could work—i.e., getting a job offer you don't want—but that's when your troubles begin! Eventually you conduct another awkward job search defending *why* you accepted that squat or inappropriate job.

(10) In qualifying for judgment jobs, show how you're an effective *subordinate.* Example: A prestigious university inquired on its admission forms whether the matriculant possessed *"leadership skills."* Surprise. The one, *repeat one,* young person who acknowledged she was unsure of her leadership but certain she was a good follower was the first student admitted. At last report, she's a great success on the job, too! And subordinating—that is, submitting to expert authority—is a necessary ticket to enter the world of work. So maybe, if this is your first time around in the job market or the first time in twenty years, *the job after this next job* should be a judgment job.

Effective leaders were once effective subordinates. They coped with authority, bureaucratic structures, and the perennial people problem. On your job search (and on the job), stake out leaders you can learn from and, in some cases, someday might wish to be like. Imitation (aside from being the sincerest form of flattery) is the way we learn to become the people we really want to be. Make these leaders your mentors; learn from people who are effective. As for the rest of the ineffectives, remember: When you're the boss, what you learned in coping with them will be worth a lot to you as a manager. Managing people for effectiveness means working with people of every condition and circumstance.

(11) Learn to live with and learn from your mistakes in the job search: trying to qualify for jobs you don't really want, letting an interviewer put you down, passively accepting the first salary figure offered, refusing to evaluate employers, and so on and so on. The people who have the most difficulty finding judgment jobs are perfectionists, people who don't permit themselves to make mistakes. Since the job search by definition is sloppy, irrational, comical, and capricious, perfectionists customarily self-destruct and back off the self-managed job search. Since no job search can ever be perfect, the perfectionist job seeker feels like a failure.

Unless we learn from our mistakes, we go on repeating them our whole lives. Why? Well, for starters, we don't like to admit mistakes. The point is to be perfect, isn't it? But, of course, mistake making is as much a part of life as a baby taking that first step and falling flat on her face. No, making mistakes is how we learn to correct for tilt.

Second, mistake making often becomes a pattern of behavior, similar to a child's coping mechanisms that are no longer appropriate as an adult. For example, many young people back off conflict situations at home and then—after growing up and going to work—can't confront the boss and discuss problems. It doesn't matter whom you work for, what you do, or for how much, invariably these mistake patterns follow you into every job, through marriage (and divorce), into child rearing, and on into senescence.

Nobody likes to change. Personal change is painful. But nobody likes to continue making mistakes either. A beginning, a big beginning in thinking about your job search, is admitting your mistakes and wanting to change. Recognizing that your attitude might need changing before you can change jobs is reaching a level of self-awareness without which you cannot find happiness on or off the job. Many people confess to me, "I don't know what I want to do when I grow up!" It's said jocularly and with some embarrassment. What people are saying is that they are *ashamed* of not knowing what they want, that they are not grown up, imperfect, that being unsure of what they want is immature. Nonsense.

When we act on what we want and find it, we don't retire from life. Thinking through next steps on the basis of desire, never duty, allowing ourselves to become happier, growing on our current job, or looking for another career where we can grow larger is perfectly natural. And that's because no healthy person is entirely grown up. The child, maybe the genius inside us, is saying that life isn't necessarily a race against *other people*. It's more likely a contest with ourselves. The responsibility rests with us in hiring an employer. And if it is a race, the losers are simply those who have failed themselves.

(12) Learn to feel free on the job. "Feelin' free" simply means you are more *effective* than folks who consider work a pain, a joyless occupation.

So on that first job, ask yourself: "What do I *like* to do?" Money is not the most important thing in a job; that's what follows becoming truly expert at some skill. For your first job, therefore, aim at what taxes your imagination, physical stamina, intellectual capacity —a job that stretches you as a human being, a challenging job. In the process of growth it may cause some manageable anxiety, some pain, and a good deal of disappointment. That's why judgment jobs cause pleasure *and* pain, why people who succeed know how to bounce back, why we openly admire a person who does what she wants *despite all the setbacks*. It is our setbacks—the idea rejected, the report unread, the books unbalanced—that give us that sense of achievement and then, by God, the idea *is* accepted, the report *is* read, and those pesky double entries *do* balance. That's what we mean by a challenging job.

(13) Learn on the job not to *compete* with anyone except yourself. No matter what you do, you alone are the best judge of how well you're doing. If you measure up in your own eyes, chances are good you've got a good job. Don't be, in David Riesman's phrase, an other-directed person, who measures his progress against a group, not his own standards; accepts received opinions as his own; moves no faster or slower than the mass about him. "The masses are asses," someone once said. And you're an ass, a jackass, if you

let your boss, your peers, or your investment counselor decide how well you're doing. That's something you'll know if you are in touch with your values. Life is not a race—there are no winners and losers. There are simply people who love what they do and those who don't. Don't be a winner. Be a lover; the world loves a lover.

(14) Learn to invest your emotions in your job. People who care about what they do, do so because what they do touches their feelings; they are involved, they care about the consequences of their actions. Whether you work as a claims adjuster, a bank clerk, a teacher, or bridge-toll collector, get involved. People who care about their jobs feel anger, joy, distress every working day. That's because their emotions are engaged.

(15) Learn on the job how to cope and cooperate with all kinds of people.
A lot of people are going to resent you on the job. Especially if you are young, educated, ambitious, and they are older, not so well educated, and maybe no longer ambitious. On the job, you might be surrounded by people who no longer care, those who wrong-headedly perceive life to be a race that they have lost.
The world has more people of this unfortunate disposition than people like you. As such, middle managers might put you down, try to intimidate you with their experience, age, occupational street savvy.
Your job is to win them over. And that means hearing them out. There are a lot of good talkers on the job; few good listeners. Be patient with those less fortunate. Suffering fools gladly is not the message. My message is that the world of work is composed of more people who hate what they do than those who love it. Working with them and not becoming like them is a full-time job in itself.

(16) There are not many managers who really *care* about what they do, care enough to teach you to do your job better, push you beyond your ability, or even ask a day's work for a day's pay. Such employers are often *not* nice people; but they are effective. On your first job, look for that man or woman who is tough, demanding, and from whom you can learn. It's worth a graduate degree in

business management. And you'll learn to care about your work and push people who work for you.

(17) Learn on the job not to be *afraid*. A lot of people fear failure. "How am I doing, Mom?" they ask. People on the job who never run risks run a far greater risk of never being considered for risky jobs—i.e., judgment jobs on the line where qualities of leadership are demanded.

But before you take risks, you've got to feel free. And what's the worst risk you can take on the job? Why, being fired, of course! And what's so wrong with that? It's men and women who risk being fired from time to time who keep organizations alive and well, because they care enough about themselves, what they do, and the organization that employs them (and its objectives) *to make waves and raise rows!* Chances are you won't be fired, but spotted as a leader, and if fired, what's so bad about that? Who wants to sustain a nonworking relationship? Now you're free to go out and find the job you want, free to leave one organization for another. In many countries around the world, freedom of occupational choice is unthinkable. The state assigns you a position; it's yours for life. And life on the job in those countries seems so dreary, so bleak . . . so *secure.* Small wonder. People are *not* free and cannot pursue happiness, which, as Americans, is our constitutional *right.* Human happiness is simply a matter of feelin' free. Nobody and no organization can *guarantee* your happiness. That's not a constitutional right, nor should it ever be. What is promised is the chance to feel free and happy on the job, and therefore be effective. But the responsibility is yours, *not* the organization's.

(18) Learn how to separate life from work. Part of feelin' free is feeling separate. Sure, it's great to throw yourself into a task, invest your emotions, see a project through to completion, and feel pain and pleasure in the process. But while work is a joy, so's the rest of life. Many successful men and women put the job before everything else in life. My hunch, not carefully documented, is that workaholics have *no other life!*

No working person will go full term without being touched three or four times by workaholism. Remember, it's a contagious disease. You carry the dreaded bacillus home and contaminate thy spouse. The antidotes are many: hobbies, good sex, mini-vacations, climbing down the ladder of responsibility, self-awareness, therapy, jogging, executive sabbaticals. But above all, another job or another working way of life might be necessary. Moreover, a little-discussed aspect of the problem is that most workaholics don't *want* to kick the habit—not because work is wonderful, but because their home life is hell. Workaholics often become managers; working, for them, is a twenty-four-hour-a-day assignment. If you value your life, say no to the boss and find other means of employment.

So endeth the sermon. A lot of what I preach is what you learned in Sunday school. The trouble is, you don't believe it because you learned it in Sunday school.

The theme of this book is how to become competent in the job hunt and how to make that competence carry over on the job. The thrust of my advice is how to identify what contribution(s) you can make to potential employers, how to act on that information, how to become self-aware, confident, poised, and prepared to hire yourself an employer.

The methods outlined in this book are for people with strong egos (or who want them). Job seekers who feel powerless feel so out of an inappropriate sense of insecurity (people must become their own security—nobody owes you a job). "Powerless" job supplicants need to address these problems before they qualify for judgment jobs. One choice is to find a grunt job (any income-producing job) and start the necessary, and finally fulfilling, task of self-analysis. Nor are the approaches described here particularly useful to those people—mostly young people—who have an altogether unrealistic sense of entitlement. Remember, the Declaration of Independence guarantees "life, liberty and the *pursuit* of happiness." There is nothing that says we are *entitled* to happiness (or even a job).

I believe it is in your power to change the character of your employment life, to step out of roles foisted on you by mother, father, placement counselors, friends, and employers. My central point is to look upon employers as someone you hire to give you the means to develop into the person you are.

As such, this is a how-to manual. Nobody learns to make love, repair a car, or hit a baseball by reading a book. But everyone usefully supplements existing skills with improved techniques and self-knowledge. Learning on the job, I believe, is the only sensible way to learn a trade; looking for a job is the only way to find a job.

This book is for those unhappy in their work, people who want to change their occupations, people who are competent and want to become more competent, people with strong egos who need important work for self-expression, people who do things and do them very well, people who recognize that their skills transfer from one career to another.

So go hire yourself an employer!

Work consists of whatever a body is obliged to do, and Play consists of whatever a body is not obliged to do.

TOM SAWYER

PART ONE

Question: What should a normal person be able to do well?

Answer: Lieben und Arbeiten (love and work)

SIGMUND FREUD

ONE

Staying Put or Buying In

"What exactly are transferable skills?"

Every year there is a 20 percent personnel turnover in jobs. Job seekers must stay in touch, as they say in tinsel town, with themselves and with that market of jobs where the skills required are being constantly redefined. Skills, aptitudes, and experience gained in one field have a definite crossruff in newly coalescing fields. And plenty of jobs simply disappear, to be replaced by other jobs fulfilling newly identified wants. Learning how to be fast on your feet, recognizing how what you do at Company A might fit Organization B is acknowledging that what you do at A can be transferred to B. Switching careers two or three times in your life and changing jobs within a field five or six times (even if you work for the same organization) isn't all that uncommon and can indeed be desirable. And education might have nothing to do with your success.

For example, where I work our top Mexican-American expert doesn't speak Spanish; our best financial vice-president majored in political science; our boss (my firm is a management services firm) is a trained city manager; our best programmer, an immigrant Englishman; our best project manager, a woman liberal-arts major and ex-secretary; our marketing expert, an aeronautical engineer, and so on. . . .

The same is true with everybody; our skills are portable, we carry them from job to job, we can't help doing something well no matter where we work or what we are called. The trick in thinking through either first steps or next steps is defining your flair, genius, or talent and its application to many fields.

"But don't the rewards go to those who stay put and work up to the top?"

If by rewards you mean money and increasing responsibility, I agree. If by rewards you mean the Worth Ethic, then I also agree. But everyone is different and we are changing every day in every way. Accordingly, welcoming change and planning for it is part of the human condition. And that means planning on changes both within yourself and in the world of work.

"What about shelf sitters?"

Since people and institutions are always changing, what about those who don't change jobs *or* even function and remain with the same organization for a lifetime? Shelf sitters: they work in order to finance other activities. They do, off the job, what they really want. So long as they are able and willing, there is a definite place for the constructive shelf sitter in every organization. Shelf sitters trade liberty for security.

"What's the difference?"

Corporations, mega-governmental agencies, and even universities can't avoid becoming bigger and thus more bureaucratic. The trade-offs for the job seeker are liberty or security, creativity or control, self-direction or other direction. Big organizational types frequently confess to the frustrations they feel working for large, impersonal organizations. On the other hand, one-man and -woman bands admit to occasional loneliness and insecurity working for themselves.

The happiest people in the workplace—no surprise—are the self-employed and those who manage their own businesses. Usually they don't make much money and the money they do make has a way of going back into the business. Accordingly, we must decide about next priorities when looking for new jobs. And priorities change. All the more reason why knowing how to change careers is a lifetime skill.

"Is there a case for job security?"

There is no such thing as a permanent job.

Still, some jobs are less insecure than others. And folks with large families, elderly relations dependent on their earnings, or essential financial obligations (e.g., school debts to repay) search out jobs that provide more stability than others.

Maintaining a vacation cottage on the Cape, socking away funds for a child's education, moonlighting at a second job to pay off your second mortgage are clearly not abstract obligations. The tricky factor is distinguishing in your own mind between what's obligatory and dutiful and what is desirable and pleasurable. Supporting your children or your elderly parents, if that's your free will, is not so much a duty to perform as a joy to fulfill. The resentment begins if you feel obligated and unfree.

Solving problems takes time and can't be done alone. Someone besides yourself must help you think through what you want. And the outcome might mean divorcing your spouse, kicking your children out of the nest at age eighteen, giving up friendships based on obligation rather than desire. Or the outcome might be the opposite: reinvesting yourself in your marriage, planning a future to take into account money needed for your daughter's law-school education, renewing friendships based on desire rather than habit, and staying put rather than changing careers.

Simple, but not easy advice, and impossible if you can't focus on yourself. You can't establish what you want if you don't know what you're feeling. Self-awareness is the best security.

"What do you mean, 'there is no such thing as a permanent job'?"

Excepting jobs with tenure (and even in academia there is a movement to abolish lifetime tenancy), there are surprisingly few secure positions. And a good thing, too. Therefore, in planning the job campaign, look for work, not a job.

Insecure?

A little insecurity makes life bracing. Its synonym is freedom. Don't expect a job to provide security—even civil service employment. The government won't fire you, to be sure, but even it is constantly reorganizing and eliminating people.

"What's the ideal size of an organization?"

Don't work for an organization where you must relate to more than fifty people. Nervous systems overload when dealing with too many people. In plain fact, most people are not occupationally happy in departments of more than fifty. In larger organizations, *effective decentralization* can postpone giantism (or elephantiasis), but not eliminate it entirely. Many large businesses are, instead, opting for smaller profit centers, a trend that takes into account people's natural predilection to want to know (as well as work with) each other.

Hire yourself an organization (or department) where you learn the job on the job. (Your skill is learning *how* to get jobs and learning *from* them.) One of the best ways to ensure this is to be sure the organization is *human size*.

"But aren't all the available jobs with the big corporations?"

Another myth about employment is that all the jobs are with huge corporations, government, and through the labor unions. Ninety-four percent of employers have fewer than fifty employees, and 53 percent of the jobs in this country are with these employers.

The more complex society becomes, the more kinds of judgment jobs develop. In these fields the so-called unskilled, liberal-arts majors maneuver best: They know how to learn on the job (their skill, in fact, is learning on the job), they have the imagination to change jobs, and *the good judgment to know whether a job is worth doing in the first place*. This is the difference between an intelligent generalist and a bluestocking expert.

"What's the connection between work and education?"

The purpose of education is not training a person for *a* job; the classical aims of a liberal education are preparing us for *leisure*. There is, however, plenty of room for *trade* schools. Law schooling is *trade* education, so is medicine, hotel management, computer science. This is not so much education as work training. Moreover, graduate (and increasingly undergraduate) education causes many students to feel locked in to a career. Both those with degrees and those without, furthermore, complain that what employers want is experience. What needs repeating to employers and job applicants alike is that (a) no one is unable (a man with a strong back who likes lifting things is skilled), (b) motivation and ability are more important than experience and education, and (c) skills are transferable.

A liberal education, which trains students for leisure and teaches them at the same time how to *think, write,* and *speak* (in more than one language) and acquaints them with the values and principles governing the physical and human universe is still the best education for life and work, too.

In picking trade schools (barber colleges, schools of pharmacy, conservatories of music), understand we are simply refining skills we probably already possess. Choosing a trade education unrelated to our abilities on the basis of what's in demand shapes us for jobs predetermined by education and not motivations. Many people are schooled for the wrong reasons (they need a job) and feel trapped (in their own minds) in a career path prefigured by educators or the job market. Many graduates, therefore, feel unfree, and nobody who feels unfree is going to be particularly effective either looking for a job or on the job.

"But aren't diplomas admission tickets to jobs?"

Certainly for lawyers, CPAs, engineers, operation-research types, B.S.s in civil engineering, and court stenographers. Certainly not for business people, diplomats, management consultants, public administrators, and marketing people.

Going to school or going back to school to acquire additional "hard skills" is often a chimera. Thus, the obvious failure of manpower-retraining programs and professional schools that don't take into account the fast-changing labor market. (Do we really need any more urban planners, linguists, librarians?) It's time-consuming, expensive, and seemingly inevitable: Graduate school in some industries seems no longer an option so much as an occupational necessity. For many undergraduates, the worrisome matter is not whether grad school is the *right* decision, but whether they have a right to a decision. That's the catch: People who feel trapped don't make free decisions.

"But won't grad school help me think through what I want to do?"
Maybe.

And since a majority of graduate students don't know what work it is they want, they attend grad school to find out. That's why grad school is time-consuming and expensive.

There is another less expensive way: working at a craft, trade, or profession *before* studying it in school. Thus, an *employer pays you* while you ponder a career in the law, economics, or social work. Graduate school, on the other hand, is something *you pay for* while deciding whether you have what it takes to be a journalist, foreign-aid specialist, or operations analyst.

Best of all, by taking a job at the bottom of the ladder, many young people learn lessons about work that no school can teach. And may discover that going back to grad school isn't necessary at all.

"But won't working for a few years wreck my prospects in going to grad school later?"

Most admission directors in the best professional schools *prefer* applicants with considerable on-the-job experience. Such students are more mature, focused, and motivated.

Working now and considering graduate school later (or perhaps never) is being practical if you're unsure of what you want to do. The point, however, is finding work that pays the bills, gives pleasure, and provides a *feel for a certain function.*

"But if I work for five years, then take three years for grad school, won't I miss out on the fast track?"
Life in the fast lane.

What most younger people don't realize is that in mature organizations, promoting younger people over the heads of men and women ten, twenty, and thirty years *older* isn't going to happen. Thus, many young people, climbing the organizational ladder, feel enormous frustration waiting for those above to move up in the organization . . . or out. But able people with or without graduate diplomas are bound to move up at the same *pace.* Everyone invests time on the line before being raised to the executive suite.

And age is still the single most critical element in anybody's career path.

"Why is age such an important factor in the hiring process?"

Chances are better than even that most employers won't hire anyone their elder for a position beneath them in the chain of command, that you'll hesitate accepting a job working for someone your demonstrable junior, and that both you and your employer might feel awkward if you're the same age.

As we grow older, we're more flexible about age; oddly, it's the young who are more inflexible on this issue. But your best stance is to ignore the age issue in the job search, since for some it isn't an issue at all.

"Going to grad school seems more responsible."

Working at what you want could cause guilt; doing what you *should* (going to grad school), leaves you guilt-free. Thus, many students in school feel no guilt, but are miserable.

Dilemma?

Not necessarily. Sometimes doing what you want arouses feelings of guilt. Therefore, learning how to cope with guilt is part of growing up. Avoiding feelings of guilt by doing what others want makes no sense. And certainly doesn't help you grow up.

Often grad students who study impractical subjects feel irresponsible. But the good news is that these students habituate themselves to doing what they want at a formative age. Career decisions are likely to come easier later in life.

Keep in mind that an advanced degree in astronomy, anthropology, or archaeology won't necessarily lead to a job in the field. And college teaching prospects are dim in every discipline except engineering. But if studying an impractical subject is a free decision, based on desire rather than duty, it's bound to be the right decision.

"What about credentials?"

That's my point.

Experience is the best credential in finding work. If employers must choose between experienced (but undereducated) job candidates and educated (but inexperienced) job seekers, the nod goes to the former every time.

As for breaking into a field where you have no credentials (experience *or* education), the going is tough. But there is room *at the bottom* in most lines of work. These are paraprofessional jobs in social work, law firms, economic planning organizations. Working as a volunteer, subsistence paraprofessional, or low-salaried entrance-level trainee is a ticket some employer will punch while you *test* a certain line of work. It's what academicians call field experience.

Two years in the Peace Corps is just the thing if you fancy a career in international development; selling a line of industrial products as a manufacturer's representative is a front-line business job; writing up high-school sports for your county newspaper tests whether you have what it takes to make it in journalism.

"Whatever I do, I want to be certain it's the right decision."
Whoa.

Uncertainty is a part of all major decisions: Whom you marry, vacations you take, property you buy. There is always a nagging sense that any decision might be *wrong.*

Whether you go to grad school or go to work, there's a chance you'll feel it's a mistake. But what's wrong with making a mistake?

Successful people (i.e., those who do what they want) make mistakes. That's because they make decisions. If things don't work out, they take their lumps, and move on. Mistakes are disappointing, but don't destroy you. And making a free decision means living with the consequences. The biggest mistake is feeling that you have no choice, that events control you rather than that you control events. Feeling free to go to work or go to grad school is the message.

"But won't grad school help me on the job?"
A first-rate graduate school trains students to meet deadlines, work under pressure, think on their feet—not inconsiderable factors in the world of work. Moreover, grad schools *certify* you to be a lawyer, economist, or social worker. But there is a big difference between being certified to do a job and being motivated to do it. The two most important predictors of success on the job are motivation and ability. But schooling doesn't motivate students, and ability is something students bring to grad school. Thus, profes-

sional schools can certify students, but can't forecast their success on the job.

"Any tips on who should go on with graduate training?"

Those people who should do nothing else except go on to school are invariably those who have something original to contribute: dancers, scientists, economists, medical researchers, people who are not so much students as thinkers, not passive receptacles of learning but active progenitors, men and women intending to add to the sum of human knowledge. Yes, it's best for people with this special flair to continue schooling; they are clearly in touch with their talent.

The problem with talent is knowing it when you see it (particularly in yourself). And overcoming the resistance such self-knowledge causes. Most men and women of talent are generally recognized by other talented people.

"Why don't grades predict success?"

Grades are important, but unless the graduate wants to be a scholar, grades are a poor way to predict on-the-job performance. Grades measure how well we take examinations; but how many jobs require us to take exams? Grades are no predictor of how much money you'll make.

Some employers believe that grades in elective subjects are important. That's because electives are freely chosen by students and reflect will and motivation.

"Do many corporate employers back off from young people coming out of graduate schools?"

Studies show that most young men and women quit or are terminated from their first professional jobs within three years. Plenty of employers, therefore, let the big banks, accounting houses, and blue-chip industries do the hiring and then raid or pick off those younger people who truly want work, say, as a food-packaging engineer for United Brands.

Big business buys young people by the boxcar the same way it buys raw materials: A lot goes on the scrap heap. And younger graduates themselves, unsure about what they want, become disillusioned. This is particularly true of those who believe academic achievement predetermines success in business, government, and the professions.

Moreover, so many entrance-level jobs are simply highly structured screening sieves (i.e., industry is screening out those who don't fit) that the best and the brightest grow bored with the lack of responsibility and look elsewhere. That's when second-tier market-oriented companies hire them and give them real work. Finally, some younger people search for mentors on the job and rarely find them in octopus organizations. Indeed, middle managers in large organizations are often hostile to the young, particularly younger people strong on theory and short on line experience.

"What about attrition rates?"

Entry-job turnover is cyclonic the first five years. Expectations of success are greater and the disappointment sharper. Yuppies don't so much job-jump to a better job as they job-hop to a similar disappointing position. And job hoppers rarely move up the salary ladder as job jumpers do. The best-compensated young men and women are those who remain with the same organization and job-jump within it.

"What's the major reason some people succeed in judgment jobs?"
People.

How well you lead, enlighten, praise, chastise, judge, accept, reject, understand, and learn from people are the chief factors in being successful in judgment jobs. Schooling people for trades, skills, and occupations should take this central fact into account. (This might be the most practical justification for a liberal education, but test scores and examinations never reveal this ability.)

"So what you are stressing is the importance of starting at the bottom?"
Yes, in the boiler room.

Down in the pits young people learn how to cope with resentment and frustration. All of which is schooling in interpersonal behavior—so important in reaching top management.

"Don't most organizations train on the job?"
Some do—and most that do, fail. The best training is a real job with staff or line responsibilities where you are accountable, where

what's accomplished is easily distinguished, where the organization rises or falls because of what you do.

The important things in life we teach ourselves: how to read, swim, make love, play Parcheesi, balance the petty-cash fund, raise money, spend it, teach, talk, and haul for lobsters.

Same at work: To get a good education, get a judgment job.

"Is it necessary to become computer-literate?"

There is an enormous computer-education movement in this country. Its message: Computer literacy is the wave of the future. But the sound you hear is the tide moving *out.* Computers are big, dumb typewriters that have speeded up and greatly simplified our lives. The printing press and the typewriter had similar effects in their day.

But the question "By the way, do you do programming?" will cause job seekers a generation hence to bristle in much the same way that "Do you type?" raised women's ire as they entered and re-entered the workplace during the women's movement. In other words, this morning's computer programmers will be this afternoon's clerks. And truly, the status, salaries, and promotional prospects of most computer programmers are not much better than secretarial-science majors.

Worse, according to the Bureau of Labor Statistics, in predictions of new job openings expected to surface in America, computer programmers rank *thirty-first* behind—you guessed it—secretaries (700,000) and other occupations such as janitors (501,000), kitchen helpers (231,000), and physicians (135,000). By the nineties, it's thought we will need only 112,000 new programmers per annum.

Computer literacy is not to be despised. It helps when *entering* the labor force. But the judgment jobs of the future belong to those who hire and supervise the programmers. The jobs most of us want will go to those men and women who don't so much know *how* to program as *why* we program in the first place.

"So the person who knows how to do a job will always work for the person who knows why we do it in the first place?"

That's right, and that's the definition of the importance of a liberal education. Skill-based training has created a glut of expensively educated people whose most important skill—sound judgment—hasn't been challenged. The best education, pre-professional, liberal, or otherwise, teaches you the *why* of it all. So liberal-arts types need to *learn on the job* and skill-trained people need to take two steps backward and understand *why* they are doing the job in the first place.

The problem with young, skill-trained people is that they think they can't afford the time, money, or imagination to take those two steps backward; the problem with liberal-arts majors is that they don't think they can do *anything*. Both groups need to recognize that *everything* worth learning about work cannot be learned in school.

"Isn't it true, however, that there's a vast and growing number of educated proletarians to be kept off the job market?"

Many authorities maintain that American society in its dynamism builds in the kind of dropout reaction some young people feel today. They see the adolescence of the young as deliberately prolonged, grad schools as head-start or transition centers for the professional classes, and alternative jobs as a temporary expedient to keep millions out of a seemingly saturated professional job market.

Probably because of my own lack of depth perception, I don't share the sinister establishment conspiracy the above analysis suggests. But if you believe that even half of it is true and can't settle on what row you want to hoe, maybe the thing to do is nothing.

There's nothing stopping you.

"What do you mean, 'Do nothing'?"

Some people need to buy time to think through and accomplish what they want to do. Sometimes it takes a decade. Becoming a psychiatrist, for example; accumulating capital to buy a small business; marketing a complex idea or project; raising money for some wacky project—all are examples of people with realizable objectives, people who care enough about themselves to spend money; time, and imagination on the number-one person in their lives.

But these people really aren't doing nothing. They are paying their dues, coming to grips with reality, accepting the terms and conditions of what they want to do. And that's the major qualification: understanding, coping, and cooperating with reality.

"How can I be sure I really want a job?"

One way is to imagine you've struck it rich—say, you've won a million dollars in the state lottery. Chances are you'd quit your job. If people don't have to work, they usually don't, which says something about work in America. But if you keep a job after you've won the lottery, you know you want it. Many rich people who don't have to work do find jobs, and are successful, i.e., happy. This is because working is natural, like playing, sleeping, eating.

A new job (like a new girl- or boyfriend) generally has a salubrious effect on your personality. Whereas most job seekers are sullen, ineffectual, and incompetent, the new job holder has a brisk gait and the certain knowledge he has chased a falling star and caught it. The question thereafter is whether our star catcher can hold it.

"Why do people stay at jobs they hate?"

Deprogramming people from going to work at jobs they loathe is my foremost mission in life. Having studied the problem for many years, I find that the chief reason we do what we don't want to is because we feel obligated to other people. Needing to stay put and do one's duty is a plague; it's part of our Calvinist heritage. But the job of each new generation is shaping our heritage. These past twenty years, many maturing Americans have managed to shake the Puritan ghosts. In fact, some younger folk, alas, have gone to quite the opposite extreme: They work only if it feels good, forgetting that work that doesn't raise a sweat won't raise their self-esteem either.

Routine, repetitive, reflexive behavior is a component, a major nucleus of any job, whether as president of an engineering firm or manager of the firm's janitorial services. Learning to live with and being proud of one's coping capabilities, whether it's homemaking chores or working as an advertising space salesperson, is the first essential *any* employer should discover in *any* job applicant for *any* job.

"I don't understand what you mean by labor."

By labor I mean something I'm *obligated* to do, dumb work that gives me little pleasure (no matter how much lucre I earn).

The idea of "labor" was brought to a productive boil by Lord

Calvin and other Swiss theologians who preached that we labor because it's our duty, that God's grace anoints those who press the grapes and winnow the chaff. Labor was a pleasure in one sense: It got the awful monkey of obligation off our backs. Until we rose again the next morning to fervently welcome another ton of Karma. An endless cycle of labor/obligation, of obligation/labor.

This interpretation of God's will formed the ideological basis for capitalism; it sanctioned wealth as an indication and measure of God's grace and signaled our election to heaven and eternal life: a reason to labor at a dumb job.

I mean, people really busted ass.

"How can institutions function if they don't impose obligatory tasks on their people?"

They can't.

What they can do—in filling judgment jobs—is pick men and women who labor for love. I mean it. People who perform work out of a sense of obligation function much less effectively than those who work out of a sense of pride and accomplishment.

Often we work best when we are least expected to. That's because we feel free with ourselves. Working when we are not supposed to eliminates the sense of responsibility. And, thus, we work more effectively.

"Surely there are other reasons we don't leave jobs we loathe?"

Plenty of middle-aging Americans can't give up feeling trapped by their retirement benefits. The point of work being to retire from it. A clear majority of Americans work for money, out of need, and so stay at a job for what it pays now and for what it will pay at retirement. Don't cry in your beer when they complain about their jobs.

Another reason, curiously, is that people fear they might succeed if they change jobs or careers (fear of failure is greatly exaggerated). A successful job search means giving up either a bad opinion of themselves or of their new employers. These folks fear losing their identity and sense of self when, of course, they will actually be uncovering it.

A huge factor in people's staying put these past years has been inflation. Whenever we think next year is going to be worse—

price-wise—than last, it causes us to stay put, button our lip, and swallow our sorrow. A price-stable society is essential for a truly free labor market.

There are other reasons: physical disability, the lack of capital to start a business, opposition from key family members—all of which can undermine determination to find occupational fulfillment. But we should be responsible only to ourselves when we look for work. Everyone has a free will, but most people won't admit it. To do so is to take responsibility for our own happiness, and that means giving up blaming other people for our unhappiness. Taking responsibility for our happiness has its price: *Happiness* (take notes on this) *gives pleasure.* The price of pleasure is guilt. It follows, if we feel no pleasure on the job, we won't feel guilt either. The perfect way to avoid paying the *price* of pleasure is to do what we "should."

"What about 'dropping out' and using unemployment benefits?"
First a few facts:

—Employers, not working stiffs, pay for it.
—It was established to finance reemployment.
—Unemployment insurance was never designed to trap people into lines of work no longer needed or to keep people in places where there are no jobs.

Today's unemployed are unlike their grandfathers of the thirties. Most use unemployment insurance not to find a job but to avoid looking for it. The whole system has become a national disgrace and fiscally unsound. (Many state unemployment-insurance programs are now funded from general revenues—that is, your tax dollars and mine.)

Unemployment insurance, particularly for the young, has become a trap; another government scheme that prolongs adolescence ("I'll find a job when my benefits run out"). It destroys self-esteem —the beneficiaries are not required to earn their benefits. And it prolongs and increases the chance for continued unemployment because it provides the means to avoid ending it. If unemployment benefits were cut back 50 percent tomorrow, the rate of unemployment in the United States would drop substantially.

Moreover, unemployment, while an imposition, is not a personal tragedy. Willingly or unwillingly, the unemployed do find jobs.

The seven million unemployed people today aren't the same as the six million unemployed this time next year. In other words, a great many of the unemployed are simply frictionally unemployed.

"What's frictional unemployment?"

The greatest percentage of out-of-work people represent what Dick Lathrop, author of *Who's Hiring Who,* calls "frictional unemployment." That means it's just a matter of *time* until they find a new job. Trying to reduce the time it takes to find a job should be a government priority, since unemployed people don't pay taxes. Reducing the time it takes to find a job decreases the unemployment rate and correspondingly increases governmental revenues. Yes, some of the unemployed are victims of *structural* unemployment (steel workers, for example) or *cyclical* unemployment (winter-wheat farmers), but the vast majority of unemployed are simply paying their dues and taking the time every job search requires. Accordingly, if the government helped the unemployed find jobs (i.e., job-*search* training), it would significantly reduce the rate of unemployment, all of which is financed through increased payroll taxes. The idea makes so much sense government is bound to oppose it.

"What about doing your own thing?"

A sentimental, pervasive, and largely self-destructive national delusion.

The dream of every American over the age of fifteen.

But few of us—in isolation—do our own thing. Oh sure, there are independent lawyers, consultants, and myriad professionals, but they are no more independent than their big-organization counterparts.

Why?

Because independent people depend perforce on clients, and clients are heavy taskmasters. So think twice about running your own business—whether it's a string of hardware stores in Westchester County or a bike shop in Vermont. There's nothing wrong, of course, with running your own business. But don't think you will be independent. You'll be more dependent than ever on the need for business.

"But isn't starting a business the American dream?"

Ours is an age of entrepreneurship. The number of businesses being incorporated far exceeds the number of those going out of business. Noteworthy, women are now starting businesses at a pace slightly greater than men—a fact every mid-career woman might take into account. But while starting a business is an option, it's worth remembering that far more businesses fail than succeed, that many ongoing operations are only semi-successful and that making money—really big money—isn't necessarily the objective. But yes, starting a business is the dream of many Americans. The desire is to become independent. My point is that far too many people fly from salaried, bureaucratic, and hierarchical jobs without taking into account the *price.*

"Are big-company people necessarily good bets to run a successful small business?"

It all depends. (Everything important in life *depends.*)

Plainly, many high-salaried corporate types would love to become self-employed. And they do it, if they *have the confidence.* That's the kernel of the nut: Do they have the ability, conviction, and desire to do what they want alone? Do they give themselves a vote of confidence?

Keep in mind, most business advisers strongly caution us that most small firms fail because of (a) too little capital and (b) poor management. So, in thinking through your capital requirements, when writing out your business plan, *double* your capital needs. That's painful but realistic. And remind yourself that entrepreneurs are generally great idea men and women, but terrible managers. Hiring the management expertise—particularly in the money-management department—is essential. More new businesses fail because the founding genius of the enterprise simply can't understand the first law of business administration: Cash in must exceed cash-out.

"Should I use my own money to start a business?"

Rule #3: Never use your own money. The whole point in starting a business is using other people's money to establish yourself.

But a lot of people who want to do their own thing can't bear being in debt to others. That's an entrepreneurial disqualification.

Reason?

Lots of us hate being *dependent.* The responsibility to others (creditors, partners, banks) defeats us. In other words, people who go into their own businesses feeling responsible to other people aren't going to be successful. Being your own boss means being responsible to the self. An entrepreneur understands the necessity of using other people's money, for which she later pays) on her own behalf. Effective entrepreneurs know how to make money using other people's money.

"Why does starting a business mean a sharp reduction in income?"

The self-employed plow back their earnings. Real income is often drastically reduced. People accustomed to high incomes often disqualify in business start-ups because of plummeting self-esteem associated with a lower income. If earnings are the chief measure of self-esteem, then many entrepreneurs should feel like failures. But the whole point in being self-employed is psychic: Being self-reliant is worth more than a paid vacation on someone else's payroll.

"What are some other factors to keep in mind before becoming self-employed?"

First, the vast majority of small business people *underprice* their product or service. Second, entrepreneurs must make tough decisions every day. A lot of business decisions are mistakes. Making mistakes and learning from them is *qualifying* for self-employment. People afraid to make mistakes never make decisions and are unqualified to be entrepreneurs. Third, hang a safety net: a second mortgage on the house, a working spouse, a job, trade, or profession to go *back to.* Analyze your business with a view to it failing; ask yourself, "What happens then?" Fourth, having analyzed the risks, learn to live with the pleasure of being self-reliant and its pains. Many have illusions about being their own boss, and when the inevitable disillusionment sets in, they give up. Disappointments accompany small business start-ups; it takes time to accustom yourself to the new you. Fifth, remember that the sheer pleasure of being independent might cause *guilt.* Indeed, many people—functioning freely for the first time—think they are losing their identity and feel correspondingly guilty when they succeed in small business. Not being miserable at their work and truly enjoying it must mean they are doing something *wrong*. Of course, it's the attendant guilt that is wrong. Finally, a little-recognized factor in self-employment is the type of loneliness of long-distance runners. They miss the sociability and politics of larger enterprises.

Another little-known fact about potential entrepreneurs is that many were fired (or otherwise hit their ceiling) where they were working. An imaginative exit from a dead-end job is simply to start up a new firm. But if the fledgling entrepreneur is often more excited about leaving a job than starting her own business and if she doesn't understand how to run a business that works . . . she's in big trouble.

Think twice, therefore, about hanging out your own shingle. At least a third of the résumés many employers are seeing these days are sent by consultants, the self-employed, small businessmen and -women, and entrepreneurs all hoping to wend their way back into the mainstream. And there are plenty of them: over three million new incorporations each year; the number of self-employed people has jumped to ten million and is rising.

"So success can be a problem in small business?"

Plenty of people who become their own boss can't handle the sheer pleasure of it. To work at something and enjoy it, to work for themselves and not somebody else, to be self-disciplined and not disciplined, makes some people dizzy. They feel they are losing their grip, when of course they are actually taking hold. Becoming their own boss means coming to terms with the people they really are. Aspiration, anticipation, and ambition are the preconditions of being your own boss.

Another trendy aspect of entrepreneurship is the increasing promotion of innovation *inside* an organization. Established firms are fostering new products and services by creating an "intrapreneurial" climate, the so-called skunkworks where the most imaginative ideas in corporate America are developed. The point for entrepreneurial job seekers is not so much to look for a job as to sell ideas; let your employer put you to work doing what you would otherwise do and pay for yourself.

Now, the danger in selling ideas is that an employer might buy the idea but not you. Your idea can be ripped off and assigned to someone in-house. Some ideas are worth copyrighting or patenting; consult a lawyer about how to protect your idea from corporate raiders short on imagination and business ethics and quick to see a potential blockbuster.

"Okay. Think carefully before going to work. Beware of the snare of grad schools. Don't think running your own business is easy. What's worth doing in the job mart?"

Most job seekers suffer from a bad case of the disease to please— putting the employer's interests before their own. The point of hiring yourself an employer is for you and the employer to establish congruent *interests.* Both parties to this business transaction are fifty-fifty shareholders. Thinking, as so many job seekers do, that they don't count, that employers are more important than they, putting other people's interests before their own is plainly destructive to a judgment-job campaign. Selfish? But there is nothing at all selfish in a productive business relationship—it might last a lifetime, like a durable marriage. Look carefully, therefore, at any employer whose interests you would be glad to serve because his interests serve your own.

"What are some examples of putting one's own interests first?"

ITEM: Finding a great job, knocking yourself out, sizing up your fellow workers (and finding them wanting), and a month later . . . asking for a raise. Putting one's interests first means employers come in first, too. If your goals and the organization's are congruent, then both parties are winners.

ITEM: Rejecting a good job offer everyone envies you for, because you want to do something else.

ITEM: Investing your imagination in a job (another definition of a judgment job) and welcoming more responsibility, never shying away from leadership, visibility, and public recognition, and being comfortable with increased self-esteem. No joke: Some folks feel terrible when sensationally successful; they feel like impostors!

The trick in putting your interests first is knowing, in the first place, what your interests are. How can you invest emotion in a job, feel good about your performance, and welcome the gratitude of your superiors, the respect of your peers, and the admiration of your staff, if you don't know what your interests are?

Tricky, yes?

The toughest work in the world is mounting an authentic self-image. But for judgment-job seekers who make it (find what they want), it's the only objective.

"Do specialists have more difficulty than generalists in finding judgment jobs?"

Yes . . . and no.

Specialists, if demand is fair to good, can usually find jobs easily within their specialty. But if demand is poor to nonexistent, they have enormous difficulty.

Most specialists lack imagination in understanding how skills transfer from one occupation to the next. Like graduate students, specialists feel locked in and perceive a dim future, or no future at all, if their training/experience doesn't precisely fit an employer's specifications. All the more reason for specialists to give up explaining themselves by way of degrees/jobs and focus rather on skills and accomplishments.

As for generalists (and who isn't?), people who confess to being a jack-of-all-trades and master of none are confused. Everybody is a specialist if he thinks long enough about his talent. Thinking we are generalists (and that's all) is a recipe for self-defeat. The knack is analyzing those few activities we do as well as or better than anybody else. Presto, the generalist is now a specialist. As for writers, statisticians, architects, designers, photographers, most are looking not so much for a job as for work. Finally, specialists never go on a job search without a portfolio.

"Could you give me a breakdown of types of judgment jobs?"

There are five categories of judgment jobs: (1) general-management jobs usually held by people a long time in the same or similar outfit; these managers are the ones who run the place; (2) technical positions, in which one functions as a specialist; (3) shelf sitters more concerned with employment security than mobility; (4) entrepreneurs, the enterprising self-employed; (5) consultants.

All judgment jobs require talent. Estrangement from our talent makes us uncomfortable. Skills are our strengths. Analyze skills. Knowing what we can do is knowing what we want to do.

ITEM: A professor of English is nominated to be his college's president. In his new job, he feels strangely dissatisfied and unfulfilled despite an increase in income, power, and visibility.

ITEM: A crackerjack production whiz is promoted to a group vice-presidency. He works on government relations and is unhappy despite an enormous increase in pay and privileges.

ITEM: An expert family counselor accepts an important policy-making job in the government. She much prefers the satisfaction of her lively private practice.

Working people need to guard against unwanted promotions: teachers who become administrators, consultants promoted to managers, craftspeople appointed as administrators often complain inwardly about their jobs. They "should" like their jobs, but they don't.

To separate people from their skills, to promote them to a job where they can't exercise their abilities, to reassign the competent to areas where they feel incompetent is no uncommon thing. Something dies in us. What we were "meant" to do isn't what we are doing.

"So everybody someday hits a ceiling?"

That's right.

The plain facts are that everyone *someday* is Harry Hasbeen. For plenty of people, the day we know we won't replace Lee Iaccoca at Chrysler is the first time we realize the inevitability of our occupational mortality.

For others, who love their walk of life—that is, they like selling, soldiering, and managing—rising to the ceiling of their institutional environment is not like walking the plank. In, Up, and Out is half true—it keeps up the body tone of the institution. But there is a place for conservative shelf sitters able to change with changing organizational objectives so long as top management is frank about their promotional prospects. That way neither party has unrealistic expectations of the other.

"What happens if I begin a job, and the job I really want is offered two months later?"

Quit and take the second job.

It's crackers to be obligated to employers. Betcha your current boss will congratulate you on your good luck.

Rejecting the job you want out of a sick sense of obligation or loyalty is eliminating yourself. Martyrdom's hardly a constructive outcome of a successful job search.

"How about money rewards? Which of the five judgment-job categories pays best?"

Well, it's in order of the jobs named. The general manager's position pays most; the maverick consultant or entrepreneur might earn the least.

Specialists are well paid but usually hit a salary ceiling in mid-career. Entrepreneurs do well but never have any money because they plow it back into the firm. Shelf sitters are paid adequately to very well, but it's the pension program and the job security that keep them punching the time clock.

"But doesn't everyone want a judgment job, and isn't the competition cutthroat?"

Yes and no.

No, not everyone wants a judgment job, and only a small percentage of the work force is going to do what I recommend. Moreover, plenty of people simply don't grasp that they are as important as employers in the job search. If you can act on your own interests and put yourself first, you'll succeed or at least get on the track to success.

Working with ten thousand or more people unhappily employed or unemployed people these many years has led me to a composite of the typical job seeker. If you are anything like this person, you

—feel incompetent, except among your network of friends and colleagues, in creating job leads

—find it difficult to be enthusiastic about job interviews, fearing rejection

—have trouble understanding the connection between undertaking a successfully self-managed job campaign (increased self-es-

teem, vitality, and confidence) and making what you learn work for
you on the job

—experience difficulty sorting out job titles and understanding
new career jargon

—fail to grasp how skills transfer from job to job, career to career
and how to express it in a door-opening résumé

—feel awkward to downright impotent when negotiating salary
and benefits

—seem shy about taking people's time who will help you obtain
the information you need

—back off using perfectly ethical and successful sales techniques
in finding a job

—feel clumsy talking about a challenging job, i.e., a judgment
position

—are unable to evaluate employers, often accepting the first job
offered, out of a malignant sense of gratitude

—seem cloudy about long-term goals

—are stymied by your seeming lack of experience, whether you
are young or middle-aging

—are easily intimidated by reading the want ads

—lack the self-confidence every job seeker must generate

—are indecisive because of a rich variety of options, believing
any decision prefigures your whole occupational life

—panic at the thought of quitting your current job and being
unable to find another

—feel trapped in current employment patterns and unfree to
think of new directions

—hate the idea of being dependent on employers

—are frightened of failure and/or success

—secretly envy people who seem to love what they do for a
living

—like working for authorities who are not authoritarian

—inwardly feel unqualified (compared to other candidates) after
accepting a job

—botch interviews for jobs you need but don't want

—feel an unaccountable sense of elation and potency when truly
effective on the job

—practice Masonic secrecy looking for another job

—privately believe all employment interviewers are powerful people to be appeased

—are accustomed to being miserable on the job, since that is, you believe, the nature of life and work

—try not to qualify for judgment jobs, the top jobs

"So go after the 'top job'?"

If it meets half of your criteria or more, yes. It's a cinch you will make a better impression. Don't compromise and go second-class when going first brings you closer to the captain's cabin. You'll feel greater self-esteem, which carries over into your interviews.

"Isn't aiming too high a certain invitation to failure?"

It's an invitation to disappointment but never to failure. Failure is the state of mind of people who never took aim or aimed too low. And many successful people often think themselves failures. That's because they cultivate the happy habit of doing what they want, satisfying objectives, developing new agendas, breaking new turf. Probably a definition of civilized man: His reach exceeds his grasp.

Discontent and dissatisfaction are common character states. The difference lies between those who try and fail (or try and succeed) and those who don't. The latter are always discontented and dissatisfied.

"Why is there less competition at the top?"

Most people don't want responsibility: more risk, more chance of being fired. Most people prefer job security rather than challenge and adventure. They want safe jobs. To go after the top job is to qualify as a risk taker.

"So be ambitious?"

For a lot of complex reasons, many of us suspect ambition in other people and especially in ourselves. Some think our hypercompetitive culture makes ambitious people monsters. At the same time, lack of ambition (i.e., desire) is frequently found among the unemployed. But what is really lacking is a sense of potency, of being able to do a job and, moreover, to enjoy doing it. So ambition when it's clothed in the garments of the main chance, the fast buck, and the inhuman use of human beings is something we all should oppose. But if our opposition to this kind of ambition also masks our own healthy desire *to do something,* it is equally reprehensible.

What we need (instead of ambition) is a sense of potency. Potency is knowing who we are (our values), what we want (our goals), and what we can *do* (our abilities). Becoming potent is the first block you lay in building self-esteem and launching a judgment-job campaign.

"But doesn't it depend on what each of us defines as success?"

My definition of success is being happy, productive, self-expressive, and fulfilled in whatever line of work I do; I've found it working on a loading dock, starting a business, teaching, writing this book. Self-serving ambition and selfishness seems, though, to be the popular definition of success. In becoming self-reliant and fulfilling our talents, we help ourselves and our employers at the same time, whereas the merely ambitious individuals are always and only looking out for number one. Naturally, people unable or unwilling to be self-managed unwittingly take on the coloration of their environment; they have no goals except those professed by the system —money, power, status. Poor substitutes for a sense of self. And a tragedy, too.

"So looking for a job means being assertive?"

Most people are never assertive enough. It's a glittering half-truth that women fail on the job because they aren't assertive. That's true of men, too.

And assertive people are never aggressive—i.e., disagreeable, pushy, autocratic, domineering—all defective characteristics. Being assertive, on the job search means persuading other people that you want the job and showing them you can do it.

How we admire people who say what they want; it frees us to say what we want. But employers and job seekers who can't are confused. Neither party, in this often hilarious transaction, is in touch with himself; neither person is putting himself first. Neither one knows what he wants!

"Do women seek out male approval on the job?"

People on the job naturally *want* the approval of authority. Most authority exercised in the world of work is male. Accordingly, whether you are a woman working for a man, a man working for a man, a man working for a woman, or a woman working for a woman, it's healthy to want his/her *approval.*

So it's not strictly true that women seek male approval. It's far truer that people want the approval of their boss.

Period.

"Yes, but why are women so prone to follow the rules?"

Well, if you mean the conventional rules about finding a job, are women any less savvy than men? Women, as a whole, seem in this respect—job hunting—to be as dim-witted as men. If you mean that women tend to be nicer and more respectful toward institutions, well, that's surely changed in the past decade. If you mean that women on the job tend to be less assertive, more inclined to protect other people's interests, more ready to obey than command, then that's also true of *most* men.

That's because only 10 percent of the jobs in any place of work *count.* Women still have these jobs in less proportion than men. But there are more men than women working, and, accordingly, far more men (than women) who have jobs that don't count. In any case, be you man or woman, being nice while looking for a job (or even on the job) is not nearly as important as being *effective.* The fact that plenty of ineffective men manage institutions should encourage effective men and women alike to go after their jobs.

Institution building is the final step in women's liberation. Not until the owner and managers of one half the organizations are women will there be complete equality in the workplace. Networking women's organizations is another way younger women these days are penetrating the hidden job market. The old-girl network is as effective as the old-boy network, especially at junior and middle-management levels.

"But don't men really want women to become subordinates?"

For *non*-judgment jobs, perhaps. That would be true, too, if they were interviewing men for the same position.

If you *feel subordinate* or that you *should be* subordinated, then why try to qualify for a judgment job? And some subordinating—that is, *submitting* to expert authority—is a necessary ticket to enter the world of work. So, to repeat, if this is your first time around in the job market or the first time in twenty years, *the job after this next job* should be a judgment job.

"What's wrong with hiring nice people?"

An unadmitted but pervasive factor in the workplace is the incompetence of "nice people." We business theorists call this the Klutz factor. Nice people adapt quickly to the environment and become part of its coloring—the bland leading the bland. Many firms are literally choking on nice types: people who don't make demands, don't work for change, don't act unless led. In short, the vast majority of the human race.

The problem of nice people is easily solved.

Decide that the nicest people in the world are effective people. It might change your whole life!

"Why isn't job seeking a rational process?"

It should be, but usually isn't. It's irrational because job seekers don't know what they want or what they do . . . a lost sense of direction. It's psychological dispersion, and the result is frustration and greater incompetence.

My advice is to do market research on yourself. Find out what you want, and then go after it. This means dollars and time. Usually you won't find the ideal job the first time around; you simply accept the second or third best. Often the best among us must create our dream job on the job.

"What about the trade-off between what you do and where you work?"

Big question.

I generally shy away from younger job candidates who say, in effect, "Who I am is where I work." Still, in mid-career especially, plenty of people are backing off from judgment jobs that mean a drastic change in living location.

If young, however, I would go anyplace to do what I wanted and let considerations of place become central in mid-years.

Foreign-currency traders happily practice their craft in Hong Kong or Hollywood.

Saxophone players gladly make music in Carnegie Hall or Covent Garden.

Baseball players rejoice in shagging fly balls in Three Rivers Stadium or the grubbiest playing field in the Texas Panhandle.

"Who is the happily employed person?"

The happily employed person is one who feels a sense of partnership with the boss instead of subordination. That person says, "TGIM!" Work is something to look forward to, not be apprehensive about.

A judgment job is never stagnant; it's always changing, and so are the lives of employed people who like themselves and their jobs: They know they are accountable, and manage time, money, and people as contributing factors to an organization's progress. But they work out of wish or desire, not out of duty or obligation.

Every morning the happily employed person gets out of bed unemployed!

"Every morning when I get out of bed I'm unemployed?"

That's right: whether you're the executive vice-president of Ingersoll-Rand or six months unemployed. It's because work is simply a series of assignments that must be satisfied before a job can be said to be done. And every morning, whether we are employed or looking to become employed, we must identify what our objectives are that day.

More reason to put personal objectives up front on your job search, understanding that people with jobs are unemployed if, on any given morning, they are unable to match personal objectives against organizational goals.

"Isn't it utopian to expect that you can always do what you want?"

Only for those who think it is. It's scary knowing you can become a self-managed, powerful personality—utopian. It's safer, less disappointing to believe you are shaped by your environment, determined by events. It's also unhappier and unfulfilling. You are partly determined by outside forces, but you also shape your environment.

Doing what you want takes courage. And choosing to continue to do what you are doing might take the most courage of all. Making up your mind to stay put *or* to find another job is a decision. Making a decision to stay is qualitatively equivalent to the thinking that goes into a decision to change jobs.

At all events, the decision *is* rational because it is based on desire and self-fulfillment, not on habit. Every working day I decide to buy, sell, or hold stock I own. If I hold it, that's a decision.

Same with you on the job. If you went to work today at the *same* job, you've made a decision.

Pity the poor chump, however, who stays at his job out of habit, not desire.

"I buy doing what we want, but every job requires doing things we must."

Sure, every judgment job contains elements of pleasure, pain, disappointment, triumph, and frustration in about equal measures. That's what job candidates mean when they say they want a challenging job. But do they really mean it? A few thousand interviews on both sides of the table have convinced me that most people don't. Most job candidates are unprepared to accept the terms and conditions of tough judgment jobs. All the more reason for you to make a list of conditions you want in a job, in a boss, in an organization.

"Well, don't you think employers have a duty to upgrade and enrich jobs?"

The worst result of the fun ethic is the establishment of these new work rules:

(1) Work should not be painful.

(2) My work, which is sloppy, is as good as your work, which is excellent.

(3) Uniformity, therefore, of pay and privileges to me is more important than rewarding you with higher pay and more privileges.

(4) Any work that is boring, frustrating, or tedious is bad and exploitive.

(5) Practice never makes perfect—it's simply a bore.

(6) Inspiration is worth more than perspiration.

(7) Work must always be fun.

"I go along with a judgment job never being permanent, and I like the idea of its being fun, but how can a job both be fun and at the same time tedious, monotonous, and frustrating?"

—The entrepreneur who takes over shaky businesses and puts them back on their feet.

—The social counselor who works patiently with a school dropout, an alcoholic, or an addict, and sees progress, backsliding, more progress, another step backward.

—The legislative aide who painstakingly nurtures a piece of legislation through hearings, committee, reports, amendments, deletions, more hearings, conference committees, and finally sees it signed into law.

All excellence demands pain, tedium, frustration.

"Does it make any sense to volunteer, for no pay, to work in a field you want where you have no qualifications?"

You bet.

Half the political hotshots in the country started off as unpaid canvassers in some obscure campaign. And advertising geniuses often begin by stacking mailbags for free.

People volunteer for many reasons: personal growth, to meet other singles, to win recognition, and to be first in line when a hidden job opens up. Volunteering is particularly recommended with a few qualifications to those who want work in glamour fields: museum management, investigative reporting, electronic journalism, political campaigning, advertising, PR, stage, screen, and radio. It's experience we can represent on our résumé (be sure not to indicate it was a volunteer position) and is especially recommended to the young, who are repeatedly told they would be hired "if only you had some experience."

The exponential growth of student co-op programs testifies to the pragmatism of student volunteering. Students are exposed to the workaday world (and job offers upon graduation), introductions to men and women who can open hard-to-open doors, and—above all —help students decide whether the working environment of, say, an international bank is the turf they wish to plow.

Another fringe benefit of volunteering in tough-to-break-into fields is the experience of playing personal politics on the job:

learning how to confront authority, follow directions, cope with difficulty and frustration—all of which are truly learning experiences.

Volunteer work makes the volunteer, especially if he or she rapidly becomes indispensable, highly visible to decision makers who in turn are often quick to recognize and promote competence.

"Does volunteering make sense for older people?"

A third of all Peace Corps Volunteers are now over fifty-five. Indeed, for people in a pre-retirement holding pattern, volunteering to work in a field you wanted to plow in your youth makes sense. First, you overcome the reservations of the younger, salaried middle managers by showing you're a producer. Second, like a younger person, you are first in line when a salaried job opens, and finally you banish feelings of uselessness felt by many of the newly retired.

Qualification: Both young and older volunteers should try to negotiate. Establish hours of work, reporting authority, function, title, and even—in black and white—insist employers give you a shot at the first professional job opening. Plenty of volunteers are exploited. A letter of agreement protects your interests and spells out employer obligations, which might include bus fare, babysitting fees, and an expenses-paid trip to the annual company meeting.

Another payoff in volunteering is practicing a skill; anyone who wants to write for a living (but lacks a portfolio) can test his skill by writing news releases for a state legislator or preparing a friend's marketing plan.

"What about going to work as a temporary?"

The biggest growth area in jobs has been the wildfire expansion of temporary-employment agencies, that hire out the highly technically adept and specialized workers for three days to three weeks. An effective way to wend your way into the judgment-job stream is to sign up with these agencies, float from one temporary assignment to another, check out the vibrations at this firm compared to that, and make your mark where you want work full-time. Often employers are recruiting temps (after paying the agency a hefty fee) to use as something more than designated hitters.

Working as a temp is similar to volunteering for important work or being a student intern. Both the employer and the employee have a chance to look each other over before either signs up for the long cruise. Working as a temp, student intern, or volunteer is much like understudying stage and screen stars; if they take sick or are otherwise unavailable, guess who the casting director puts in their place?

"Who shouldn't volunteer?"

Full-time professionals working at tough jobs should back off civic and volunteer jobs. Fulfilling other people's needs and not their own makes no sense. In a word, never volunteer for anything out of *guilt.* Many people in mid-career are set up by organizations who prey on their sense of guilt. Learning how to say no to others means saying yes to yourself.

Volunteerism, yes, is a chance to be of help to others; but don't forget yourself in the process. Otherwise you simply job-hop from one volunteer gig to another without ever making a professional connection, leading to a decline in self-esteem.

"What about not so much looking for a job as searching for a mentor?"

Many young employees (women in particular) make it an article of faith to identify a successful person, attach themselves to this rising star, and rise to king or queen of the hill.

Mentoring is an emotional minefield. Often "mentors" simply exploit "mentees' " ambition—a good source of squat labor, much as a college professor uses grad students to research what he should be doing. For women, the mentoring relationship often carries with it the stigma of sexual innuendo. "Appearance," as the French say, "is everything." Mentoring can also cause peer resentment—teachers' pets are no more desirable in the workplace than the classroom.

Finally, a large minority of "mentees" are fired by their benefactors or quit when expectations each has of the other are not realized. Hitching your wagon to a rising star works fine. But stars have a way of falling as well.

A better approach in using mentors is to "apprentice" yourself to them. Keep what you want and throw away what you don't want in their leadership style. Remember, workplaces are not established so you can work out problems you had with your mother or father. In all events, to conduct a job search on the basis of seeking a mentor rather than a job is a confession of impotence and argues strongly against your sense of self-worth. So, on the job, let other people seek you out as a mentor! But remember, treat them like apprentices.

"How about accepting a job you don't want with an organization in a field, or with a person, you do like?"

This is an effective strategy for people new in the job market, recycling into another field, or returning to the job market after a long hiatus. It's not recommended for those who want to continue to practice their craft in the same line of work, who are in mid-career, or those past the age of thirty-five.

Looking for mentors might be desirable in the young, but suspect in the middle-aged. Taking such a job in mid-career in an entirely different field suggests that you don't know, or don't know how to identify or represent, your transferable skills (for more responsibility and pay in an alternate field). Working at a *hopeless* job for an organization that you love in middle age is not protecting your own self-interest.

"What about working with relatives, in-laws, and close family?"

Not an easy decision.

Many of us are recruited into the family business, it being the line of least resistance. Others irrationally rebel against working for the family firm. What's wanted is a freely formed decision where you treat the family business like any other potential employer.

A first-rate career counselor or even a therapist might help you work it through. My only point is that choosing (or not choosing) to work for your family's firm should be freely willed. And that kind of decision usually can't be made *alone;* seeking the help of an outside professional is recommended.

"Do all employers share some characteristics in common?"

Yes, a few.

They all have hidden jobs and hidden agendas, and find people in the hidden manpower pool. More on this later.

They love to talk about themselves.

They all have problems.

They come in every shape and size. The more you know about what they do, the better chance you have of landing a job.

"Any last words on what you don't do on the job search?"
—Don't try to be *liked* by everyone on your job search or on the job. The most popular people in organizations are generally elevator operators, guys in the traffic department, and jolly ladies in staff services.

—Don't go looking for Big Sister or Mom and Dad on your job search; eschew a family atmosphere. What you want to hear is the hum of the lathe, not a teakettle boiling over.

—Don't expect keys to the executive washroom. Those perks belong to those who were winning their first job when you were playing stickball.

—Don't bring the job search home with you. You won't work effectively nor feel free to have fun. Home is the fun place, not the workplace.

"What are your guidelines about promotion on the job?"
If after nine months on a job you haven't been promoted, something's wrong:

(1) Every year you should receive a cost-of-living increment.

(2) You should be generously compensated if *you* bring in new business or responsibilities to an organization, or if you manage what you do so well that organizational capability is augmented.

(3) Again, get yourself together and define what to do *next*. You are a better judge of your own capability than your boss is.

(4) Think twice if offered a raise. Does someone else deserve it more? Push to have him or her promoted; that's putting the organization and your own feelings *first* and winning a helluva ally.

(5) So if promoted, ask yourself, "Do I deserve it?" Justice is important—as important as your ego. So spread it around, like money and manure. A lot of justice makes living things grow. Namely, human beings.

TWO

Will and Work

Okay.

Let's look at some ways job seekers identify talent and use this information to hire an employer.

The best exercise, whether you're a Rhodes Scholar or a high-school dropout, is to list those positive activities that turned you on to yourself, where you impressed yourself, and felt 100 percent *effective.* Did you feel a sense of self-expression and self-fulfillment? And did these events give you self-confidence? The job search, keep in mind, is something we do for the *self.* Believing you have something to contribute to an employer and feeling good about revealing it is essential in appearing qualified both on paper and in person.

Take five nonconsecutive hours to accomplish this exercise. Don't write a long-winded explanation of what these accomplishments mean; a sentence or two is all that's necessary. And don't list simply events that impressed *other* people. Make sure you list accomplishments that came *easily,* but don't hesitate to describe activities where you overcame frustration and difficulty and were equal to a challenge. Finally, don't worry about a strict chronology: What happened at age eight is as significant as what was accomplished yesterday.

Randomly, what follows are some achievements I recall from talking with hundreds of people I've worked with who were changing jobs or careers. (Parenthetically, I've noted the jobs they eventually took and the relationship between what they *did* and what they are now *doing.)*

——Collected postage stamps from an early age and became a recognized philatelist by my mid-teens. (Told to me by an unhappy life-insurance salesman who now insures postage-stamp collections worldwide for a large international insurance company.)

——Cared for stray cats and dogs all my life. (Told to me by an unwed mother and school dropout who found work as an animal attendant with a veternarian.)

——Conceived and wrote a well-received paper on the origins of the First Bulgar War, cited by my professor as the best term paper he had ever graded. (Told to me by a graduate student now the chief foreign affairs assistant to a senator on the Foreign Relations Committee.)

——Managed the campaign of a shy girl in our school for the office of school secretary——she won the election. (Told to me by a political consultant for three successful candidates for public office.)

——Completed the income-tax forms for my father's landscape-design business. (Told to me by a Ph.D. political scientist who later became treasurer of a major corporation.)

——Failed every college course except art, where I received the highest grade in the history of the school. (Told to me by the director of a major American art gallery.)

Now, the point is to start a list. Tell yourself what the consequences of an achievement were——a promotion, recognition, winning over adversity? Note, too, that achievements are not necessarily accomplished on the job; flair, talent, ability are exercised usually when and where there's opportunity. Your ability is ubiquitous and flows naturally. And, I repeat, don't think accomplishments must always be *difficult.* Some events come so easily we don't associate them with *work,* which we have been trained to believe is always tedious, difficult, and frustrating.

Somewhere, in the back of the room, someone's saying, "Yeah, but what about my weaknesses?" But of course, by listing our disappointments, misfires, incompetencies, and plain old-fashioned ineptitudes, all of us would be writing *forever.* Everybody alive can't do millions of activities: downhill skiing, analyzing a financial statement, writing a complex report. Forget what you *can't* do and focus on what you *can* do!

Having talked to hundreds of people about jobs, I am struck by the importance of feelings of *achievement* as *the* factor in assessing relative job satisfaction. It makes absolutely no sense to study weaknesses except as they are the reverse side of your strengths. Nobody hires you because you can't learn the new math or jump rope or were disciplined for not rising for reveille in the Army. If you have real weaknesses, the chances are good that you have recognizable strengths. You drove a Maserati convertible nonstop across Utah's salt flats for twenty-four hours, performed as an operations clerk for a dump-truck company in the Army, and worked through college as a taxi dispatcher. Chances are you should work in the transport field.

Rather, make a list of what you've done *right*.

How do you learn to know yourself? Simple.

Take pencil and paper, take the phone off the hook, turn off the TV, and warn everyone in your household to stay away. Go back as far as memory allows and list every accomplishment, achievement, contribution that made you feel proud deep down in your tummy. Spare yourself not—no matter how modest or otherworldly, everything listed may have relevance to the job you *want*.

Study each accomplishment—i.e., that positive activity that gave you a sense of self-fulfillment—and give this experience a name. At this point, take a pair of scissors, cut out each accomplishment, and stuff it in an envelope marked "Management" or "Mediation" or "Agricultural"—categories of skills are as infinite as your accomplishments. Now examine the contents of, say, the "Agricultural" envelope and rethink whether the skills are strictly "Agricultural" or, rather, "Agricultural Planning."

If you can identify and name fifty accomplishments or more, you'll establish five or more generic skills. The point is to clarify your skills, asking yourself again what you call them.

Now you have the raw material for a résumé. Think through each category, mesh it with more appropriate categories, and establish no more than five (no fewer than two) distinct generic skill areas. Review your work by category and discard every accomplishment (or category) that does not, repeat *not*, support what you *want* to do. Plenty of people's strengths are weaknesses if they don't support the job they want. Singing in your college choir is a strength if you want to be a performing arts manager and unimportant if you are trying to qualify for a geological expedition to Patagonia.

Now you have two to five generic categories and from three to fifteen accomplishments within each category. Establish which category is most important in your being considered for the job you want (and which is least important). Rank the other categories in between. Whether or not you know it (and you won't), yours is the guts of an extremely effective written presentation.

Human activity in the world of work is broken down into the following: data, things, people, money, and nature. Of the five categories, where do your skills lie?

Answer that question inductively. That is, beginning with a list of your accomplishments, giving them a name, segregating accomplishments by genre, ordering each category in accordance with how it supports jobs you want—having done all of this work—it's duck soup figuring out where your talent lies. And it's foolhardy to think about jobs outside your abilities, no matter how romantic or well paid or highly regarded they are. (My secret fantasy is to be a fireball relief pitcher for the Philadelphia Phillies. The reason I keep it a secret is that Tug McGraw has already fulfilled my ambition, I squint at distances over fifty feet, and my fastball has three speeds: slow, slower, and slowest.)

There's a big difference between dreams and fantasies. Constructive dreaming precedes every self-managed job search; it helps thinking through intermediate and long-term goals. Fantasies, however, are childish speculations. Dreams, if rooted in reality, are important; fantasy, which is out of touch with reality, is often destructive. The question becomes, therefore, "What is reality?" And since much of reality is what you're feeling about yourself, separating constructive dreams from destructive fantasies is a first order of business.

Now, these are just examples. And selection is editorializing. By no means do all accomplishments exactly relate to the jobs you want. But the habit of analyzing your past in positive terms—seeing where you've been a potent human being—is the secret to understanding who you are and what you do well.

Let's look at a sample list of a young man and see if we can figure out what his accomplishments "mean."

ACCOMPLISHMENT EXERCISE

Learned to operate a letterpress and in a short period produced three beautiful poetry broadsides; presented my own poems, one a German poem and my translation of it.

My doctoral dissertation deals with four major European novelists and two important theorists in psychoanalysis and anthropology; it was enthusiastically praised by my readers as "one of the finest I've seen in years," as one "that should be published soon," and as "fascinating, very impressive" by René Girard, one of the most influential critics in the field in which I was working.

Learned to sail easily and quickly; I was particularly good at delicate docking and landing maneuvers in a small boat.

Several times while living in Germany, people I met mistook me for a native speaker of the language; the first time this occurred, my acquaintance with the language was all of six months old.

Drove with a friend from Princeton, New Jersey, to Los Angeles in three days, in December, in an old Dodge Dart.

Participated in an open poetry reading in a coffeehouse in Seattle at a time when I had been writing poems for three or four weeks; an accomplished local poet who has since become a good friend told me my reading was good.

Got a job in one of the best bookstores in Berkeley, California, and won the respect of the very seasoned, shrewd, nonconformist staff and regular customers.

Learned an Eric Clapton guitar solo by ear from a record.

I've read and understood the work of Jacques Lacan.

Spent a winter on a small island off of Kodiak, Alaska, working in a small, family-run fish-packing business.

Taught myself how to paint with watercolors; did several fine landscapes of the northern California coast.

Received the grade of "1" (highest grade) in the philosophy class of the German gymnasium I attended.

Achieved a high degree of mastery of the French language in a short period of time, working mainly on my own.

With two friends I climbed Mount Stuart in the northern Cascades in Washington; judging the descent of the same face to be too difficult, we hiked and climbed for twelve hours to get back to our base camp.

After submitting a translation sample, I was selected as co-translator of René Girard's *Des Choses Cachées Depuis la Fondation du Monde*

Was a good dramatic actor in junior and senior high school, and played major roles in *Mame*, *Dial M for Murder*, and *The American Dream*.

Acted swiftly and decisively in a potentially dangerous situation: While sailing on Tomales Bay in fresh wind and whitecaps, the tiller snapped; I got the sails down quickly, reassured two inexperienced friends on board, and when the outboard motor wouldn't start, paddled toward shore until someone came out to tow us.

Wrote a twenty-page paper on E.T.A. Hoffmann that was praised by my professor, who himself had written on Hoffmann, as "one of the finest pieces I've seen."

Conceived and co-taught a senior-directed seminar, "Literature and Psychology," at the University of California at Santa Cruz.

Gathered friends together for an all-night reading of Frank Stanford's epic poem *The Battlefield Where the Moon Says I Love You*.

While living in Germany and attending a gymnasium, I enrolled in and successfully completed a course at a major German university in the area.

At the invitation of my former thesis adviser, I conducted two successful colloquia (one on Kafka, one on Thomas Mann) in graduate seminars at Princeton University.

As a high school student, I conceived and co-wrote an environmental handbook for our community.

After a trial reading for my wife of a paper written to present at the 1985 Modern Language Association convention, I decided the paper had serious flaws and rewrote a much improved version in one night.

Okay. Let's reorganize these accomplishments functionally, forgetting chronology, and write them up as they might appear in a first-draft résumé. Clearly, this individual has demonstrated *public presentation, linguistic, analytical,* and *self-management* skills. We sense he is sensitive, deep, responsive, and extremely intelligent. So . . .

PUBLIC PRESENTATION:
—Learned to operate a letterpress and in a short period produced three beautiful poetry broadsides; presented my own poems, one a German poem and my translation of it.
—Conceived and co-taught a senior-directed seminar, "Literature and Psychology" at the University of California at Santa Cruz.
—Acted effectively as dramatic actor in junior and senior high school, playing major roles in *Mame*, *Dial M for Murder*, and *The American Dream*.

LINGUISTIC:

—Achieved a high degree of mastery in French, both written and oral, working largely on my own and living with a French family. For example, read and understood the complex writings of Jacques Lacan.

—After six months in Germany, was often mistaken for a native in the language.

—My doctoral thesis was praised as "one of the finest . . . in years," "should be published soon," as "fascinating, very impressive" by a well-known French critic.

—After submitting a translation sample, selected as a co-translator of a difficult work by René Girard.

ANAYLTICAL:

—Received the grade of "1" (highest grade) in the philosophy class of a German gymnasium.

—Rewrote a flawed paper overnight, which was well received at the 1985 Modern Language Association convention.

—Wrote a twenty-page paper on E.T.A. Hoffmann, praised by a leading authority on Hoffmann "as one of the finest pieces I've seen."

—as a high-school student, conceived and co-wrote an environmental handbook for our community.

SELF-MANAGEMENT:

—Spent a winter on a small island off Kodiak, Alaska, working in a small, family-run fish-packing business.

—Learned to sail easily, particularly skilled at delicate docking; once when the tiller snapped, got the sails down quickly, reassured two inexperienced friends on board (and when the outboard motor didn't start), paddled to shore for help.

—Learned an Eric Clapton guitar solo by ear from record.

Now, not all of our accomplishments are included in a résumé—only those that support our job goals. So before writing the second draft of a résumé, try winging a tentative, hesitant statement of goals. For example, based on this person's accomplishments it seems he might write:

PROFESSIONAL GOALS

Qualified for a position of major responsibility as an editor, proofreader, bookstore manager, teacher, or writer where demonstrated use can be made of my analytical, public presentation, and communication skills. Fluent speaker and writer in two languages (German and French). Would welcome work in international publishing, curriculum development, textbook and fine-arts publishing, or in highly specialized graphics work. Would also consider work in customer relations for a sailboat builder, working as ship's broker, or in international education. Self-directed but a good team player. Welcome long hours, hard work, and satisfactory compensation.

Well, a mouthful . . . and probably not focused enough, slightly contradictory. But not a bad effort for the second draft. Try to do as well in your drafts. Remember, good writing is a product of clear thinking. And these exercises help you think clearly.

The point of these activities is to compel a definition of those events that made you feel *effective*. Those events predict how well you fit certain jobs, because achievements that fostered confidence are translated into transferable skills that predetermine job objectives.

Employers, of course, say they prefer experienced people when what they mean to hire are able people. The trick, if you have no on-the-job experience, is to establish your *ability*. And if you have both experience and ability, so much the better.

No one reading this book is lacking in ability. But job seekers will continually put themselves down by citing a lack of experience when what they are really telegraphing is an impotent human will.

After this exercise, you're able to represent strengths to potential employers. Remember, however, that a strength for one employer is a weakness for another. You might, for example, feel comfortable and productive working in an analytical capacity, and bomb in a job where you must meet many people face to face—and vice versa.

Knowing what you've done well and quarterbacking your past for real success is the name you'll eventually give your objectives. Once you've thought through this list, expect to feel the first stirrings of ambition.

A second exercise, aimed at putting you in touch with your desires, is projecting forward into time and seeing yourself thirty years from now by writing your obituary. Pretend that we are well into the next century and that you have just expired; the New York *Times* is writing your life history. The obit will be a legit version of events up to the time of your writing it; everything henceforward is what you *want* your occupational and personal life to become. The operative word is *want*. The aim of this exercise is to switch on that old dream mechanism, freeing yourself to imagine the impossible, making yourself aware that in dreams begin responsibilities.

Writing your obituary, as if this were the year 2030, is a way of seeing yourself the way you would want the world to remember you. And it's an exercise in reviving those grand goals and glorious prospects that made adolescence worth the rites of passage.

For middle-aging and elderly people, writing one's obituary is a way to recover the confidence of youth, ignorance, and innocence. It makes you want to *dare* the gods and furies and reveals, as nothing else can, a job hunter's hidden agenda.

For many, it's a difficult exercise; we can't face the prospect of our own demise. However, for rich imaginations stimulated to think deeply about the future, this exercise exposes your dreams . . . and wishes are the fathers of deeds. The problem, of course, is that our wildest dreams often come true (with apologies to Oscar Wilde). That's a subject for another book.

What follows is a sample obit. It seems wild and woolly and won't correspond to what you'll write, but note how this young man projects the future on a screen, writes a lifetime scenario.

KUALA LUMPUR, MALAYSIA. UPI

The remains of L. Roscoe Milestone were found early yesterday morning by local tribesmen in the jungle highlands of western Malaysia. Missing and feared dead for the last three weeks, he was found, say preliminary reports, sitting with his back against a bo tree; there were no signs of foul play or attack by an animal.

Though an autopsy will be performed tomorrow, it is thought that a lifetime heart condition was the cause of his death. When asked why he was alone so far from civilization at the time of his death, his wife answered that "he every so often felt the need for complete solitude, away from all people for a few days." She also added that some twelve years earlier he had hiked the particular trail upon which he was found.

Born and educated in the United States, a graduate of Harvard and Johns Hopkins, Milestone worked alternatively in private business and government. His last job with a major firm was as the Far East director for the T.I. & I. Corporation, which he left in 1996 when he formed, with three other men, an investment consulting firm. From this point on he was primarily involved in work as an intermediary between large U.S. corporations and the government-owned national corporations of many of the countries of East and Southeast Asia. He had been with this firm, which has grown only modestly since that time, from its inception, though leaving it for substantial periods of time on three separate occasions. The first of these was in 1996–97 when he started as a special adviser to and observer for and was later appointed vice-chairman of the U.S. delegation to Tientsin, the company which negotiated the compensation to be paid to U.S. firms for properties expropriated during the previous year's occupation of Taiwan by the People's Republic of China. Later he was to serve for two and a half years as the U.S. ambassador to the then newly formed United Federation of Malaysian States, leaving that post with the change of administrations in 2009. Finally he took a fourteen-month leave in 2012–13 to live and study in a Japanese monastery. He was one of five Westerners who remained in Rangoon throughout the fall of the capital and the installation of the present regime, and it is reported that his friendship with the current prime minister, who was then one of the leaders of the revolution, may have helped in stopping the indiscriminate killing of foreigners immediately after the fall of the city.

Despite his lack of a Ph.D., his name was known among scholars in the field of comparative theology. Two small works on the Taoistic influences on Chan Buddhism and on Zazen meditation have been well received within the discipline, as have his translations of Theravadic liturgical texts. He is best known for his writing in this country, however, for the three volumes of Yuan and Sung dynasty poetry he compiled and translated and the two slim volumes of his own poetry published under the pen name Larry R. Hayward. The second of his own books, *Rites of Passage,* received the Wendall Prize for Poetry in 1999, and pieces of both his own work and his translations have appeared regularly in anthologies over the last quarter of a century. Mr. Milestone is survived by his wife Wyoma Lou and two children. In accordance with his wishes, he will be buried Friday in an unmarked grave, upon which a sapling plum tree will be planted.

What you don't know because you don't know him, is that Roscoe conducted his job search not in this country but in Hong Kong, and, yes, got three job offers. At last report he was, in fact, a published poet; no doubt you'll be reading about him.

Sure, no employer is going to hire you for your dreams, for heaven's sake, but when the question "Where do you see yourself in five years?" arises, your answer will be rooted in reality. And your answer is likely to be more plausible, sensible, and impressive than that of the competition who haven't thought through the general outline of their lives. Writing an obit is particularly recommended to those who (a) are futurists, (b) like to write, (c) have situational objectives quite unlike those of their friends, and (d) wish to establish immediate, intermediate, and long-term goals.

Employers, too, like to probe to find out whether your long-term planning fits their organizational goals. If yours do, that's a qualification for employment. And qualifications mean, in the following order:

(1) Motivation: "Does this guy want the job?"

(2) Ability: "Does this person have the talent?"

(3) Experience: "Has this woman ever done anything like this before?"

(4) Training: "Does this person have any training to prove he/ she can do it?"

Qualifying for a job, therefore, means really wanting it, being able to do it, showing that you have done it or have been trained to do it. Few candidates for any job will be able to muster affirmative answers to all four questions. The one question you must say yes to is #1: "Do I want this job?"

It's no surprise, but those who say yes to the last three, usually for excellent reasons, can't say yes to the first. That's because they have accomplished the job—it no longer *tests* them. The job, therefore, is no longer challenging. What's so strange about that?

Developing realistic job goals, sweeping away manifold self-delusions, therefore, requires a hard look at yourself. Here again, putting yourself in the employer's shoes, asking yourself *why* you should be employed, what you offer an employer, is an exercise in realism.

Your worst step forward (and the commonest mistake of the first job search) is *not* defining goals in comprehensible, realistic, and concrete terms. This fact surfaces early in an interview situation. "This guy doesn't know what he wants or what he does. And he wants *me* to give *him* a job?"

Since I've done a fair amount of employing myself, I fancy I can see the *process* whereby one person offers another a job from both vantage points. A central truth of the whole process is that nobody is hired for her weaknesses—it's her strengths, her capacity to make meaningful contributions to an employer that decide whether someone's offered a job.

During the past decade I've also worked for about ten variously remarkable people, men and women, effective and ineffective. The striking characteristic of all employment relationships is that there is no such thing as the *wrong people;* there are only people matched against the *wrong jobs.* And that's fundamentally both the employer's and the employee's responsibility and loss.

Most judgment-job candidates should have three or four job goals. Each goal will relate in terms of function to the next. Not to reveal your goals causes employers to think you don't know what you want. Moreover, revealing what you want causes employers to confess what they need. By being particular, a job seeker frees an employer to be specific. Another reason motivation is central to the employment process.

One happy result of establishing what you want is qualifying for hidden jobs, because an employer has more knowledge about you. Hundreds of judgment-job candidates have told me about finding great jobs that they did *not* define in their résumés but which fit their skills and values, because they took the pains to discover their skills and objectives and let employers describe similar jobs that were also available.

A third activity that helps photograph professional goals is to put yourself in the employer's shoes and imagine him writing a want ad that meets most of your desires. Write three longish help-wanted ads as they might appear in the trade press or the daily newspaper. Pretend that you are a chief executive officer of an organization writing up the requirements for a position. List the qualifications, training/experience, and kinds of personal motivation you are searching for in a candidate. Make sure you write up the essence of what is to be *done* and something about the work environment, salary, etc. Zero in on the special contributions successful candidates must make to the organization, the strengths the employer seeks in job candidates, the flair or talent required for the job.

The aim of this exercise is to focus on the contributions you'll offer to an organization. A secondary objective is to acquaint job seekers with the jargon of job descriptions, taking the words employers use to describe jobs and transmuting these same vocabularies into a description of who you are, what you can do and—above all—what you *want* to do.

Let's look at a young woman—an attorney—who does *not* want to practice law and an example of an imaginary want ad she wrote.

POLICY & PUBLIC EDUCATION

National organization of (governors) (community colleges) (housing advocate groups) (municipalities) (businesswomen) (manpower agencies) (county chairmen) (or whatever) seeks director of education & policy. Requires excellent writer w/public-affairs background. Administrative experience. Develop alternative recommendations for consideration at annual meeting. Based on policies adopted, prepare white papers for distribution, conduct direct lobbying efforts, develop strategies for mounting public pressure on appropr. agencies for needed govt. actions. Develop strategies & materials for public ed. Assist local units in drafting bylaws, statements, proposals. Assist natl. officers w/speeches & documents. Downtown location. $45,000.

Now let's see how she translates this ad into an expression of professional goals.

Welcome a position of major responsibility as a director of education and policy for a national or regional organization of governors, community colleges, housing-advocate groups where my demonstrated report-writing and public-affairs background would be useful. Such a position would require unusual policy, analytical, community outreach, membership development and fund-raising capabilities. Would be especially useful in mounting legitimate-interest lobbying efforts, developing strategies for influencing designated government agencies, and preparing public-education documents, drafting bylaws, and proposals.

Also qualified to work as a speechwriter. Prefer downtown location and a salary in the mid-forties.

Writing your achievement list suggests what you *can* do.

Writing your obituary suggests what you *wish* to do.

Composing three or four job advertisements indicates what's *realistic* to do.

And it's only after spending a goodly amount of time and heart searching that you're ready to interpret what all this homework means.

It's much easier, of course, for those who simply want to change jobs than for those who are changing careers. If you *want* to do what you have already done, great! If I, as an employer, must choose between two people—one who is motivated and able and one who is motivated and experienced—I'll go with the latter every time. But the major point is: All of us are experienced.

Why?

Talent, ability, flair—what we mean by experience—are rooted in childhood. These events are individual accomplishments, experiences that made us feel effective, potent. All of us have too few of these positive activities to be proud of, but nobody has none. If, as a job seeker, you can demonstrate some examples—in the interview and your résumé—of being a self-starter, a decision maker, an entrepreneur, then it's not necessary to *proclaim* it; let your accomplishments speak for themselves. Back off, therefore, from sweeping generalizations about your abilities. For example, how many job applicants are authentic "self-starters," "decision makers," or "problem solvers." Far better to give examples of decision making, problem solving, and innovative accomplishments. Establishing ability is your responsibility to the employer, who will push you, as he should, hard on this point. So if you're experienced and able in a line of work you still love, sell *both!*

The fourth exercise (and the toughest) is to think about work not as labor, which makes for certain job dissatisfaction, but as something *desirable.*

"If I had one million dollars I would . . ."

Write out what you would do if tomorrow you were the recipient of a fat inheritance. Most people work out of a sense of obligation and constraint; far fewer from a sense of joy and desire. If money were no object, what would you do with your life?

As you probably expect, I just happen to have an example lying about.

> If I won the state lottery jackpot for a cool mil, I would:
> —put my unemployed brother-in-law through grad school
> —pay off my mortgage
> —settle two educational trust funds on my children
> —buy a new wardrobe, a Porsche, and waterfront property on the Lake of the Ozarks
> —quit my job
> —invest $500,000 in tax-free municipals
> —Then I would use the remainder of the money in association with two or three other venture capitalists and start a new firm to fund biogenetic research to the end of having a net worth of $100 million by the year 2015. My time would be spent in new-product development and backstopping products and processes that could revolution-

ize medical care worldwide. If successful, I would use half of my earnings to financially backstop talented but impoverished inventors to realize their dreams.

Not bad.

Note that this person isn't going to stop working; she is simply quitting her job to work at what she really wants. What this exercise reveals is a keen interest in biogenetic research. But why does she need a million dollars? Don't ask me; ask her. The idea that we need a million is how we defeat ourselves. What's wanting is not money, but a *will*.

Freedom is a frightening experience. It's why so many people in the flush of retirement collapse psychologically and physically. It's the reason the rich are often more interesting than the poor—they have the means to make or break their lives.

If you can't figure out what you want (now that you no longer need to work), *not to worry;* many people can't. It might take years to free yourself from doing what you *ought*, to doing what you *want*.

Another activity is understanding that a judgment job means working at what touches your emotions. To be 100 percent effective on the job, more than intellect is required. No one is truly potent until he does what engages the emotions. The passionate response to jobs is a certain satisfier—the whole person is engaged.

The aim of the next exercise is to list those things that stir your emotions. This exercise identifies a passionate *caring*, so obviously absent in the psyches of most job holders.

For example:

TEN THINGS THAT ANGER ME AT WORK

(1) Career types treading water on my time.
(2) Addicted smokers.
(3) Minimum-productivity time-clock watchers.
(4) Women being treated as secretaries.
(5) Wishy-washy decisions or decision makers.
(6) Being too far from the ocean.
(7) Office politicians, gossipers, backstabbers.
(8) Not being able to speak my mind freely without fear of reprisals.

(9) People worried about territory and privacy, secrecy, jealousy.

(10) Fragile people in a competitive environment.

A second exercise that helps establish values in the workplace is "Ten Things I Want in a Job." Let's look at this same person's list.

TEN THINGS I WANT FROM AN EMPLOYER

(1) An open work environment.

(2) To be surrounded by competent and committed people.

(3) A chain of command where access to all active participants is direct and encouraged.

(4) Excellent salary and benefits and the chance to move up quickly on merit.

(5) To report to someone who moves, makes decisions, and wants results.

(6) Authority and responsibility to intervene wherever my skills are appropriate and requested.

(7) To be challenged to perform at all times.

(8) To be evaluated in writing and face to face on a regular basis.

(9) The opportunity to travel but to be based somewhere near the ocean.

(10) To work at an ass-busting pace while on the job, but having time for my family as well.

Now, scan this final version of this individual's "Professional Goals."

Project Management
International Development
Construction Management

Require demanding position as a project manager, chief of party, director of development, program designer/administrator, or director of construction for an internationally oriented project-development group, international construction company, real-estate developer where use can be made of my demonstrated management, technical, and communication skills. An attractive salary and benefits package where performance is rewarded with new responsibilities and mobility is preferred. Particularly qualified by my construction management expertise to direct construction and technical projects, internationally or domestically, from an on-site or U.S. headquarters base. Position should require and welcome a confident, poised, energetic executive comfortable with technical and managerial responsibilities who is results-oriented. Seek the opportunity to travel and use foreign-language skills and extensive overseas experience. Desire an open and aggressive work atmosphere in a coastal location.

And, on the fourth page of his résumé, note this final profile statement. Both his statement of goals and the profile were partially gleaned from his "What Makes Me Angry" and "Ten Things I Want in a Job" exercises, drawing on his emotions and clarifying his values in positive terms.

PROFILE

Sharp, aggressive, open; interested in results and human concerns. Equally at home in corporate pinstripes or work boots and a tool belt, on an ocean-racing yacht or in a cabinet minister's office. Dedicated, communicative, responsive. Works hard and plays to win. Enjoys life most when everybody wins at what they are doing.

Let's suppose your list reads something like this:

WHAT I'M LOOKING FOR IN AN EMPLOYER

(1) An opportunity to work in the transportation field.

(2) A chance to exercise my marketing and analytical skills.

(3) A position leading to major responsibility.

(4) An organization that is growing.

(5) A chance to feel a sense of achievement.

(6) Recognition for outstanding performance.

(7) The companionship of people who love their jobs.

(8) An opportunity to work for a leading authority or expert in the transport field.

(9) Frequent opportunities to work under pressure and/or deadlines.

(10) A salary related to work performance.

(11) An ethical work environment.

(12) A chance to travel some of the time.

All that's needed is the necessary follow-through, writing a definition of what's wanted and making it part of your "Professional Goals."

For example, scan the list and read how it might appear in a résumé.

> Welcome position at a professional entrance level leading to major responsibility as a marketing-research trainee, salesman, or analyst with a growth organization in the transport field (e.g., airline, transportation consulting firm or government regulatory body). Qualified to work in any marketing arena that can utilize my demonstrated public speaking, marketing, and analytical skills. Value an occupational environment where recognition is extended for work well done under expert leadership. Am especially productive under deadline conditions and work optimally where pay is related to performance. Especially desire ethical and productive work environment among professionals who like their jobs.

Utopian?

Not in the least.

Note how many characteristics surface as part of your goals, how pronouncedly focused you seem, how discriminating you are in sizing up what you *want.* Any employer would say, "This guy knows what he wants!" And that doesn't happen enough in the world of work. Employers, remember, often complain that job seekers don't seem to have a mind of their own.

A sixth exercise is writing a biography of someone you admire. Write three one-paragraph biographies that suggest why you are like that person. No one really knows why we learn *this* and can't learn *that.* But if we imitate those whom we admire, chances are we'll be like that someone, someday.

Another way to get inside your own head and connect to what's out there is to interview five admirable working friends to find out their career paths, identifying the key switches, the out-of-work times, the smooth transitions, what they like and dislike in what they do.

A variation on this activity is listing public people, living or dead, you admire.

"Gee, I could be like her, too!"

Everybody is a hero worshiper. And staking out people we

would like to be says to our secret selves that we could be like them. Reading the biographies of celebrated achievers in any walk of life puts you in the shoes of men and women, usually long dead, who continue to mold the future through the dreams of people like yourself.

Still another activity is keeping a file of advertisements, want ads, and news stories. Unconsciously your psyche is self-selecting what interests you. Tearing out and filing every item you find yourself reading identifies products, services, problems, and target populations suggesting certain lines of work.

As part of your general accomplishment list, or as a separate exercise, focus on every job you had—paid and unpaid, no matter how disagreeable—and identify one, two, or three aspects of the job you *liked*. Is there a pattern of *likes* that threads itself throughout all your jobs and experiences? What is the genre? What do you call it?

What I really loved as a . . .
—soldier
—student
—teaching instructor
—bartender
—babysitter
—door-to-door salesperson

A part of any job seeker's bedtime reading is the trade press. Outside reading that informs you how people make a living is valuable. Often you stumble across stories that cause star shells to go off, "Hey, that's a business I would love." Well, pick up your duff and go out and talk to the folks who turned you on.

Finally, some people who want to investigate the mainsprings of motivation can skip the previous exercises and simply write out their life story in prose. A close reading by yourself and by intelligent outsiders reveals a wealth of undetected skills and talents.

It's particularly recommended to people in mid-career and those making a radical career jump. Compose your background as if for publication, as an anonymous journalist would for a news-magazine profile. The aim, like listing your accomplishments, is to make participants focus on real events and to show you why, as William Faulkner said, the past is never past, and that the future is now. If all else fails, see a psychiatrist. No kidding. That's why we pay them

$90 an hour. Cheap, if it helps you overcome the resistance to figuring out what you want. And—without wanting to prejudice the verdict—not doing what you want will, ten to one, have a lot to do with Mommy and Daddy. (Old Sigmund Freud had an idea or two.)

THREE

Writing Winning Résumés

"So these exercises are what you mean by putting yourself first?"

That's the toughest chore of all. Focusing on ourselves *first*—knowing what we want—is especially difficult for all of us carefully trained by school, church, and state to put organizational goals before personal objectives. Moreover, this indoctrination is so effective that millions of people are unwilling to separate the two.

"Will these activities help me to choose a graduate school or trade program?"

Sure . . .

It means you build on strengths, skills, accomplishments in choosing a trade or graduate program. The chances of your returning to school for the right reasons are much enhanced. Besides, in completing grad-school applications, describing real accomplishments (rather than glib generalizations) will make your submissions stand out from the pack. So these exercises are the raw material for a whole series of applications, and one protypical application will service, with a few alterations, almost any school.

"How do these exercises differ from aptitude testing?"

These activities are less expensive and measure motivation as well as ability. Moreover, nobody in a long white coat is going to declare, chapter and verse, that your fortune lies in "restaurant management, organizational development, or probate law." It leaves the interpretation to you (and your friends), not to a machine or an expert.

"If these activities help me to decide what to do, will they help me answer any more questions?"

They should reveal answers to the following:

—what level of responsibility you want inside an organization: entrance level, middle level, senior management

—the kind of surroundings you desire: competitive or collaborative

—what consequences you expect from your work: money, recognition, promotions

—what values you bring to the job

—the kind of people you work with best: children, customers, colleagues

—where in this country or abroad you want to work: East Coast, New York City, the Middle East

—the *kind* of organization you want to work for in regard to *your* and *its* objectives: profit, government, independent sector

"What makes us so anxious when we focus on ourselves?"

Anxiety is irrational, fear rational. The fear of a gun at your head is natural and rational. But the anxiety about doing what you want (and the accompanying paralysis) is irrational and disabling. From parents to peers to professors, people discourage us from having minds of our own. Job seeking is an act of will. And the chances are good that the job either exists or can be created. And who's the winner then? But going after what you want often causes anxiety. Focus on *why.*

"How do I know my own mind? How do I know if I have or can have a mind of my own?"

Do the exercises.

A pattern of recognized accomplishments—dreams, treasured experiences, etc.—will surface. This information is an encyclopedia of your skills. In those skills you are expert.

"How do you become an expert?"

Start calling yourself one; we are expert at many things, but hesitate saying so.

People tired of being expert in one field need to stop calling themselves experts in *this* and start calling themselves experts in *that.* Now that you understand that skills are transferable, chances are excellent that you won't hesitate to jump into another line of work. "Education" and "experience" are terrible traps to self-fulfillment if we allow work experience or training solely to program our futures.

That's why, in a résumé, what's revealed are accomplishments that support objectives. And why you want to downgrade experience and training if it doesn't support the job you want. And why you build on both ability *and* experience if you want to continue doing what you have done.

"Yes, but isn't it true that some people with little or no talent succeed?"

Remember what Leo Durocher said about Eddie Stanky, the old Brooklyn Dodger second baseman: "He can't hit, he can't run, he can't field. What he *can* do is beat the hell out of you!"

True, but most people feel most pleasure and are most competent doing something *well.* Straying too far from one's ability is risking disappointment and failure. At the same time, not straying far enough might risk not being considered for judgment jobs. Again, the onus is on you: What do you instinctively feel about a job? Try to quantify and qualify those instincts; gut reactions are great, but we need to rationalize, know the reasons we accept or turn down a job. If you hate exercising authority, are shy of visibility, back off from competitive situations, chances are that those reasons are arguable. If you feel uncomfortable about a new job's responsibilities and more pain than pleasure at the prospect, if you sense that you can't *grow* on the job or will rarely exercise your abilities, well, chances are that you should nicely say no.

"Is talent God-given or acquired?"

Damned if I know.

My hunch is Freudian; we acquire our flair, talent, ability—call it what you will—somewhere in early youth in the family nexus while acting out our parents' desires (or reacting against them). Otherwise, how do you explain the uniformity of success among the Strauss brothers (music), the DiMaggio brothers (baseball), the Kennedy family (politics)?

What I *do* know is that everyone has gifts—hundreds of skills, in fact—that transfer into many lines of work. Often, those who have the most talent are least aware of it.

A clinical reason for success, both in the job search and on the job, has to do with either our mother (if we are a boy) or with our father (if we are a girl). A woman who was the pride of her father's life, his confidante in business, and his glory at home is a candidate for success. The same with little brother who was the apple of his mother's eye. The biographical evidence of this is overwhelming.

For most of us who had simply good enough parents, the business of being successful is acquired. It won't come naturally. Guilt, depression, despair, and lower back pain are to be expected. It takes time to unlearn certain patterns of conduct induced in childhood and adolescence. Buying a new attitude about ourselves isn't like purchasing a new wardrobe.

It might mean unscrambling mixed messages sent by Mom and Dad: "Be successful (but don't show me up);" "I need you (but don't help me);" "I love you (but you look terrible in that dress)." Years of these signals leave children with a fairly gloomy view of the world and of themselves. It takes time to repair the damage, and the scars often remain for life.

"Why is writing my professional objectives so difficult?"

Most people wrestle with what it is they want to do. Describing what we want is the central problem in the job search, marriage, life itself. *It should be difficult.* Think about doing the body of your résumé first—i.e., establishing skills and accomplishments—then working on values and interests, doing everything but writing out job goals.

Finally, take pen in hand and sketch two or three goals. Since nobody is absolutely certain of what he wants, don't put yourself down if you alter your job goals well into the job campaign. What's happening is that the job search is changing what you want to do based upon "what's out there."

Again reveal what your will is in precise terms: no windy statements about a "challenging job in upper management working with creative executives to maximize profits." Employers properly choke on such pap. Better, "Welcome long hours, hard work, and good pay as a mass-pectometrist with a Beltway consulting firm to the pharmaceutical and hospital supply industry. Also would consider . . ."

"What's an example of how to represent grunt employment in your résumé?"

As a manager of a twenty-four-hour-a-day 7-Eleven in a university community was responsible for the inspection, delivery, acceptance, and payment of all deliveries; dealt with vendors, hired and fired cashiers and clerks, oversaw cashier's accounts for each shift; resolved customer complaints and did weekly inventory and price checking; responsible for opening up and closing and making accurate accounting entries. Regional supervisor complimented me on managing the tightest-managed store in his territory. Financed 100 percent of my education with earnings.

"How about some examples of winning résumés?"

And that means looking at real people, both like and unlike you. Let's see how they shape their backgrounds, putting that best foot forward, to qualify for the jobs they wanted. Keep in mind, all of these people accomplished the self-assessment exercises described in the previous chapter; the résumé didn't print itself—some gut-wrenching effort was involved. First, the résumé of a middle-aging homemaker, an Oil of Olay type, without a college degree but scads of "volunteer" experience (by the way, never describe work strictly as voluntary; forget you weren't paid to do what you did and focus on what you accomplished).

Mary Anne White
1919 Elm Street
Newfield, Indiana 45678
Telephone: 555-4567

VOCATIONAL OBJECTIVES

Customer-relations manager or administrative assistant. Qualified for a position that requires communication and management skills.

SUMMARY OF BACKGROUND

Attended Indiana University and studied business administration in night classes, specializing in business application of computer science. (1)

Worked for three years as secretary to manager of sales division, XYZ Company. Was promoted to administrative assistant, and coordinated schedules and data flow for forty-five salespeople. Left to raise two children. During last ten years, coordinated annual United Fund drive in my neighborhood. (2)

MANAGEMENT SKILLS

Organized ninety volunteer fund-raisers into statewide task force for United Fund's Golden Anniversary drive, which raised $375,000 and exceeded any previous year's contribution by 20 percent. As member of day-care center board, helped revamp federal funding guidelines, increased community participation on board, and headed search committee that hired new director. Revamped salesman husband's chaotic filing system so that part-time and temporary employees could understand it, and oversaw installation of microcomputer in his office. (3)

MONEY-MANAGEMENT SKILLS

Have consistently managed a tight family budget so that we annually save 10 percent of our income. When I received a small inheritance, I studied investing and invested it for a 20 percent annual return. To raise money for son's class trip, devised scheme whereby all class parents agreed to collect money-back supermarket coupons; raised the necessary $500 in two months. (4)

COMPETITIVE AND TEAM SKILLS

An avid athletic participant, I've finished among first twenty women runners in local marathon for past five years. Organized a bridge club of players who love the game for its analytical qualities and am usually top scorer out of eight players. Sing in church choir for pleasure of the music and collaborative effort. (5)

NOTES:

(1) She went to college for only one semester, but who cares? If anybody does, they can check.

(2) At forty-two, she's had only three years of salaried employment, but by focusing on her achievements in that job and in volunteer work, she presents herself as competent and productive.

(3) Though her interest in computers was largely motivated by a need to assist her husband in his business, she wisely recognizes that any skill she's picked up may be marketable.

(4) Any initiative that leads to concrete results is of interest to smart employers. It doesn't have to involve millions of dollars.

(5) Even the things you do for pleasure teach certain skills.

Turn bad news into good. Everybody has had disappointments in work. If you mention yours, look for the positive side. A woman who lost her job as a teacher's aide due to a cutback in government funding wrote:

> Principal of elementary school cited me as the only teacher's aide she would rehire if government funds became available. Feel most effective in organizations that recognize my dependability and initiative on the job.

Never apologize. If you're returning to the work force after fifteen years as a parent, simply write a short paragraph (summary of background) in place of a chronology of experience. Don't apologize for working at being a mother: It's the hardest job of all. Simply stress in the heart of your résumé any accomplishments that support the job you want. No need to write that the work was unpaid. If you have no special training or higher education, don't mention it.

The main purpose of a résumé is to generate interviews. Most résumés are the familiar tombstone type that list schooling and where you've worked in chronological order. The second kind is functional—topical, fun to read, unique to you, and much more likely to land you an interview.

It's handy to have a tombstone résumé for certain occasions—for example, if you get an interview through a personal contact and that person wants a background statement. But prospective employers don't read obit résumés, preferring to interview the quick rather than the dead.

What follows are tips on writing a résumé that will get read—a résumé that makes you come alive to employers. Each résumé should be as different as your thumbprint.

Put yourself first. A woman once told me about a cash-flow crisis her employer faced. She'd agreed to work without pay for three months until business improved. Her reward was her back pay plus a 20 percent bonus. Asked why that marvelous story wasn't in her résumé, she answered, "It wasn't important."

What she was saying, of course, was "I'm not important." In order to write a résumé others read with enthusiasm, first feel important about yourself.

Traditional housewives often enter the job market because the family needs the income. Often they are underpaid because what they make is "pin money" whereas their husbands earn a "salary." Some traditional housewives returning to the job market are poor negotiators in obtaining the money they deserve. So homemakers returning to the work force need to put themselves first and focus on what they want. True, it might be necessary to accept a grunt job earning the cash to finance the search for the job you want, not to mention the grocery bills that need to be paid. But the point is to keep your eye on the ball (the self) and use a stop-loss job (stopping the loss of income) as a base to find a job you do *so* want.

Sell what you can do, not who you are. Practice translating personality, character, and accomplishments into skill areas. There are at least five thousand skill areas in the world of work. For example, if you've a flair for saving, managing, and investing money, yours is a money-management skill; if you've shown yourself to be effective at designing curricula or developing church and school programs or raising money, you have (among others) program-development, problem-solving, and conference-management skills.

Toot your own horn. Many people choke when asked to think about their abilities. Some think they have none at all. But everybody does, and one of yours may be just the ticket an employer would be glad to punch—if only you show it.

A shy woman convinced a colleague to apologize to his boss for misconduct on the job. She quit hiding her conflict-resolution skills under a basket. After a few drafts she wrote this paragraph:

> Counseled alcoholic employee and persuaded him to apologize to employer and join AA. He then devised several proposals that improved the bottom line. His boss informed me that had I not mediated the problem, this valuable man would have been fired.

Be specific, be concrete, and be brief! One résumé included the following:

> Invited by my supervisor to straighten out our organization's accounts receivable. Set up orderly repayment schedule, reconciled accounts weekly, and improved cash flow 100 percent. Rewarded with raise and promotion.

Notice how this woman focuses on results ("improved cash flow"), specifies how she accomplished them ("set up orderly repayment schedule"), and mentions her reward—all in thirty-four words!

"How do employers read a résumé?"

(1) First, employers don't so much *read* résumés as skim them. As in an interview, when the first twenty seconds are vital (appearance in those first seconds is *everything),* so in scanning a résumé: "How does he *look?"* employers ask themselves.

(2) Employers read between the lines; they are as often concerned about what an applicant leaves out as what the job searcher includes. Accordingly, many employers start at the end of the résumé, thinking the most essential information is at its conclusion: indifferent work record, interrupted education, and conjectural personal information.

(3) Employers are increasingly put off by sloppy functional résumés containing no dates of employment. With some honorable exceptions, almost everyone, no matter how contradictory his work experience, should include a chronology of employment on the first or last page of the résumé. Résumés without chronologies often suggest a cover-up.

(4) For profit-oriented employers, showing a bottom-line orientation is important: Demonstrate how you saved money, improved

efficiency, increased sales, or otherwise enhanced efficiency. This qualifies you for market-oriented organizations.

(5) Hobbies, interests, values, and special-situation experiences are best incorporated so as to project an "accomplished personality"—not a dilettante. Include nonoccupational information as an organic part of your résumé; don't necessarily separate out this information from the body of the résumé.

Revealing human-interest examples that don't directly support job goals makes sense. For example, a young man looking for his first professional job without significant work experience did a first-rate functional résumé aimed at industrial consulting. After praising his résumé, I scanned his accomplishment list to make certain no significant accomplishments had fallen through the cracks. Number seventeen on his list simply said "rowing."

"Tell me about it," I said. And what he told about was crewing at Harvard, captaining the team, winning the intercollegiate championship, and then competing against Oxford and Cambridge. Well, after some persuasion on my part, this stellar job candidate composed three lines, and subsumed them under "Leadership" in his résumé. Guess what? On an interview, at the Arthur D. Little Co., his first interviewer was the crew captain of the 1948 Harvard crew. And guess again who had himself a job offer?

(6) Résumés that contain qualifiers such as "knowledge of . . ." or "exposure to . . ." or "hands-on experience in . . ." suggest résumé enhancement easily spotted by sharp employers. Focus on accomplishments and, if consistent with job goals, experience; lay off the wax and polish.

(7) Education: Employers are suspicious of lengthy educational statements and seminars attended. A solid educational background statement—and no more—is what's wanted. If you don't have it, don't include it.

(8) No sour grapes: Any suggestion that past employment experiences have been unsatisfactory is unacceptable. Since no one reading this book hasn't at least one unsatisfactory employment episode, the least you can do is shut up.

(9) A sloppy résumé doth a bad impression make. Every résumé —no matter how short and targeted—should go through four drafts, an editorial review by an outsider, and thorough vetting by a graphic arts expert, printer, or layout artist.

(10) Employers will read favorably more into a résumé than is actually there if its appearance, content, and cohesiveness add up to more than the sum of the parts. Show a logical consistency between your objectives, abilities, experience, and education and a neat dovetailing of interests and values to project the kind of person you are.

(11) Any employer is deeply interested in someone who loves to work hard. The plain facts are that executive productivity has been in a free-fall since circa 1968. Another reason hard workers get the job and not the laid-back competition.

(12) Go to a stationer or printer and look over some stationery samples. Order 500 or more sheets of 8½" × 11" plain, professional-looking stationery with your name, address, area code, and telephone number centered at the top of the page.

Order an equal number of matching blank sheets for second pages of letters and for résumés. Matching #10 envelopes with your name and address on the upper left-hand corner make an effective impression. Off-white, light blue or gray paper is professional-looking, and ecru or light cream-colored paper is also acceptable. Other colors are silly for job hunting. Choose a quality of paper that feels good when you hold it, nothing cheap, heavy, or fancy.

(13) Be stingy using adjectives, especially describing skills and values. Strong explicit nouns and verbs rarely need a string of adjectives or adverbs. "Analyzed" leaves a vivid image in the employer's mind. "Documented analytically difficult policy papers" clouds that picture and is redundant. And keep the résumé in the active voice; use action verbs: "advocated," "briefed," "catalogued," "drafted," "estimated." Effective résumé writing punches the reader—it aims to grab his attention, not somatize him.

(14) The layout should be simple—no gimmickry, binders, fancy folds.

Don't date your résumé; thus, it won't "date."

Avoid using "etc."; it's implicit that you did more than you wrote.

Don't give reasons for leaving a job; be prepared, however, to make explanations at the interview.

Mention military affiliation, fraternal, religious, or political organizations only if such associations support job goals.

Forget height, weight, and Social Security number; always redundant and sometimes adversely assessed.

Be wary of using acronyms: "OMB" . . . "NATO" . . . "FTC." Always spell out, in toto, "Office of Management and Budget" . . . "North Atlantic Treaty Organization" . . . "Federal Trade Commission" . . . and thereafter revert to the shorthand acronym.

Another delicate matter: Unpronounceable first and last names cause employers to back off otherwise enterprising job candidates. Some second-generation Americans have anglicized and legally changed their names, shortening and phonetically improving on the pronunciation. For those of you with difficult-to-remember or -pronounce first names, think about using nicknames (even in your résumé). Some job searchers, in parens, give the reader a clue on how to pronounce names, e.g., Richard Irish (Eye-reesh).

"How do you represent campus volunteer jobs?"

A lot are filled by insecure students anxious to pad their résumé with important associations. Employers are suspicious of this kind of window dressing. The best way to represent such activities, when meaningful, is to focus on your major accomplishment, say, with the debate team and represent under "Public Presentation Skills":

> Joined university forensic society as freshman and successfully reached first string by my junior year; honored by being elected vice-president of the club in my senior year; participated in annual collegiate debate competition at Georgetown University and captained successful defense of the proposition "Fair Trade, Not Free Trade."

"Surely you don't need a résumé to get volunteer jobs do you?"

It can help . . . especially focusing on why and what you want to do volunteering. A targeted résumé is preferred. For example:

PROFESSIONAL GOALS

As a newly graduated liberal-arts major, seek exposure in a top-of-the-line campaign consulting firm working on issues development, phone bank management, canvassing, and telesurveying. Some experience in telemarketing for college annual giving campaign (personally responsible for contacting three hundred alums who gave in excess of $500,000). Welcome long hours, hard work, and tough assignments. Dependent on my performance and business activity would wish to discuss (after a few months' volunteer experience) a salaried entrance-level assignment.

The idea is to let employers know why you want to volunteer, what you want to do, and what the employer can expect of you. Some volunteers with a bad case of the vague-ies make a poor impression on employers (and give volunteerism a bad name) by showing up at the workplace door with nothing much in mind except to come in out of the cold.

"But I've read that résumés don't get people jobs."
Plenty of people ignore résumés altogether.
But these job searchers know what they want, know how to cold-turkey interviews, have a knack of connecting with people, sense that jobs are hidden and become part of the hidden manpower pool. A résumé for these folks is a waste of time.

But résumés are still valid. A first-rate functional résumé, a product of three weeks' work and four drafts, disciplines people to answer three questions: (1) Who am I? (2) What do I do well? (3) What do I want? Developing a résumé answers those questions. And the document serves, with some alteration, the remainder of your occupational life. Moreover, effective résumés generate more interviews. Interviews produce more employers to interview. And employers produce job offers.

"What about résumé-writing services?"
Which cost $50 to $250. And every employer senses when a boiler shop puts its impress on you. A résumé is a personal reflection, a self-portrait. Hiring a stranger to write up your biography guarantees a loss of personality and is a confession of impotence.

So eschew résumé-writing services, résumé books, and form résumés. Play with the functional formula to mesh form and content. And never compare yours with other résumés (especially those reprinted in this book). Try to make your functional résumé at least as different as you are from every other job seeker.

"So don't use the one-page description of background they told me to use in college?"

Certainly not off campus.

A résumé is valuable for two reasons: (1) It makes you focus on who you are, and (2) an excellent résumé generates interviews and opens doors to judgment jobs that an obit résumé never does.

"What's an example of a descriptive (or traditional) résumé?"

This kind of résumé is used by 50 percent of the people looking for jobs, and for all I know, is a product of the Eisenhower years when Ike wanted everything said "on one page." What follows is what one job seeker used for her on-campus interviews.

Janet Ruth Martin
3766 Spring Drive
Summit, New Jersey 32260
Telephone: (576) 555-2316

VOCATIONAL GOAL

I enjoy working in a situation where I can be of assistance to the general public. I like the atmosphere of a busy office and am capable of making visitors feel welcome and assured that they will be helped in every way.

PERSONAL

Born: November 20, 1963   Health: Excellent
Marital Status: Single   Weight: 118

EXPERIENCE

Summers of 1981 and 1982

I worked in my father's automobile dealership. I helped out in the bookkeeping office, greeted customers, and did inventories in the parts department.

September 1982 to May 1983

I worked part-time at St. Bonaventure University as a language-lab assistant. My duties were to monitor the students, hand out language tapes, and help out in any way needed.

September 1983 to May 1984

I worked part-time as a shift manager for a student-operated grocery store. My duties included supervising the cashiers, stocking shelves, keeping track of change, and dealing with customer complaints.

Summer of 1984

I worked as a front-desk clerk for Ramada Inn. I was responsible for checking in customers, writing up reservations, operating the switchboard and reservations computer, and some filing.

EDUCATION

Georgetown University, Washington, D.C., School of Foreign Service.
    B.S.F.S. in U.S. history and diplomacy.
St. Bonaventure University, Olean, New York. Fall of 1981 to spring
    of 1983. President of Women's Council, member of Campus
    Dorm Council.

HOBBIES AND INTERESTS

Flying, basketball, tennis, golf, cooking.

Let's look at an effective functional résumé. Same gal, same background, this time for her real job campaign.

Janet Ruth Martin
3766 Spring Drive
Summit, New Jersey 32260
Telephone: (576) 555-2316

VOCATIONAL GOAL

Customer-relations manager, administrative assistant, or constituent liaison representative. Qualified in a position where use can be made of communication and management skills, and special abilities in effective organization and coordination.

SUMMARY OF BACKGROUND

Graduate of Georgetown University; spent first two years of undergraduate study at St. Bonaventure University; one summer of intensive study of French at Laval University, Quebec City; worked at the front desk of Ramada Inn, often filling in for the general manager; worked as a manager of the Georgetown Student Corp. grocery store —a position that entailed responsibility for the effective operation of a store servicing hundreds of students a day; research consultant for author; worked in the customer-relations department of a Datsun and Mazda dealership.

SOME AREAS OF EXPERIENCE AND INDICATIONS OF POTENTIAL VALUE

ABILITY TO SOLVE THE PUBLIC'S PROBLEMS AND COMPLAINTS

Evidenced by my work at the front desk of Ramada Inn, first and often only contact the public had with the hotel. Made decisions and acted on all complaints received; helped customers to find alternate lodging when there was no vacancy; responded quickly in all emergencies—electrical fire, extensive flooding from broken water pipes, and quarrels among guests. Evidenced also by my solutions for customer complaints concerning products purchased at the Georgetown Student Corp. grocery store. And by my customer-relations work with customers at Wilson Auto Sales: speaking with potential buyers until a salesman was available, ensuring the comfort of a customer waiting for car service, and handling complaints both in person and over the phone concerning bills.

MANAGEMENT SKILLS

As a manager of the grocery store, was responsible for the inspection, acceptance, and payment involving deliveries; oversaw cashiers' accounting procedures for each shift; price checking and customer satisfaction; apprehension of shoplifters; and the responsibility of making accurate accounting entries and locking up for the day. As student manager of the language lab, was involved in ordering supplies and new machinery, setting up employees' work schedules, hiring and training of lab instructors, and conducting demonstrations.

LEADERSHIP SKILLS

While attending public schools, was elected president of my class for six consecutive years; was selected from among 500 girls to represent my high school in the 1980 New York Girls' State Convention—a weeklong seminar entailing in-depth study of local and state government; also captained three varsity athletic teams my senior year in high school: basketball, volleyball, and track.

COMMUNICATION SKILLS

Demonstrated ability in communications with peoples of diverse foreign backgrounds; while studying in Quebec City, was asked by the visiting Cuban Olympic water polo team to act as their guide during their stay; also aided several French-speaking families in securing accommodations while working at Ramada Inn; proficient in French; possess survival knowledge of Spanish.

ORGANIZING AND COORDINATING SKILLS

Organized the research process for a book about Charles de Gaulle. Coordinated the landscaping of an automobile dealership. Represented my high school at Empire Girls' State, was elected party chairman, and organized caucuses and election campaigns. Coordinated the first fund-raising fashion show for Women's Council involving participation with several local merchants.

INGENUITY AND IMAGINATION

Devised an effective voting system for the Campus Dorm Council, eliminating much time, effort, and wasted meetings. With no previous experience, wrote the commentaries for a fashion show.

COMPETITIVE SPIRIT AND PERSEVERANCE

Am an avid competitor in both athletics and academics. Have won several golf championships; hold two Section III New York State track and field records; have been a member of championship basketball, volleyball, and track teams. Have also competed in several English and journalism contests, winning Daughters of the American Revolution Excellence in History Award.

EDUCATION

B.S. in Foreign Service, 1985, Georgetown University; two years undergraduate study at St. Bonaventure University; one summer's study at Laval University; elected to Pi Delta Phi (National French Honor Society); elected dorm representative; social activities chairman of Women's Council; coordinator of intramural sports program; overall grade-point average on a 4-point scale: 3.2.

PERSONAL DATA

GEOGRAPHICAL PREFERENCE   East Coast
SALARY   Negotiable
BIRTH DATE   11/20/1963
POISE AND APPEARANCE   Have modeled in numerous fashion shows and seasonal collections; have appeared in advertisements in a national magazine.
MARITAL STATUS   Single
DATE OF AVAILABILITY   August 1
HEALTH   Excellent
TRAVEL STATUS   Willing to travel for short periods of time.
Writing samples on request

REFERENCES:

Warren A. Stansberry, Chairman, W&D Enterprises: (713) 555-2605
    1986 Woodthorpe Drive, Elizabeth, New Jersey 55667
Richard K. Irish, V.P., Transcentury Corp. (213) 555-4567
    6464 Wilson St. N.W., Washington, D. C. 23456
Margaret Weller, Director, WBC Inc., (416) 555-5507
    46 Alchester Blvd., Troy, New York 20794

"What about employment history?"

Many employers back off the functional format since some badly advised job seekers omit employment history. With a few exceptions (homemakers returning to the marketplace, academics making the plunge into the "real world," military folk reentering the economy), an employment history—if only in small type—is essential. Otherwise employers think you are covering up three years of playing the ponies at Saratoga.

So list last employers first: dates of employment, job title, organization on one line and MAJOR ACCOMPLISHMENT exactly underneath. Try to pick an accomplishment that best supports your job goals even though it wasn't central to your work as an international credit analyst at Chase. Please don't recite DUTIES AND RESPONSIBILITIES. Boring. Irrelevant. Unreadable. Résumés are marketing documents, not boilerplate job descriptions.

"Can you recap the order in developing a functional format?"

(1) Vital facts: name, address, city, state, Zip and phone number, top center page

(2) Professional goals

(3) Summary of background or employment history

If you have no supportive work history, summarize nonvocational achievements in one hundred words or less and compress into a bare, hard-hitting synopsis.

If you have significant supporting employment, retail (last job first) each job, DATES, ORGANIZATION, JOB TITLE and, if appropriate, SALARY HISTORY.

Immediately underneath each heading write MAJOR ACCOMPLISHMENT on each job. For summertime, squat, and nonsupportive stop-loss jobs, a paragraph at the end of the linear chronology summarizing these jobs makes sense.

(4) Skill areas (with examples)

(5) Education

(6) Personal data: health, geographical preference, travel, date of availability, special licenses, birth date, etc.

(7) References: no more than five, no fewer than three

(8) A personal statement: personal profile. Rewrite job goals

with different words, this time stressing values, philosophy, and what you want from work besides a paycheck.

Don't overlook military service. Did you serve in the Army? Don't say it quite that way. Instead:

> Managed a complement of one thousand men in developing communications system for brigade-wide organization using miniature circuitry, field telephones and radios, light airplanes, and carrier pigeons. Cited by unit commander for managing the best communications system in I Corps.

Don't try to include everything in a résumé; use headlines for each category, set off with plenty of white space, striving for readability, graphic impact, and internal coherence—don't jam up captions, descriptions, and conclusions. Remember, wide margins, double-spaced, headline captions (obit résumés are for the dead), making every word count.

Edit.

Edit again.

Take it to a stranger (you respect).

Remember, strangers are looking at it as an employer will.

Take it to another. Act on their criticism.

Don't show it to friends.

No pride of authorship, please.

Now, look at the final document.

Will this résumé win you interviews?

Mail out a hundred, follow up by phone, and find out.

So far we have reviewed three kinds of résumés: a purely functional résumé of a middle-aging woman with no recent work history, a traditional résumé typical of most college graduates that is satisfactory for on-campus interviews and nothing else, and the same woman's different résumé for an off-campus job campaign.

Now let's have a look at another young person, trained in international economics but without the slightest interest in that field. His real obsession is to be a public-relations flack for a professional athletic team (a big ambition—jocks and the children of athletes are preferred). Note that his biggest problems are (1) overcoming his considerable youth, (2) downplaying advanced degree, (3) playing up motivations and abilities, and (4) getting the interview. Remember, the content of his résumé was gleaned from the exercises previewed in the previous chapter. The final result:

Mortimer Youngblood
3205 E. Jones Avenue
Princeton, Maryland 20785
Telephone: (301) 555-8668

PROFESSIONAL OBJECTIVE

Qualified for a responsible position in athletic/recreation-oriented organization, especially in public/community relations and front-office management. Particularly qualified in communications (promotions, press relations, advertising) and organization (traveling secretary, scheduling, recreational programs). Desire to use strong sports orientation in conjunction with such demonstrated abilities as marketing, public speaking, and innovative approaches to problem solving. Welcome high pressure, long hours. Willing to travel and/or relocate. (1)

SUMMARY OF BACKGROUND

B.A. and M.A. in international relations. President of student government and advertising editor of yearbook in high school. Interests and activities, including volunteer work, focusing on sports.

Extensive background in black culture and history, and in cross-cultural communications. Worked in community for telephone company during summers. Despite specialized background, my education and outside activities have developed flexibility and skills applicable to fulfilling most requirements of a sports PR position. (2)

SKILLS AND INTERESTS OF POTENTIAL VALUE

SPORTS ORIENTATION

Active participant and informed, compulsive spectator of all sports. Accepted as member of sports-oriented fraternity, Phi Gamma Delta, although not a varsity athlete; active participant and organizer of interfraternity league teams. Organized and supervised a sports club for fourth-, fifth-, and sixth-grade boys on volunteer basis; developed educational programs and activities relating to their interests. As volunteer, helped coordinate and conduct recreational activities during summers at church Bible school; also bike hikes for elementary-school students. Have always given the highest priority to sports activities, enabling me to devote myself full-time to a vocation in this field. (3)

Addressed assemblies of up to 2,500 people in both prepared and extemporaneous situations. Conducted meetings for wide spectrum of groups, including both parents and students, at local, county, and state levels. Interaction with other student government groups in seminars, meetings, student exchanges. Direct relationships with business community in soliciting and developing advertisements for yearbook. Effective cross-cultural communication in Europe; while proficient in French, was also able to communicate effectively with people of German, Italian, and Spanish origins. Able to communicate confidently with both large groups and individuals in both business and informal situations. (4)

LEADERSHIP AND ORGANIZATIONAL SKILLS

Elected and appointed to many positions throughout school, such as president and financial secretary of student government. Organized and coordinated schoolwide candy sale grossing approximately $10,000.

Initiated and supervised new orientation format in high school; served on orientation committee at Hopkins. Elected council chairman at Maryland Association of Student Councils workshop. Chosen as school representative to statewide American History conference; sole Hopkins representative to nationwide Naval Academy Foreign Affairs Conference, 1980. As advertising editor, developed national award-winning ad campaign for yearbook, including soliciting, planning, designing, billing, and collecting for ads. Coordinated student housing program for Johns Hopkins summer program in Geneva on extremely limited budget, which taught me to be effective both as a leader organizer and as a participant in varied projects at all levels. (5)

SPECIAL ABILITIES

Work well under intense pressure. Able to meet specific deadlines and work long hours if needed. Met every deadline for yearbook, some with extended hours. Do well in timed examinations.

Able to work with details. In physical sense, built own stereo receiver and carved wooden ship model; drawing ability. Otherwise able to remember and deal with minute details in organizing and executing projects, such as coordinating travel in Europe, both individually and in groups.

Able to work with figures. Financial accounting in student government, church, and personal accounts. Scored 770/800 in SAT math, 34/35 in FSEE quantitative reasoning. Highest grades in class in advanced math, probability and statistics in graduate school. Designed own scorecards and kept score of every All-

Star baseball game during childhood, and every other game attended. (6)

EDUCATION

Accepted for five-year B.A.-M.A. program at the Johns Hopkins University, leading to M.A. from School of Advanced International Studies in 1983. Included summer of 1980 of study and independent travel in Europe. Full fellowship at SAIS; B.A.-M.A. and Maryland Senatorial Scholarships at Hopkins. Many scholastic awards, including National Honor Society (1976) and National Merit Scholarship letter of commendation (1977).

PERSONAL DATA

Born August 9, 1959; single; excellent health. (7)

WORK EXPERIENCE

Summers of 1978, 1979, and 1981, worked for telephone company as frameman and installer repairman.

Volunteer work at Wilchester Elementary School as organizer/leader of sports club, 1982.

Part-time work selling art supplies at Woodward and Lothrop, winter of 1982-83.

REFERENCES AND WRITING SAMPLES ON REQUEST (8)

NOTES:

(1) His objectives are sufficiently precise and run a gamut so that an employer has a "feel" for his abilities and what he wants. He sums up his "demonstrated abilities"—marketing, public speaking, and problem solving—all of which he proves in the body of his résumé. Note, too, his willingness to work hard. Not a bad qualification for any judgment job.

(2) Yes, he does mention his education and degrees, but only once and does *not* elaborate. In a word, what he leaves out of his résumé or barely mentions is as important as what he includes. Finally (and in the entirety of the résumé), he stresses his cross-cultural skills; preeminent qualities for work in a meritocratic environment.

(3) Every accomplishment in the SPORTS ORIENTATION portion of this résumé is drawn from his accomplishment list. Again, he searched out his abilities, which are facts (not fantasies); no employer is in doubt about his commitment.

(4) and (5) Significantly, he stresses quantifiable accomplishments: "addressed . . . 2,500 people." Whenever possible use numbers to back your case. The schoolwide candy campaign might sound like peanuts, but the child is the father of the man, remember. We often telegraph in our earliest youth what our talent will be in later years.

(6) SPECIAL ABILITIES is where he puts all those specific and impressive achievements that don't, as such, support perfectly his job goals, but that indicate intelligence, character, and perseverance.

(7) Note how he buries his age, concealing his extreme youth.

(8) For most judgment jobs, writing skill is a *sine qua non.* In government, especially. But there are different kinds of writing: descriptive, analytical, reportorial, social, scientific, technical. Tell an employer what kind. As for references, with no work history his referees—mostly college professors—are satisfactory, but no need to list them.

"Why would you want to interview this fellow?"
Well, for openers:
Mine is a PR job, and of 150 résumés on my desk, only five are

adequate public-relations material. Since this candidate markets himself, the chances are good he will market my client's organization.

This fellow seems inexpensive—twenty-three years old. Chances are he won't want $35,000 per annum.

He knows what he wants. His vocational objective fits my job 90 percent.

The résumé, while clearly promotional, isn't slick—no acetate cover, no cutesy photographs and mindless blurb seen so often in the résumés of public-relations people.

The guy is clearly a compulsive sports freak.

The outcome is that this résumé gained him interviews, despite his having no experience, with a score of professional sports teams. His youthful experience didn't help, and he was rejected for plenty of jobs. But, finally, the Baltimore Orioles hired him as assistant public-relations director. Another example of someone putting his best foot forward, exactly the kind of characteristic any employer would look for in a public-relations type.

Now let's study a so-called targeted résumé: one page, one goal. This kind of résumé—the shortest—is often the hardest to write, since the person usually wants do just one job. But it's easy to skim and digest.

As you read this, notice that his objective is up front: Values, issues, and interests are short, pithy, and transparent. Instead of concrete accomplishments, he gives us a snapshot of his strengths and sums up his background in one paragraph. What you can't know is that, as a Ph.D., he also has an eighteen-page academic curriculum vitae complete with publications history.

Now, a résumé this short can't be comprehensive. His aim is readability. Unavoidably, he must generalize about his skills (there is no space for exact examples). Finally, a targeted format works best if you're truly obsessed with doing one thing. Employers are surprised and astonished by your precision.

Oscar Meyer
617 Chase Parkway
District of Columbia, 20015
(202) 555-5678, 555-3945

JOB OBJECTIVES

Old-fashioned Democrat, prairie populist, cold-war liberal, and unrepentant Vietnam veteran seeks responsible, decision-making position in Washington, D.C., area in or out of government that is consistent with the goals of what's left of the New Deal coalition, viz: equity and opportunity at home and opposition to totalitarianism abroad. Particularly qualified in the human dimensions of military preparedness, the reduction of unemployment, and the minimization of unnecessary human suffering. Discretionary authority a must.

STRENGTHS

Work well in a crisis atmosphere and in fluid situations. Effective pulling diverse factions in an organization together. Demonstrated ability to win the confidence of strangers. Articulate, presentable, perceptive, good writer, logjam breaker, and extricator of smoldering chestnuts. Big-picture generalist and qualitative analyst. Effective leader, and a good follower of strong and competent leadership. Excellent teacher. Effective at bringing out the hidden strengths of others and putting those abilities to productive use.

BACKGROUND

Post-academic, published anthropologist (Ph.D.). Also recent experience (1983) in improving work productivity on large construction projects. Did anthropological fieldwork among (1976–79) and worked to provide educational and employment opportunities to the Cree and Ojibwa Indians of the north woods of Canada. Seabee headquarters company commander, battalion weapons and communications officer, 1968. (Assistant company commander, 1967.) Coordinated the activities of 180 men of widely varying military occupational specialties. Supervised installation and maintenance of best battalion-level communications network at Quang Tri. Executive officer, 300-man Seabee detachment, Okinawa, 1969.

AVAILABILITY

Immediately

TRAVEL STATUS

Some travel welcome

"Do you have any examples?"

I just happen to have a few lying about in my sample case. The first is culled from some traditional résumés I've reviewed recently; the second series of job objectives represents the same people after going through these self-knowledge exercises.

> Seek human-involvement work utilizing my interest in applying community-development techniques.

Everyone wants to work with human beings. And nobody can define community development, much less apply its techniques. Let's look at his objective after three days of *hard* work:

> Qualified for a responsible, decision-making position with organizations fostering self-development in the fields of education and community control among American Indians, utilizing my skills in teaching and cross-cultural communication. Welcome adverse working environment, long hours.

An improvement. But he doesn't tell us what *kind* of organization he wants to hire (e.g., a tribal council, the Bureau of Indian Affairs). Moreover, he has but one job goal: teaching. Why not counseling, management, and curriculum development? And he mentions only one kind of population he wants to work with; why not Micronesians, Eskimos, itinerant farm laborers?

What did this chap's homework reveal about him that improved the clarity of his job objectives? Many achievements were accomplished in a minority context. He was the only gentile in a Jewish Boy Scout troop, the only Protestant in a Catholic boys' school, and the only college graduate on a summer job. He will feel right at home on an Indian reservation.

Let's look at another, a young, well-traveled woman who writes:

> Seek position in suburban school system where my interest in music qualifies me for a responsible position.

No dice.

I'm *interested* in ballroom dancing. My problem is I have a peg leg.

Nobody hires a person just because he or she is *interested* in doing something. Are you effective? That's what you speak to in your job objectives.

> Qualified for educational research in modern languages and/or music on an international scale (UNESCO, African-American Institute); mass-media communications and creative writing involving the dissemination of above educational materials and programs (Voice of America, United States Information Agency, and such organizations). Particularly qualified in educational research of Africa, specifically East, Central East, and French-speaking Africa.

Much better. But again, she usefully could add two or three other objectives. Music-camp director? Editorial assistant? Publisher's representative?

And what did she find out about herself between her first and second efforts? That she was especially proud of "collaborating with Radio Malawi in producing several programs of cross-cultural music . . . performed in song recitals with the American cathedral in Paris . . . was the features editor of her school newspaper . . . developed music exhibitions favorably reviewed in the European press," etc., etc., etc.

The point is that she was indubitably qualified for a European job in the field of modern languages (she speaks five languages) and music. Maybe not director of the Bayreuth Festival. But that did come up in 2024 in her obituary.

As for her original job objective (teaching harmonics in Darien), that's an evasion. That's what she thought she should do, what Mom and Dad thought was sensible. Not what she wanted to do or what she is doing.

How about a middle-aged engineer who suddenly drops everything, graduates from law school, and writes in his résumé:

> Seek position in governmental organization utilizing highly professional background in physics and academic training in law.

Well, that's great. But most employers don't have the imagination to program such a rare job specimen. Look at his second effort.

> Seek to use my qualifications as a lawyer or general counsel for private, quasi-governmental institution in advocacy, patent, or product-safety arena where demonstrated performance in management, general engineering, and applied science can be fully utilized.

Not bad. Nader's Raiders, the FDA, and a score of threatened manufacturers would like to have him on their side. A great guy to broker problems between technical and salespeople, or consumer advocates and producers, or an organization and its law firm.

So why doesn't he say so? That kind of info came out in writing up his job advertisements. And the fact that he's always been effective at explaining technical problems to scientific illiterates surfaced in his achievements list. And his obituary reports that "a grateful American government awarded him a plaque in the Smithsonian Institution"!

"Great! But I'm having trouble massaging my achievements into acceptable occupational lingo in the résumé."

Enhancing achievements is no crime, but no outright lies—otherwise you'll pass through some awkward interviews when your interlocutors ask for amplification. Résumés are advertisements, and some skillful embroidery won't hurt and might help as long as the product—you—is honest.

Here are some examples of too much sizzle, not enough steak.

Life: You were a fair field-hockey player in college.

Résumé Enhancer: Enjoy intense athletic contests both as spectator and participant.

Life: You knew about fifty people on your last job.

Résumé Enhancer: Coordinated fifty key program executives from every department to maximize efficiency.

Life: You stuck out two years in an impossible Peace Corps assignment in Africa.

Résumé Enhancer: Initiated community-action program for a small hill station in Uganda, upgrading local marketing and administrative skills and expanding horizons of inhabitants. Received letter of congratulation from the prime minister praising me for my efforts.

Life: Tend to be stopped by every street beggar.

Résumé Enhancer:	Demonstrated ability to win confidence from total strangers.
Life:	You can solve the London *Times* crossword puzzle in two hours.
Résumé Enhancer:	Commended by many supervisors for accurate recollection of miscellaneous facts.
Life:	Tend to be frugal to downright stingy with your money.
Résumé Enhancer:	Prudent manager of organizational funds; able to account and justify all cash and credit disbursements.
Life:	You fell in love with every male teacher from the eighth to the eleventh grade.
Résumé Enhancer:	Am especially able to work under senior decision-making executives. Have been cited for loyalty and efficiency.

Am I putting you on?

A little bit of résumé enhancement is okay, but too much apple polishing does turn off employers. The point is to represent strengths effectively. If you're comfortable with what you represent, you can defend and build on these skills in an interview; if your skills and strengths are untrue or exaggerated, this will surface in the interview, too.

Résumé expansion, the black art of making ourselves sound on paper a good deal more effective than we are, is kith and kin to being altogether too cute. Robert Half, who heads a New York search firm, cites in *Forbes* the following examples of come-ons that are real turn-offs:

> "Will relocate anywhere—except Russia, Vietnam, or New York City."—Cleveland computer programmer.
>
> "I want it completely understood that my objective is money. If there were two jobs available, one as corporate treasurer, and the other shoveling horse manure . . . I'll pick up the shovel if it pays more."—Chicago assistant treasurer.
>
> "I am the best-qualified candidate for any positions that may be available. I have no reservations about stating this."—St. Louis financial analyst.

"I can type, pitch hay, and shear sheep. I am also skilled at ground-hog hunting and ballroom dancing."—Seattle financial analyst.

"I am a notary republic."

"What other items shouldn't be included in a résumé?"

No employer needs to know you are a philately buff or a member of a Greek-letter sorority. If, as a member of an organization or in pursuit of a hobby, you achieved something (e.g., captained an intramural lacrosse team, integrated your sorority, or were elected national stamp-collecting champ), then functionally represent this information under SUMMARY OF BACKGROUND, generic headings, PERSONAL DATA, or SELF-MANAGEMENT SKILLS.

At all events, like writing a research paper, what's left *out* of a résumé clarifies job goals and focuses on strengths. This means that you leave a lot of interesting (but not supporting) material on the cutting-room floor. The aim of an effective résumé is clarity and brevity: You focus on what you want and can do. Any information that detracts from this photograph weakens your qualifications for a judgment job. Here are some personal facts you should detail in your résumé.

(1) **BIRTH DATE:** Extraordinarily important in the employment process. Generally an employer courts disaster if he employs someone in his twenties to supervise someone in his forties. So give your birthdate on the last page of your résumé. Generational conflict is real. Looking younger or acting older helps, but the plain truth is that age (rather than race, sex, education) is a major factor in employment discrimination today.

Legally, you're no longer required to report age in a résumé. That doesn't mean you shouldn't. Most people who don't, however, are extraordinarily defensive about it (too young, or too old.) And defensiveness, wouldn't you agree, is hardly a characteristic that endears us to employers. Thus, volunteering this information shows a lack of defensiveness and might endear you to an employer. In all events, it's the worst kind of job-hunting strategy to take umbrage if someone asks your age, marital status, number of dependents, and so forth. Employers are trying to come to grips with whether your personal condition is appropriate to the job. No one is necessarily trying to discriminate against anybody. But employers are being discriminating; there's a big difference, and it's what employers are paid to do. Where your discriminations and a potential employer's coincide is the point of sale in an employment relationship.

Anyone who hires discriminates by definition.

But in the final analysis, the decision is yours. If for strong ideological reasons you object to stating your birth date, then leave it out. Conversely, if for strong practical reasons you include it, that's fine, too.

(2) **PHONE NUMBERS:** It's ridiculous, but at least 150 job candidates I've wanted to hire failed to give me phone numbers (or gave ones where they couldn't be readily reached). I never employed them, *because I couldn't reach them when I needed them.* Put telephone numbers up front on the first page of your résumé. More than one if possible.

Think about buying an answering machine or hiring an answering service. It could be the same organization that stuffs and stamps your envelopes and types your cover letters. Being professional in the job search means spending money on it, which is to say, on yourself.

(3) **GEOGRAPHICAL PREFERENCE:** Nine out of ten jobs are filled by applicants who already live where they are considering their job searches. Don't try to find a job in New York City if you live in Anaheim. It *can* be done, of course, but job finding is tough enough right where you live—so start there.

If you won't work in New York City under any conditions, flatly say so. How many fruitful interviews (on the point of breathless consummation) abort because Johnny Jobsearcher didn't say—on his résumé—that his sinus condition precluded employment in a wet climate. This rules out every state but Arizona, John babe.

(4) **TRAVEL STATUS:** Sticky Wicket, Inc., wants Suzie Liberation, superwoman, to promote its United Way program at three plants in the Northwest. She'll be traveling for three months. Suddenly, Suzie, mindful of her three tiny tots, says she can't go. But she didn't put this in her résumé—and guess who's called a male

chauvinist pig for not hiring her? Always level with your employer on what your travel status is: some time, half time, full time? Do you like it? Say so! Abhor it? Say so.

I once hired and fired a woman for a traveling consultant's job because she forgot to tell me she was not licensed to drive. Did she think she was going to use the Greyhound bus? At $264 a day?

(5) SALARY: "Negotiable."

Or establish a range within which you'll consider negotiating ("$31,000–$36,000"). It's true you reveal your salary requirements *before* the interview, but it's also true that you're screening out employers you can't afford.

Also, under DAILY RATE indicate what you cost per day as a consultant: $75, $125, $269.50 (currently the U. S. government's maximum), $500, $1000.

(6) PREVIOUS EARNINGS: If yours is a progressively upward salary history, enumerate it. Personnel directors breathe heavily, and operating people—who do the hiring—can figure out if your salary history is in their ballpark.

(7) NAME: You think I'm joshing? In twenty years in this bodybroker business I've received more than ten résumés in which the name of the applicant was *not* included.

(8) SEX: If you happen to be called Francis, Leslie, Carol, or any of a hundred other androgynous names, tell the employer—again, in the résumé—whether you're a man or woman. Once I wanted to hire a freight handler for our mailroom. I interviewed a lithe lass first-named Keith, a wisp of a woman all of ninety pounds.

(9) HEALTH: Because of a slipped disk, you can't stand on your feet more than an hour. So why are you interviewing for a census enumerator's job? Tell it as it is: asthma? (You won't work out as a research librarian.) Acrophobia? (And you want a job as a consultant—with all that plane flying.)

"Just how old is 'old' these days in the job market?"

The law now defines the onset of "aging"—insofar as nondiscrimination is concerned—as age forty! This is hard on baby boomers, who but a few years ago were described as people with promise and now are thought of as over the hill. But the law, as Alexander Pope says, is an ass. Actuaries know that women live well into their eighties and men to their late seventies. Mandatory retirement, which until recently was seventy years of age, has been outlawed entirely for employers of twenty or more people. Obviously, the immovable body has met the irresistible force; the law says anyone over forty must be "protected" from employers who might discriminate while the evidence is that many people will work until age seventy and beyond.

The situation is complicated by the fact that youth wants to strut its stuff. If all these "old" forty- and fifty-year-olds continue to hang around the bullpen, there won't be any opportunity during the young's prime years.

For the smart "aging" job seeker, a bit of advice: Think about climbing *down* the ladder and working as a analyst, specialist, adviser, consultant, or small business manager and let a yuppie replace you. People in their fifties and sixties need training on how to give up control—managers have enormous difficulties sharing power, much less giving it up—but it's the only exit for those who love important work more than power tripping.

"What about video résumés?"

A sign of the coming times is the video résumé.

Chances are 50/50 within the decade we will record ten-minute cassette tapes as an introduction to interested employers. This way an employer can easily scan six candidates in an hour's time and the jobsearcher can cover more bases. Résumés will still be important. But for people who make a better impression in person than in print, it's a Godsend. And a boon to employers, too, who will now skim cassettes the way they do résumés.

"What do people who read this book and write you letters think of the functional résumé?"

Many remain unconvinced. This is because people don't believe in themselves. They still want to rely on an employer's hypothetical crystal ball to match them with jobs. But employers have precious little time on which to base the decision to interview or not to interview.

I have, however, seen hundreds of superb résumés written by readers of this book. Uniformly, people who develop an excellent functional résumé agree that *process* is more important than *product*. That is, the thinking that goes into a functional résumé resolves a host of problems other job seekers never solve.

If still unconvinced, pray and reflect and then read the next chapter. I don't give up easily.

FOUR

The Uses of the Résumé

Now what have we learned?

For starters, we now know nobody ever hired a résumé; effective résumés obtain interviews; doing a résumé compels us to clarify goals, skills, experience, education, values, and interests. Moreover, you've seen some sample résumés and know what to call them: chronological, functional, targeted. Now how to use the résumé?

Use your traditional (obit, descriptive, tombstone) résumé for:

Headhunters
Friends
At the end of an interview ("Do you have any paper on yourself, Bob?")
Placement/personnel offices
Curiosity interviews (if you don't know what you want)

Use functional, semi-functional, or targeted résumés for:

Strangers
Mass mailings
Responding to want ads and job announcements
Cold-turkey interviewing
Curiosity interviewing (when you know what you want)

Remember: If you need to generate interviews, use a functional format; if you interview without a résumé, use the traditional résumé. The practical purpose of a résumé is to obtain interviews; otherwise it's unnecessary.

For reasons not entirely clear to me, people who can't abide résumé usually love doing a comprehensive blitz letter using all the elements that ordinarily would go into an excellent résumé. With the availability of a word processor, it's a cinch to personalize a mailing campaign (altering the first and last paragraphs of your boilerplate letter to target a generic group of employers). For example, let's scan the letter of a middle-aged CPA who wants to move up to a chief financial officer job at $120,000 per annum.

D. Fred Garrison
4567 S. Barry Lane
Dallas, TX, 78910

January 17, 1986

PERSONAL & CONFIDENTIAL

Mr. Charles A. Wilkin
Wilkin and Company
4444 Shepherd Ave.
Houston, TX, 77077

Dear Mr. Wilkin:

Formerly a partner in a Big Eight accounting firm and now chief financial officer of a $200 million public company in Dallas, I'm seeking a job change to the Houston, Texas, area. I have demonstrated that I have what it takes to be a chief financial officer and, in time, to handle greater responsibilities. I'm looking for a company that has achieved success and is looking to plan and manage for long-term growth.

From my years working with a variety of organizations, here's a description of the type of business I would like to be associated with:

* It has a defined niche in the marketplace.
* It treats the customer as the number-one priority.
* It has the capacity to change with new conditions.
* Its people respond to straight talk, knowing top management cares about their welfare.
* Everybody—from the chairman of the board to the mailroom attendant—has the opportunity to share in the organization's success.

I'm writing with the expectation that what I have to offer may match up with your needs. What I want is management involvement; what I have to offer is the knowledge and experience to:

* enhance profitability and control
* improve relationships with the financial community
* increase staff productivity
* deal with governmental contracts and regulations

Because of the opportunities growth creates, associating with a growing firm is appealing. Such a firm might have a great mix of products or services, but the problems of growth have caused financial, systems, or manpower problems.

That's where I can help.

I like the idea of working with entrepreneurs who know the difference between (a) a great idea and (b) making it work. Both of us want to make the organization a dynamic and successful company.

What else do I have to offer?

Well, I know I'm an effective manager (clients and staff trust me), I like solving problems, and I recruit a staff that can and will learn to take responsibility. I know computers and data processing are important, but I know that people who know how to use information systems are more important. I know how to make financial and business plans that work, and I like the give-and-take of contract negotiations. An additional strength is my ability to translate complicated data into plain English for staff and customers. Some significant accomplishments:

* Generated $10 million in new business in a seven-year period, including single sales of $2.7 million and $1 million.
* Directed a consulting practice area that made my firm number one in the student financial aid industry (starting at zero, volume exceeded $500,000 for six consecutive years).
* Designed, developed, and installed a major pension and medical-claims system over a three-year span, managing ten consultants and solving or coping with the major problems: poor hardware performance and frequent change in client requirements.
* Particularly proud of my low staff turnover due to mutual respect and open communication.
* Director of the Office of Student Services during my senior year in college (elected to Iron Key and Omicron Delta Kappa leadership honoraries).
* U.S. Navy submarine electronics and communications officer (qualified to wear the Gold Dolphins of a submariner).

Some problem-solving achievements:

* Diagnosed and solved billing crisis for a large medical clinic through "freezing" and "fixing" contents of major files, logging daily patient calls, hiring temporary help, selecting and training new comptroller, and making timely reports to the board of directors. Radical financial turnaround was achieved.
* Recruited, screened, and employed high-quality professional staff by working closely with search firms, designing résumé-screening process, conducting final interview, negotiating terms of employment, and orienting new professionals.
* Consulting clients included the following industries: banking,

real estate, oil and gas, electronics, manufacturing, retail, health care, as well as government agencies (at every level).

* Evaluation of cost accounting, general ledger, payroll, accounts receivable, accounts payable, fixed assets, and inventory systems to meet unique needs.
* Passed the CPA exam on my first attempt.

Finally, I'm proud of my fifteen years of sales and contract negotiation experience: I know when to say yes and when to say no—and the reasons for both. I've achieved successful sales volumes at prices that permitted both high quality *and* a fair profit. I know government procurement regulations as a buyer and seller, and I know the lowest bid isn't necessarily the best.

Personally, I'm a bit of a workaholic, but I've managed to marry, be "Dad" to three kids, and design and build my own home.

I'm forty-five years old and looking to make a change. I would value meeting with you even if you don't know of an opportunity *now*.

If you are interested in what I have to offer, let's talk. I can be reached at (214) 555-1849 or (713) 555-6247

In the meantime, thanks for your consideration.

Sincerely,

D. Fred Garrison

P.S. I've included a one-page background summary.

It's often useful to include a traditional (chronological) fact sheet with such a letter. A first-rate letter, like an effective résumé, conveys abilities, values, and interests and describes goals.

But if you're still resisting a functional form, whether in a résumé or a letter, it's worth examining why.

(1) You might sense that you're losing your identity because you appear as an able, effective, motivated human being. (Rule #4: Nobody is hired for his weaknesses.)

(2) You were carefully brought up to be meek, humble, and unassuming. (Unreal. The only humble people I know usually have a good deal to be humble about.)

(3) Your best friend wouldn't recognize you. (And probably won't approve of your résumé, either. Remember, friends know your weaknesses and find them charming; that's a definition of a fraternal, not an employment relationship.)

(4) You intensely dislike selling yourself, wishing employers would sense your strengths. (Unrealistic. Employers in a twenty-second scan of your résumé or a twenty-minute interview learn little except whether they like you or not; help employers by revealing who you *are*.)

(5) You think it rude to blow your own horn. ("But if you done it, it ain't braggin'," said Dizzy Dean.) Revealing strengths that are facts is an authentic way to attract attention.

(6) You might feel you are conning a job offer. (After being offered and accepting a terrific job, do you feel like an imposter? Recall that judgment jobs go not necessarily to the most qualified but to those who know how to find them.)

(7) You might feel guilty of deception. (But a poor résumé *un*-revealing of your strengths, goals, interests, and values is much more deceiving because you conceal who you really are.)

(8) Therefore, you conduct an ineffective job search and qualify for a disappointing job. (And wonder why you are so miserable.)

(9) Then you join all the other malcontents who are unhappy, dissatisfied, and innocent. (Innocence leads to self-pity; the worst result of being unhappily employed or unemployed is to take a bubble bath in self-pity.)

(10) You wonder if you shouldn't go to law school. (A clear majority of all grad students, remember, are in professional schools because they don't know what else to do.)

A functional, semi-functional, or targeted résumé is an acceptable and ethical promotional document. Functional formats reflect ability; descriptive résumés reflect mere chronology. The obit résumé has its uses. If you generate an interview without a résumé and the interviewer wants a piece of paper, give her your bio sheet, the descriptive résumé. Functional résumés are for the job campaign and your mass mailing, love letters to employers. If you bag an interview without a résumé, you either make or break it in the interview. To use a functional résumé in this situation is communications overkill; you already have the interview. Don't gild the lily now that you've accomplished the objective. Use the bio sheet to generate interviews through friends. The functional résumé is topical, analytical, generic, and an upscale photograph that your friends might dislike.

An especially effective letter or functional résumé forces you to tell employers who you are, what you can do, thus targeting where you look. Another example of why doing market research on yourself is more important than researching the job market. No longer dispersed, distracted, and discombobulated, knowing both goals and abilities means you're job-ready.

Employers screen out job applicants; why not turn the tables and screen out employers who don't fit your job goals? Fair is fair, and you don't want to waste time following up on jobs you might qualify for but don't want.

All the more reason to be precise about a series of different (but related) jobs in your PROFESSIONAL GOALS. Plenty of people, focusing on their strengths and putting themselves first for a change, are pleasingly devastated when they read the final draft of their résumé. And friends, parents, and colleagues might giggle and put you down. (That's because they know your weaknesses and don't necessarily want you to succeed.)

Yes, employers can turn off. That's why the functional approach is risky. Obit résumés, however, leave neutral feelings and neither turn people on nor off. And that's the worst risk in the judgment job search: impressing people neither favorably nor unfavorably.

People who take *no* risks are taking the greatest risk. An effective job finder thinks on his feet and takes a few elementary risks (e.g., "being himself"), all of which means hiring yourself an employer.

The problem's attitudinal.

The bio sheet, the traditional résumé, is no reflection of effectiveness. Real accomplishments reflect ability; arid, meaningless facts mean nothing. It is far less risky to rely on a functional résumé than the bio sheet.

But, listen up: If deep down you just don't want a first-rate résumé for reasons perhaps unclear to yourself, recognize that some people *never* use résumés, generate interviews without them, and obtain terrific judgment jobs. Some people remain unconvinced of a résumé's utility. And if you're among them, try working up a cunningly crafted cover letter, attach your one-page bio sheet, and let your job campaign rip.

The tombstone résumé is a disadvantage except for people who have linear backgrounds who wish to make a simple job change rather than a career overhaul. Business people are especially prone to stick with the fact sheet plus cover letter because what they want next is what they have done.

But for homemakers recycling back into the job market, graduate students launching an off-campus job campaign, and people in a mid-career change, the functional format works best.

Some less important tips:

(1) To repeat, it's no longer legally required to reveal age, but if you do, simply give your birth date on the last page of the résumé.

(2) If you've completed the course work, but are working on your thesis, write "Completed all required courses leading to Ph.D. in biochemistry (thesis approval pending)." The same goes if you have ever declined a scholarship, award, key job: "Regretfully declined a Rotarian Scholarship (Value—$4500) to become a commissioned officer in the Coast Guard."

(3) Check around and compare various typefaces, formats, layouts, and paper quality before printing 500 copies. Don't pay the print shop until you and a friend have carefully proofread the final product. Provide clean copy, professionally typed, and carefully blocked out. So long as the résumé is neat, grammatical, with no misspellings, and easy to read or scan, content is more important than the form. Recall that an off-white, buff, beige, gray, or even light blue résumé best fits most occupations.

Some job searchers feel insecure revealing job goals, revealing only one goal, or revealing several goals. Many simply drop job goals entirely, including them in the cover letter. Do what feels most comfortable.

The results of widely using your résumé or cover letter depend on its quality, the demand for your skills, and the clarity and precision of your thinking. It's well to remember if Albert Einstein were alive and well and searching for a job in applied physics on the East Coast, his response rate to a résumé wouldn't be much higher than your own.

But since you asked, I wager:

8–14 percent of employers contacted may interview you.

40–50 percent may send "nice" no letters.

10–15 percent may send a signal: "Drop by and see me sometime."

30–50 percent may not respond at all.

To increase your batting average, *follow up by phone.* Effective job seekers could raise interview averages to 20 percent. And that's sensational.

An obit résumé, however, with the usual arch cover letter, yields only a 1 to 3 percent response. But if the cover letter is *functional,* speaks to *real* accomplishments, and zeroes in on real jobs, chances are better than even that your interview rate will rise to 10 percent.

The worst cover letters are tendentious, formal, and Victorian. The best are redundant and bland. Use a cover letter when you know the terms and conditions of a real job. That is, when you're writing to an employer about what he wants. Otherwise, a mass mailing of hundreds of functional résumés, describing *what you want,* with a note in your own hand at the top of the résumé ("I'll be phoning you Monday A.M. to discuss when it would be convenient for us to meet"), is an effective way to raise your batting average without the headaches of a cover letter. Moreover, printing in volume is cheap (a thousand résumés are three times as inexpensive per copy as one hundred). A postage stamp is twenty-two cents (or *was* when I wrote this paragraph; I wager it's more now, but still cheap). Mailing in volume is how many charities, direct-mail-order houses, and junk-mail vendors make a good living. And all you want is one good job offer.

Again, I wager my next year's vacation that the reason you back off from a volume mailing is your own displaced sense of self-worth, a fear of striking out, and/or fear that you'll succeed. No way you can possibly know of all the jobs you might want and are able to fill, let's say, within a five-mile radius of your downtown apartment. Reaching out via five hundred résumés over a five-month period to all those employers out there, one of whom may just punch your ticket, is a cost-effective, intelligent, grown-up way to find a job.

Want ads constitute a significant (but by no means the most important) source of jobs. A typical want ad attracts 50 to 150 résumés, mostly from unhappily employed folk sniffing about for a leg up in a new job. Alas, most employers are woefully inept at writing up a job advertisement.

For starters, employers rarely describe the essential function of the job. Often, too, want ads don't reveal what kind of an organization they are: Does a "trade association" represent sheet-metal suppliers, data-processing services, agricultural products? Who knows what "relevant experience" to highlight in a cover letter? For example:

AD: "Busy and fast-growing econometric firm needs billable economist.
TRANSLATION: Don't bother to apply unless you can bring a client following.

AD: Must possess an M.B.A. from a recognized school and an enviable track record.
TRANSLATION: The senior partners feel socially comfortable only with those with whom they could have gone to school.

AD: Please state your salary requirements.
TRANSLATION: We pay scut wages and expect you to humble yourself.

AD: Excellent opportunity to grow with firm.
TRANSLATION: You get a raise if you bring in more business.

AD: The company seeks an entrance-level professional
TRANSLATION: We expect hundreds of applicants grateful for working eighteen-hour days.

AD: We offer major responsibility, competitive salaries, opportunity for growth, and an attractive working environment.

TRANSLATION: That's because you'll be working for a pathological maniac.

For many job seekers, where they live and work isn't where they want to live and work. Suppose you're living in Utica, New York, but want work in Los Angeles. It's difficult enough finding a judgment job where you are, much less beyond the Continental Divide. The job search is a face-to-face activity, so the sooner you make tracks to the West Coast the better.

Go to the local phone company, which stocks phone books from around the country. Using the book (the best general resource for job searchers), make a list of three or four hundred employers, noting addresses and phone numbers on your trusty 3″ × 5″ cards. Compose a boilerplate cover letter without designating names and titles, fly to L.A., hole up in a motel room, and make your calls, asking for the name of the president (director, operations vice-president, etc.—whatever fits your craft), give your cards (with names and titles) over to a local secretarial service, conclude your letter with the phrase "I'll be calling you Monday afternoon to discuss when it would be convenient for us to meet," phone back every employer, and hope for a 15 to 20 percent response rate (which is outstanding).

At a minimum, you should have (after a week of phoning and mailing résumés) twenty to thirty interviews for the following week. Not a bad week's work. It probably means a second (and maybe even third) trip back to the coast, but that's the price you pay when you know where you want to live.

Referees?

No, they don't have whistles around their necks and wear white caps.

It's a stately name for people listed as references. While you look for a job, they are pretty important people. Choose them wisely, particularly those known in a work capacity, and who speak to your strengths *and* weaknesses. Don't use former college professors as referees; schoolmasters are okay recommending you for graduate school, but useless patrons in the job mart.

An able employer always personally checks out on the telephone —even when she's certain to hire you—the people who know your work best. That's why your referees are important; and they might blow the whistle on you.

A nice note to your referees is always in order before beginning the job campaign. As an employer, I'm suspicious of 90 percent of all *written* references. Referees are generally picked for social reasons: college chums, movement sisters, and drinking buddies. These are usually good friends. The problem is, they accept you uncritically and couldn't care less how you function on the job. (That's what friendship is.)

But referees should be objective, honest, candid, and able to analyze how effectively you would fill some employer's job. It's not who or how important they are; rather, it's how able they are in taking an occupational photograph of you.

Without your halo.

Whenever an employer checks you out, he expects an answer to this question: "Is this person effective?" Sure, there are other questions an employer might ask, especially on character, dependability, the flair you might bring to the job. In choosing referees, think about men and women who can best comment on your on-the-job effectiveness. Most employers recognize that job seekers can't be all things to all people. Choose discriminating referees who know why you do or don't fit the prospective job.

Many of us feel a teensy-weensy insecure about what our former boss will report to potential employers. Not to worry. Generally employers are too *kind*. I've done a few thousand reference checks, and 99 percent of American employers today hesitate to jeopardize someone's job offer. That's what's meant by the lack of balanced reporting and its importance in choosing referees. Almost everyone has two or three experiences in his occupational life that are sticky wickets. (I once interviewed a chap who had been fired thirteen times; he succeeded in finding another job every time!) If terminating under less than desirable conditions, ask during the exit interview for a formal letter of reference that might explain the organization's reasons for separating you. This puts the monkey on the right person's back at the right time.

If you believe a former employer is giving you the double whammy, asking a friend to sham a reading on your background is appropriate. This usually eliminates the paranoia bends if the referee's report is favorable. In the event it isn't, give prospective employers the names of a couple of other people at XYZ, Inc., who know the *full* story of your performance. Tell them, "Look, Jake Scharlach, my boss at XYZ, Inc., has some pretty strong opinions about my performance. To get a balanced picture I suggest you talk, as well, to ———————— and ————————."

Another problem for most employed job seekers is keeping the whole job campaign a secret from current employers. If you must practice Masonic secrecy in your job campaign, don't write or reproduce your résumé at the office. And the last line of your résumé should read "CURRENT EMPLOYER NOT TO BE CONTACTED WITHOUT PERMISSION."

Threaten a lawsuit if any prospective employer does contact your current boss without expressed permission. It's an intolerable violation of your rights for a prospective employer to ignore your request not to divulge privileged information.

Invent an elderly relative with a congenital heart disease who requires your frequent attendance; this story covers your repeated absences from the office for a while, but it has a fishy odor. (I know one job seeker who bumped off his grandmother five times in the process of finding five jobs.)

Finally, ask yourself: *"Is all this secrecy really necessary?"* It could unsettle future employers. (For example, marking your correspondence "Confidential and Personal" or "Eyes Only" is no way to keep a secret.) Explain *why you want out* to the person who needs to know: the boss. If you can't take her into your confidence, remember that it's going to take much more time to find that good job. But the need for secrecy is no reason not to try.

Think about discussing your job search with the boss. More employers than you think will support and recommend you, if you've been effective, to next employers. It's obviously easier finding a job with your employer's support. If you must be secret, then make it top secret, especially with your colleagues. Word often gets back if you make it known—even to your best friend—that you're interviewing off the premises.

Despite all precautions, there's a good chance you'll be discovered. Admit it—no crawfishing, please. Ours is a free country, and working people have the right to look for other jobs while on the job. Chances are, your boss is also looking. If a confrontation on this matter can't be avoided, it's time for the truth—so 'fess up.

A few DONT'S to remember in using your résumé:

Don't send a mug shot—it's cryptoracist.

Don't include your college transcript. You want a job, not a berth in a graduate school. And who the hell cares what you got in long division?

Don't bug a potential employer more than twice a month about a job for which you are being considered. Being eager is good, but salivating is gauche.

Don't say you want a "challenging" job "working with people." It makes sharp employers go glassy-eyed.

"Never apologize, never explain," said Disraeli. Deference is okay with agents of the Internal Revenue Service, but bad form in the job campaign.

Don't drop names of important people. Over five hundred job applicants have thrown this pitch at me—and are probably still unemployed. (If you happen to be a direct descendant of Samuel Adams, don't say so in your résumé. And if you went to Princeton on a scholarship and played lacrosse, emphasize the scholarship and just mention the rest. Conversely, if you attended a barber institute, don't flaunt your populist origins. Snobbery *is* snobbery.) Employers are fickle: social-register caterwauling will turn off as many employers as it turns on. And who wants to work for someone who hires you because you're a Daughter of the American Revolution?

Never send—no matter how attractive—a résumé of more than five pages. Honest to God, I've received some as thick as the Portland phone book.

Don't use the third person. Only de Gaulle and Julius Caesar pulled it off.

Don't call yourself "Doctor" if you're a Ph.D. It puts off employers and starts an interview on the wrong step.

"Reason for leaving last position" is a standard question on many employment applications. The strict truth is self-defeating. Imagine a woman writing, "Grew bored with my boss, my job, and myself. Besides, I had to work Xmas Eve." So yes, here again the strict truth in unnecessary. Don't volunteer reasons for wanting to leave. Save that for the interview. The conventional answer is that you wanted more money or responsibility. Sure there are other reasons, but no need to reveal them.

One footnote: If you worked your way through college, say so in your résumé. Almost anyone can pass from upper primary through grad school if Mom, Dad, or the federal government foots the bill. But the poor chap working his way through Siwash U.—now, that fellow has character! And character is fate.

Let's take another look at a résumé, this time that of a young person with a business background not interested in changing careers, someone trained to do what he wanted and who wants to continue to do what he's done. This kind of résumé is *semi-functional:* a combination of the traditional and functional approach especially recommended to those of you wanting to make a job change . . . and nothing more.

Richard Carnahan
60 Longfellow Street, Apt. 16-B
Belmont, Massachusetts 02345
(617) 555-8298

OBJECTIVE

Management consulting, with emphasis in areas of strategic and financial planning, and management decision-support systems. Ideal position will be in a consulting firm with opportunities for increasing responsibility and continuing professional growth; or alternatively, as an internal consultant in a firm where the potential exists to build or manage an internal service group.

STRENGTHS

Solid background and nine years of experience in multiple sides of a growing technology-based business.
* marketing and financial planning
* sales support
* engineering and product planning and development.

Sensitivity to the requirements of working on a day-to-day basis with clients and client organizations, developed through sales support and consulting experience.

Well-practiced spoken and written communication skills, ranging from presentations to customers and management, to technical report writing and preparation of user communication.

Project supervision experience directing the activities of from one to five people.

Well-developed analytical and administrative skills, building upon technical undergraduate and business-administration graduate degrees.

Extensive practical experience and research in the analysis, design, and implementation of management-information and decision-support systems.

EDUCATION

(1982–84) Sloan School of Management, Massachusetts Institute of Technology (Cambridge, Massachusetts)

Candidate for Master of Science in management degree in June 1984.

Concentration in managerial planning and control, with related courses in organization studies, finance, and information systems.

Thesis describes organizational and situational factors in the successful implementation of management decision-support systems.

Summer research assistant in corporate strategy and planning project. Teaching assistant in managerial accounting course.

(1980–82) Arizona State University (Tempe, Arizona)
Bachelor of Science degree in mathematics, summa cum laude.
Completed undergraduate work at night while working full-time.

(1973–75) Dartmouth College (Hanover, New Hampshire)
Majored in mathematics. Research assistant for Dartmouth Time-Sharing Project. Received Alfred P. Sloan Scholarship Award.

PROFESSIONAL EXPERIENCE

(1982–84) Honeywell Information Systems, Inc. (Wellesley, Massachusetts)
Part-time consultant to manager of business plan evaluation. Designed and implemented interactive computer model to support systematic evaluation by marketing and planning management of alternative product line and marketing strategies.

(1980–82) Honeywell Information Systems, Inc. (Phoenix, Arizona)
Member of headquarters marketing staff for Honeywell's 6000 line of large computer systems. Recommended market strategies (product evolution, pricing). Developed five-year sales forecasts and financial evaluations to support alternative plans.

Wrote product plans for hardware and operating-system products. Collaborated with engineers, salesmen, market researchers, and factory cost analysts to integrate their requirements into these plans. Presented technical seminars for management and customers. Co-chairman of software design review board.

(1979–80) General Electric Company, Information Systems Equipment Division (Phoenix, Arizona)
Software planning specialist in division planning group. Activities and responsibilities similar to those with Honeywell (above), for operating-system and application program software on GE-600 product line.

Special assignment as project leader for systems-engineering product-development team (five people).

(1979) General Electric Company, Information Systems Equipment Division (Bethesda, Maryland)
Directed all on-site and field technical support for test market of a GE new-business venture, the RESOURCE service bureau system. Trained salesmen and assisted customers in use of system. Installed

and maintained system software. Assisted operations staff with development of procedure and performance-measurement systems.

Extensively interviewed customers as part of test-market analysis. Recommended product and strategy changes. Assisted management with organization planning and recruiting for permanent organization.

(1978–79) General Electric Company, Aircraft Engine Group (Lynn, Massachusetts)

Member of computer center technical staff. Evaluated computer equipment proposals (factory data-collection system, microfiche applications). Prepared project plans and budgets. Developed procedures for scheduling, measurement, and analysis of computer operations. Consulted to application programmers in programming techniques and system use. Maintained operating-system software for two large computer systems.

Division representative to GE Corporate Task Force on Operating Systems. Wrote and presented major portion of final report to management.

(1975–78) General Electric Company, Information Systems Marketing (Wakefield, Massachusetts)

Applications engineer in New England District. Prepared technical proposals and made presentations to prospects to support sales of GE computer systems. Designed data communications applications with customer personnel. Prepared and taught customer-training classes. Project leader for major GE-635 system installation. Directed efforts of other application engineers in conversion of application programs, field test and maintenance of system software, and acceptance testing. Responsible to account manager for all technical support to customer.

PERSONAL DATA
  Birth date: July 4, 1956
  Married, no children
  U.S. citizen
  References on request

Yes, the résumé is a trifle long, not all that exciting, but business-like and direct. Note how he specifies objectives, sums up and generalizes strengths, and then lets education and experience reinforce his goals. There is nothing about his interests (he loves his work so much he has no interests). But his abilities come shining through in examples of accomplishments retailed under each of his jobs. An example of a restrained, professional, businesslike approach . . . and not a trace of résumé enhancement.

Finally, a last look at another semi-functional résumé. Note how this fellow builds on accomplishments under each job title, establishes his salary history representing an upward spiral of earnings, and then breaks down his background by skill area describing real accomplishments on and off the job. Result: five job offers and a salary hike of $15,000.

Note one last item: This person had no business training. But he highlighted his business skills—above all, economic planning. And, remarkably, he jumped from government to business into the package-delivery field. An excellent example of the transferability of skills.

ROBERT CRATCHIT

21 Mills Lane
Tarrytown, N.Y. 06342
Office: (201) 555-8942
Residence: (212) 555-5656

OBJECTIVE

A leadership opportunity in resource planning and development that applies substantive professional experience in finance and operations as well as education in quantitative disciplines such as financial indicators and econometrics.

PROFESSIONAL EXPERIENCE

American Science Foundation (ASF), Washington, D.C.

Assistant Study Director/Senior Economist—January 1981–July 1984 ($38,000)

Major Accomplishment:

Analyzed investment plans of President Reagan's $52 billion R&D budget as ASF project director for the Office of Management and Budget (OMB). Conducted financial analysis using IBM-PC and Lotus software. Project highly praised by ASF and OMB senior management. Supervised two economists and a statistician.

Civil Aeronautics Board (CAB), Washington, D.C.

Transportation Economist/Analyst—October 1978–January 1981 ($29,000)

Major Accomplishment:

Conducted operation/system analyses of Kodiak Western Airlines. Computed and reorganized carrier's financing and profit levels to prevent bankruptcy and maintain its vital air service to Alaska.

Department of Health, Education, and Welfare (HEW)

Education Economist/Analyst—June 1978–October 1978 ($21,500)

Major Accomplishment:

Initiated analytic research reports to project budgetary impact on Office of Education programs. Reports used extensively to evaluate and adjust program operating costs.

SKILLS AND ACCOMPLISHMENTS

FINANCIAL PLANNING AND OPERATIONS SKILLS:

Conducted ASF annual government-wide surveys of R&D budget projections averaging $50 billion. Validated R&D cost accounting to evaluate long-term investment options. Trained and supervised two economists in cost-accounting techniques.

Prepared CAB market analyses to determine essential air service for small communities under the Airline Deregulation Act of 1978. Computed financial analyses of competing air carrier service bids.

Monitored costs/revenues of carriers awarded CAB service routes with annual financing and profits to $12,000,000. Computed annual operation/systems analyses for financial adjustments.

NEGOTIATION AND PRESENTATION SKILLS:

Negotiated with ASF and OMB budget examiners to validate R&D cost accounting for savings of over $100,000,000 to the government.

Directed air carrier presidents and supervised CAB auditors to rectify accounts payable/receivable for financial analyses. Counseled CAB senior management and presented financing and profit positions as participant in carrier negotiation conferences.

Presented oral testimony before the CAB recommending carrier selection with negotiated financing and profit plans. Persuaded the CAB to adopt recommendations in all cases.

WRITING SKILLS:

Designed and wrote ASF analytic reports on impact of congressional R&D appropriation bills. Analyses used for investment planning by the National Science Board.

Initiated and wrote a special ASF analytic reports on impact of congressional R&D funding for energy-related projects. Report findings cited by Washington *Post.*

Composed and edited ASF *Mosaic Magazine* articles, *Annual Reports, Highlights,* and *Previews of Science* on R&D funding issues such as industrial performers and national defense.

ACHIEVEMENTS AND AWARDS

Won ASF's Sustained Superior Performance Award for initiating, negotiating, and managing a project with the National Planning Association to establish output measures of domestic and foreign R&D investments.

Initiated and developed ASF use of IBM-PC to enhance efficiency of investment reports. Instructed and supervised ASF senior management on software applications.

Promoted on three occasions in five tight budgetary years with CAB and ASF—a 23 percent average annual salary gain.

Elected to board of managing directors of 800-member condominium association to plan efficient use of $1,200,000 annual budget. Evaluated developer operating proposals. Approved cost-effective measures for projected savings of $200,000.

EDUCATION
University of Rochester
Rochester, N.Y.
Master of Science in Policy Analysis/Economics
May 1980

Thesis: *Small Community Air Service and Subsidy Policy*

Emphasized study in the Graduate School of Management (business and economics) and the Policy Analysis Program (econometrics, computer, and macro/microeconomics).

Designed and taught a course analyzing domestic pricing strategies.
University of Rochester
Rochester, N.Y.
Bachelor of Arts in Philosophy and Political Science
May 1974

Financed graduate and undergraduate studies through part-time employment.

PROFESSIONAL AFFILIATIONS
Association for Policy Analysis and Management, American Economic Association, and American Association for the Advancement of Science.

SALARY
Low fifties (negotiable). Dependent on location, occupational function, and size of organization.

PERSONAL STATEMENT
Born 1952. Married. No children. Wife practicing attorney. Willing to relocate and travel. Available within *four* weeks after accepting offer.

Prefer a decision-making opportunity that requires an effective *planning* executive with diversified proficiency in financial and operation analyses, report writing, public presentations, management, and instructional supervision.

REFERENCES
Mr. Philip Wilkin
Senior Vice-President–Resource Planning
XYZ Corporation
875 Glenchester Road
Trenton, N. J. 07920
(201) 555-2472
Relationship: Immediate supervisor at XYZ

Dr. James F. Bealle, Energy and Science Division
Executive Office of the President
Office of Management and Budget
726 Jackson Place, Room 7002
Washington, D.C. 20503
Relationship: Former client at OMB

REFERENCES MAY BE CONTACTED AFTER SECURING MY COMPLI-
ANCE. FURTHER REFERENCES AND WRITING SAMPLES AVAILABLE
UPON REQUEST.

Swell. Where in the world are these judgment jobs I talk about so knowledgeably? Eighty percent of all jobs are filled through a grapevine, a system of referrals that never sees the light of public day. No, you won't see them posted on a bulletin board, or registered with the U. S. Employment Service, or advertised in the Washington *Post*.

This is the so-called hidden job market.

It's the market where judgment jobs are found. The reason there's a hidden job mart is that most employers fear—quite stupidly—the unwashed masses. Employers want men and women who are recommended by friends, business and professional associates, drinking buddies—almost anybody except someone off the streets.

You say nonsense. Undemocratic. Unjust. And you're right. But only foolish job applicants don't take the hidden job market into account.

Forward!

PART TWO

Our problems in life begin when we know what we want.

JULIAN HUXLEY

FIVE

Go Hire Yourself an Employer

The name of my business is really the people game: a professional labor exchange where employers and job seekers alike discover one another, bid for each other's services, and purchase a product based on their respective requirements.

If you accept a job, therefore, you really *do* hire yourself an employer. In return for your service, the institution owes you certain dues and services, like a salary. Study the feudal system. The similarities between corporate, institutional America and the manorial system of Central Europe is astonishing. The ancient barons—the counterpart of today's corporate managers—exacted specialized services from their vassals: the hewers of wood and haulers of water, the sheriff, the wardens, and the knights. For these services, which were largely economic and military, vassals demonstrated loyalty to their masters and performed certain social acts of obeisance. The nobles, in return, guaranteed the livelihood (i.e., income) of their vassals and protected them.

Well, times have changed, but not *that* much.

We still owe our employers loyalty—though only eight hours a day, and only so long as our services are not outbid by a competitor. We still make social obeisance, though we generally don't admit it—we view our employers with a kind of American deference best defined by an anthropologist.

It's *your* responsibility, not the employer's, to identify what you *want* to do. Be realistic and find out everything you can about the job you want. Employee goals should be mostly congruent with those of the employer. When there is clear incongruence, there's certain job dissatisfaction. Identify three or four of the most suitable classes of employers. The vast majority of employers don't want you, and you don't want them.

"What's an example of job congruence?"
It's simply when work conforms to desire. Look what this woman *wants* via her job objective.

> Job Objectives:
> Qualified for responsible Health Project International Management position in the public health, family planning, medical-delivery systems, and health-care evaluation areas. Desire project director responsibilities as a planner, manager, or chief evaluator for health- or social-science-oriented institution utilizing management, statistical, and report-writing capabilities. Particularly qualified to deal on a cross-cultural basis with indigenous target populations (e.g., retarded children or geriatric programs). Welcome a continuous assignment of two years or more.

Now let's look at a job description and note what the employer *wants.*

> A contractor with the Center for Disease Control seeks experienced research manager for metropolitan office to conduct study of venereal disease incidence among inner-city residents. Qualified candidates should have five years project experience, an advanced degree in the social sciences, and strong evaluation and research skills. Report-writing skills a must; some quantitative orientation. Ability to supervise paraprofessional interviewers essential.

Our job searcher, having written out three job advertisements, converting the lingo to describe jobs into professional objectives, focused on what she wanted, which matched up against most of what an employer wanted.

Congruent job objectives mean a substantial overlap between what an employer wants and what you, as the job searcher, want. There will rarely be an *absolute* identity of objectives, and there needn't be.

"What exactly do you mean by the hidden job market?"

Eighty percent of all good jobs are concealed.

They're not listed with the Civil Service Commission or your state employment service; the personnel department is always the last to know.

Look for the good jobs in the hidden job market. These are the jobs that exist in the minds of those few people who make a place work. They have power and make decisions.

Don't look for any prepackaged job descriptions. Most operating people don't have time for such nonsense. And, like everything else worth hearing, you learn about judgment jobs through a grapevine of intelligence, an old-boy/old-girl network, or in the specialized channels of your craft, skill, or field.

"Do employers hire exclusively from the old-boy/old-girl network?"

Don't ignore networking as a source of jobs: It's the mainstream. But you'll feel better and do a better job for a stranger. That's right, someone who doesn't know you. Why? Because both you and your employer focus not on the *connection* but on the *contribution* you'll make to the organization. Keep this in mind when you start hiring. The payoff in motivated and talented people truly loyal to you (after all, you showed good sense in hiring them) is astounding.

While it's tough resisting temptation, contact friends, colleagues within the old-boy/old-girl network last. Try finding jobs from interesting strangers first, and save your friends (and friends of friends) for when you need them.

"How do you get around filling out all those company forms? I thought a résumé was sufficient."

The application forms.

Nobody knows who invented the first one. Probably the same fellow who writes the fine print on the back of your homeowner's insurance policy. A pain in the derriere, the delight of Ph.D.s in personnel administration, the most unnecessary form in any company, unless you are hiring data processors, hotel personnel, postal clerks—i.e., non-judgment jobs.

So what do you do?

I usually hire a secretarial service. I give them every conceivable bit of information any application might require: Social Security number, middle names of deceased grandparents, my rifle number in the Army.

I simply pass on the required information to them. Then I'm free to do what I should do: look for a job.

"If application forms are useless, why do organizations insist on using them?"

Application forms are not useless to employers; they are useless for job seekers. Employers use application forms to straight-arm the host of unemployed who park on their front stoop each working morning. That way, an organization proves it carefully screens all applicants. And personnel departments (who never do the hiring) justify their existence. If you are told to complete an application form, beware. Remember, especially if you're new on the job market, finding a job is the *opposite* of being admitted to graduate school. There is no admissions committee, no rational process of selection, employment dossiers are *not* compared with each other. Does anyone over the age of twenty-one and with an IQ over 90 really believe that key jobs are filled the same way a Rhodes Scholarship is awarded? And you want a judgment job!

"Don't employers scan application forms and résumés for significant omissions?"

Particularly in regard to earnings and dates of employment, all of which means a candid posture on your part. In other words, no fibbing. If you took a year off to go spelunking in Austria, say so. Did you accept a salary of $6 per hour to work with the nation's foremost semanticist and accordingly rejected a college instructorship at $27,000? Say so. Were you nabbed by the police, booked, and charged for breaking and entering the second-story window of your college girlfriend's apartment? Say so.

Concealing information or saying you have an advanced degree (when it ain't so, Joe) is certain to land you in hot water and permanently wreck your chances of ever finding a judgment job. Because lying breaks the bond of trust that binds every successful business negotiation.

"How do you break into the hidden job market if it's your first job and you're new to a city?"

Never interview someone for a job until you are sure he has one to offer.

Curiosity interviews work if (a) you can't focus on what you *want*, and (b) you don't know where to look. If you know what you want and where to look, skip curiosity interviews and start asking for jobs.

Nobody likes to have the bite put on her for a job—especially (which is usually the case) when she doesn't have one. That's why making doors open is so tough. But everyone with a normal vanity quotient loves to be consulted in *her* field. Do you know anyone who doesn't like to give advice?

And that's what you do when you're genuinely curious. You ask experts about where to look for a job that interests you, latest trends in their field, where the government is spending money, who the leading contractors are, and so on.

And don't leave any interview without the names of four more key people you can call for similar appointments. Phone them, drop a name or two, and then repeat the process. Before long you'll know where the action is and, without knowing it, become part of the hidden manpower pool. And you don't need a résumé to collect information effectively.

"The hidden manpower pool?"

Did you ever find a dentist by flipping through the Yellow Pages?

It's the same with people who hire.

If a banker is someone who lends money to someone who doesn't need it, your typical employer is somebody who offers a job (a) only to somebody who already has one, or (b) to someone who apparently doesn't need one. Employers love to steal talent from competing organizations or a whiz kid from another department in their own company. They no more rely on their personnel department to fill a key job than they phone the 7,508th person in the Boston phone book and hire him.

When curiosity interviewing, you gradually become known by people who count—the kind of professionals other decision makers rely on for help. "Say, Judson, I'm looking for a young woman with an M.B.A., making no more than twenty-five thousand a year, to begin work next week, helping me analyze interstate trucking rates." A hundred phone calls begin like this every day. Guess who Judson thinks of first? Why, that nice young woman who spent an hour asking him intelligent questions about transport problems in the Northeast Corridor—did she have an M.B.A.? What difference does that make? And isn't her résumé around someplace? Didn't she leave it with him or send a thank-you letter including it?

Pressed for time and unable to interview a whole batch of candidates, many employers will call several associates who traffic in effective people—experts with solid judgment who can recommend first-rate job candidates and/or know where they are available.

That way, since they know who and what employers want, employers are setting up a valid screening device at hardly any cost in time or money. Moreover, people like to see someone they respect find a good job. Tapping into this hidden manpower pool is the quickest way employers solve recruiting problems.

Vigorously follow this employment strategy and you become picked up by men and women whose referral counts. A kind of twentieth-century patronage system. And by being part of the hidden manpower pool, you tap into that great underground stream of jobs that rarely see the light of day.

Finally, ask people how they found their jobs.

"Why is it sensible to ask people how they got their jobs?"

First, it will confirm everything you read in this book. Second, you can test your own job-finding strategy against people who have made it work. Third, you'll see how wacky the process can be. And people love to talk about how it all happened. "It was the craziest thing, but while I was deep-sea fishing at Christmas Cove, I tangled lines with a man who manages a large wine-import business in New York. Well, we were both laughing when . . ."

At cocktail parties I rarely ask people *what* they do. How they found their job is my lead question. The answers are this book.

"You mean instead of petitioning for a job it's better to be recruited for it?"

Yes, as part of the product of interviewing about jobs in the hidden job market, you become part of the hidden manpower pool

—men and women employers want to hire because they know you, know you're available, and know you're effective. You are, in fact, recruited for the job, won away from another firm (which delights your new boss), and meet your employer on a parity—rather than on a petitionary basis.

Sure, Ms. New Employer could find another person at half the price (but only half as good). After all, you showed you knew how to sell yourself (not a despised quality in most organizations).

"Aren't employers much more leery of 'advice' interviewers?"

Alas, yes.

Because of the popularity of the idea and its wide misuse by job seekers, more and more employers, especially in highly urbanized areas, are turning off to people asking for "information." Time is money, and many busy employers find wasting money on the unemployed cost-defective. Accordingly, building information networks requires a lot more patience, time, and sophistication than ten years ago.

Precede every call with a nice letter describing why you want to see the great man or woman, try to lure this person to lunch, follow up with a nice thank-you letter, and do the same with all referrals recommended by this person. The point of a letter and a free lunch is to demonstrate that you *value* this person's advice, at the same time making clear this person will not be wasting her time. So proceed cautiously, persistently, and with sensitivity in networking employers. Curiosity interviewing still works for those willing to work at it.

"Are there any drawbacks to curiosity interviewing?"

There are only two reasons to curiosity-interview.

(1) "I don't know what I want to do."

(2) "I don't know where to look."

If, however, you *do* know what you want and *where* to look, and you're curiosity-interviewing primarily to put yourself out front and become visible to potential employers, then you are in big trouble indeed. People sense a *concealed* agenda. The result is a bogus transaction. And employers become hostile; you are trading on their time and goodwill for carefully disguised goals and are deservedly shown the door.

"What if I'm offered a job in a curiosity interview?"

Feign surprise and back off, asking for time to think about it.

Remember, you gained the interview for advice and didn't expect an offer. You'll make an excellent impression, calling back the next day and saying, "Hey, throw my hat in the ring," or politely thanking the employer for his time and gently saying no. Should an employer, upon further reflection, think back on the advice interview as a setup for a job offer, she is bound to turn off.

While curiosity-interviewing, it's in the nature of things for you to get offers; it's in your interest to show reactive good judgment. Buy the time to think the offer over, thus raising the high value the employer already has placed on you.

"What are the main reasons it's so difficult to obtain job interviews?"

(1) People don't want to reject you for a job they don't have.

(2) Time spent talking to the unemployed is money.

(3) Employers feel *obligated* to solve your problem.

Be sure, before throwing yourself on the job market, (a) you know what you want, (b) what you can do, (c) how you can help an organization. That way, you won't be wasting anyone's time.

"What about people looking for jobs? Are they good contacts for finding good jobs?"

Career counselors and placement types, please note.

Working with groups of unemployed people, job co-ops, or job clubs is an effective method of helping people to find jobs fast. Working together with twenty other unemployed people is like hiring nineteen pairs of eyes to find jobs you want. Job co-op members swap résumés, keep the interests of their fellow job seekers at heart, and exchange information on where the jobs are, who is hiring, for how much, starting when. That's why I applaud certain women's groups who provide job-finding, backstopping services. College alumni services should emulate them for mid-career graduates suddenly out of work and out on the sidewalk. And professional associations should form job co-ops to assist members in finding jobs. The trade-off for the unemployed is tremendous. Why? Job hunting is a lonely business and job clubs are "unoccupational" therapy for people who need the encouragement of seeing others find jobs. And once on the job, graduates from these clubs are great sources of job leads.

"How do you go about finding the hidden job market in your field"?
Simple.

Let's say biostatistics is your trade. You work for a small, wealthy, but stagnant firm whose management will never admit you to its ownership. You want to find a firm—the same size—with growth potential where you can own a piece of the company.

Spend your early mornings, lunch hours, or late afternoons checking out firms you might want to work with and that might need your skill. (Remember, one of your skills is knowing how to find a job.) You stake out the key people in each company, the men and women you would want to work for and from whom you can learn, and ask their advice on how to move up in your field. Always obtain the names of four more key people and companies from each person you interview, and before long you've snowballed your job campaign into fifty interviews and, I bet, four job offers.

What's happened is that you've researched your field, haven't hammerlocked anyone for a job, spread yourself (and later your résumé) around, and just happen to be the man or woman a key person first thinks of when he needs a biostatistician.

Above all, you've established what it is you *want* and asked people's help in finding it.

"How about recontacting people when you know what you want and where to look?"
Good idea.

A nice note (and your résumé) a month later to folks who have generously given you curiosity interviews is the way to let the world know you now want work in commodity investments in Chicago. Yes, if these people took a shine to you the first time around, it could be they will phone about a hidden job. In fact, why not phone them?

"So you're saying, it's not what you know but whom you know?"
Not entirely. What's truer is knowing what you know, researching the job market (curiosity interviewing), and finding out who the employers are who need to know you know it.

While there is definitely a ceiling on cunning job-finding strategies, there's no ceiling on competence and the contribution you can make to an organization. So advise a lot of people who hire (and who can help you put your assets to work) about what you do best.

"But surely important people can't take time to see me?"
Stand around a typical business at quitting time.
Five P.M.
Suddenly, a horde of the harried salaried classes drops everything and hits the elevator. Writing and then calling an important person, asking for fifteen minutes of his time, is probably the most exciting and certainly the most flattering event that will happen that day. And what else is he doing that's so important? Everyone loves to be asked for advice.
I thrive on it.

"How do you find the right person to interview?"
It's impossible to know exactly. Talk to anyone but the director of Personnel (unless you want a job in Personnel).
Looking for work in designing appliances? You'll want the vice-president for product development. Suppose there is no such position. Try research and development. Nine out of ten times, people inside an organization will know the key individual to interview. Also, try to liberate the phone book of an organization. This valuable publication lists names, titles, department and phone number extensions, a wealth of insider information.

"So asking for advice is the best strategy in finding a job?"
Always ask for it.
People give it away free.
To *ask* advice is the most flattering gambit used by the jobless. The idea, of course, is that nearly everyone is part of a job network —they know of hidden jobs. Curiosity interviewing takes the heat off those interviewed—they don't have to reject you for a job they don't have.

"How do you choose people to interview for advice?"
By asking people you like whom they admire in a field where you might want to work. My theory (hardly original and not care-

fully documented) is that we learn by imitating what we admire. Learning by simulation.

To be consistent, learning how to function on a job is simply identifying successful people and imitating them. If what you imitate is comfortable, then make it a habit, copycat. Particularly for the young. In college I chose *professors,* not courses. In the business of life pick a person you could *become,* and then learn on the job. Best education hard work can buy!

When curiosity interviewing, therefore, stake out men and women of proven success whose style you admire. If you say to yourself, "I could be like her," then be like her. Soon people will start imitating you, the highest form of flattery, and won't that be embarrassing!

"Why is the personnel department to be avoided at all costs?"

Increasingly called human resources, personnel departments are avoided because (a) they are swamped with traditional job applicants, (b) are so busy doing things your teacher made you do after school they have no time to hire, and (c) even if they have the time, personnel types—with a few exceptions—have no clout in the organization beyond their own departments.

The exceptions obviously are those who want work in human resources or job candidates in fast-growing enterprises where demand for technical people outstrips the supply. If yours is a high-demand discipline, chances are you're safe going through personnel. But just to be sure, why not first try interviewing with operating types and simply copy personnel in your correspondence?

"Why are so many want ads nothing but dead ends?"

Affirmative action in action.

Equal-opportunity programs are complicating the employment process; many employers advertise jobs already filled in order to comply with the law. Accordingly, job searchers who wage a traditional campaign responding to want ads are often bitterly disappointed to find that many job "opportunities" wallpaper over plenty of concealed affirmative-action discrimination.

If you're not a member of an established minority, bluntly asking whether a job is reserved for those who are could save you time even though it might make you furious. And if you are a minority member, build on this strength in your job search and subtly reveal your status in the résumé.

"You haven't said anything about racism/sexism. Is it still as bad for women, blacks, Chicanos, Puerto Ricans as always?"

In middle-management regions there has been enormous improvement. In my judgment—remember, I'm white, middle-class, and middle-aging—things are looking up for *educated minority job seekers;* downstairs in the kitchen, it's business as usual.

If promoted or transferred on your next job, recruit a replacement from a minority group. If we all practiced this kind of enlightened racism/sexism occupational discrimination would disappear before you could say Jackie Robinson!

So long as you focus on talent among classical minorities, this kind of reverse racism/sexism *works.* If, however, people are hustled, recruited, and hired for judgment jobs primarily *because* of race or sex, it will cause resentment, and plenty of capable women, Hispanics, and blacks are suspicious of being hired for who they are rather than what they can do.

"What if the job I want doesn't exist?"

Or no longer exists. Well, you can't know until you look for it. If you can't find it and sense that the job is needed and that someone will pay for it, invent the job and sell it. Again, the proposal-development approach. Of course, your proposal will usually be rejected, but chances are these decision makers will think of you first when they want to fill a hidden job. Also, you need a *base* to sell concepts.

"What's the proposal-development approach to finding a good job?"

Once upon a time, in the great long-ago, this approach was how people found jobs. With the erosion of the work ethic, the growth in the welfare state, and the decline in initiative, the whole approach seems positively revolutionary.

Example: Where I worked we had a street-level office with plenty of windows and lots of people traffic. One day a young street dude walked into our offices, approached me, and said, "Hey, man, how about a job?" Three minutes later he was back on the street and I was back at my desk.

A few minutes later another young man came through our doors. He was dressed in working clothes and carried window-washing equipment, a bucket, and soap powder. Standing before me and scanning our deplorably filthy windows, he announced that he would wash every window in the place, inside and out, for fifty cents a pane. "Make it forty cents and you have a deal," I said. We negotiated a forty-five-cent rate, and three hours later he walked out of the place with a check for $45.80 . . . and our thanks.

Later in the day—at closing time—I was walking up the street and saw the same young man hard at work washing a merchant's show window. "Hey, man," I yelled, "how much did you make today?"

"Ninety-eight dollars and seventy-five cents," he yelled back. "How much did you make?"

Gulp.

Think about a carefully designed concept paper(s)—three and a half pages sent to chief executive officers. And be prepared to follow up with a full-fledged proposal complete with budget, scheduling, staffing, and technical information. Selling an idea is best recommended to successful men and women in mid-career uninterested in starting their own business, unprepared to enjoy still another promotion (doing what they don't want to do), and those few who are truly obsessed.

"What do you mean, everyone needs a base to make the proposal-development approach work?"

—Your husband's salary is a base.

—A small inheritance is a base.

—A second mortgage on your house is a base.

—Moonlighting on a grunt job is a base.

—A grant from the Rockefeller Foundation is a base.

Any guaranteed income, whether earned, borrowed, or otherwise, is what you need while you peddle an idea. It takes time—often years. Researching a small business venture, developing a grant from a foundation, earning a scholarship, finding seed money —all these require organizational skills, verbal and writing ability, a persuasive knack, lots of patience, and plenty of conviction.

Most ideas fail. Some succeed. A lot depends on funding, management, and luck. But that's the free-enterprise ethic. No system can compete with it, since ideas that work satisfy human needs. If you've got an idea rolling around in your brainpan, the crazier the better, try writing it up and selling it. Moreover, it's a cinch seeing the most important people in an organization if you have an idea that helps them solve a *problem.* The proposal development approach to finding what you want is the last refuge for entrepreneurs. The Department of the Interior should declare them an endangered species along with the bald eagle, which they resemble.

"Do organizations pay travel expenses for job seekers?"

You won't know unless you ask; many companies budget to bring job seekers from out of town into corporate headquarters. Especially Fortune 500 companies and the bigger law firms. So, press an employer at a gateway interview for a shot at interviewing at the home office on their nickel. If they spring for your expenses, you can be sure they are interested.

"How do you get through the gatekeepers to the boss?"

Often called special assistants, confidential secretaries, administrative aides, palace guards. They control access: access to the boss, to power, to information, to the decision-making process.

Gatekeepers surround the boss, screen his phone calls, read his mail, write his letters, develop his agendas, compose his speeches, control information he needs to make a decision. Gatekeeper jobs are as important as the boss's, which is why they are so eagerly sought. Behind every great man or woman there are special assistants whose greatness is their anonymity, who the nobles of the realm remember with esteem and affection because these persons make their jobs easier.

But "assistants-to" should be gatekeepers, not toll collectors. Most gatekeepers, of course, are secretaries. Secretaries manage most organizations; her opinion of you is as important as her boss's. Secretaries know the score, who is paid what, who is about to be fired, who has the power, where to find other jobs in the organization, and the personality quirks and lovable eccentricities of every decision maker in the place. When you bag that good job, take her to lunch, for God's sake. Always memorize her *first name* and use it —over and over—when phoning in for those follow-up appointments.

Call her—or him—and drop a first name, which you should note on your 3" × 5" card. Always press to talk to her or his boss and—after the interview—write a thank-you letter to the boss and mention how much you liked his or her secretary. Effective secretaries are, in fact, *the* organization—they make the place hum. These are, in fact, often judgment jobs no matter what the women's liberation movement proclaims.

"What's so important about thank-you letters?"

Graceful, handwritten thank-you letters convey sincerity above all else. Try mentioning one thing learned, or some skill you failed to cover, in the interview, clear up any misunderstandings, repeat how much you value all referrals, send something of interest (e.g., a newspaper clipping), and finally thank the interviewer and say you'll stay in touch. At the conclusion of your job campaign mail a programmed letter of thanks to everyone who helped or talked with you during your job search. Take it from me: People like to be remembered and will cheer your success. That goes for everyone you interviewed who didn't offer a job, friends who offered tea and sympathy, and colleagues back at work. Be sure to add a nice, handwritten personal note to your announcement, especially to your former boss (and other key people). Who knows? Your ex-employer might want to hire you and your new firm!

"How important are job titles in attracting effective people?"

So much so that job titles conceal more than they reveal, cause institution-wide identity problems, and hobble effective communication. All in the name of stroking the ego.

Yesterday in America, we called people "clerks"; today they are "administrative technicians"; yesterday we called people "salesmen"; today they are "marketing engineers"; garbagemen have become solid-waste technicians; ticket takers are ramp engineers; and press agents are public-information specialists.

All are products of the industrial imagination. Note how many titles are pseudo-technical.

In addition to corrupting language, obscuring communication, and generally deluding postmodern man, playing games with phony job titles represents a good deal of the management manipulation younger people so rightly complain about.

Once upon a time I needed a full-time person to repair a hundred commodes at a summer camp I managed. I had no luck advertising for plumber/janitor/maintenance types.

So when I rewrote the ad, I said:

"WANTED: A HYDRAULIC MECHANIC."

Four applicants called the next day.

Well, it was my first experience in playing games with titles. And if God is just, I'll pay in the hereafter. Be sure you make prospective employers define your title before accepting employment.

"Where do I find the information to conduct a job campaign?"

Most judgment-job seekers, many with advanced degrees and highly refined research skills, play dumb when they think about this question. If a bright historian can research the origins of the Boer War, she certainly can research how to break into investment banking. Unfortunately, she doesn't think about it.

Having interviewed a few thousand people who have found marvelous (and not so marvelous) jobs, I like to find out how a job seeker bird-dogged the employer in the first place. What follows is a capsule summary of written sources, most of which every job seeker could use:

—libraries (the bigger, the better)
—placement offices (usually have all the standard references)
—trade associations (great for lists of employers)
—college placement directories
—company annual reports (the best overall view of an organization), capability statements, and brochures
—Christmas card lists (use your parents' and your own list)
—Dun & Bradstreet Reference Book
—Federal Phone Book (the best single guide to finding a job in the District of Columbia)
—Poor's Register of Directors and Executives
—Congressional Staff Directory (for those with a political penchant)
—all newsletters (try to buy their subscription lists)
—listings in the lobbies of office buildings (quickly scanning

these handy directories is ammunition for the cold-turkey interviewer)

—alumni listings (the best single source for curiosity interviewing. A few progressive colleges and universities maintain up-to-date, computerized printouts of alumni addresses, professions, names, titles, and phone numbers)

—MacRae's Bluebook

—Thomas's Register of American Manufacturers

—Moody's manuals

—All chambers of commerce (often have libraries and photocopying facilities)

—people mentioned in trade journals (announcements of promotions, transfers, new accounts are lead-ins for job seekers who know that business activity usually means new job opportunities)

—trustees (usually know the chief executive officer and can arrange an interview)

—Fitch corporation manuals

—bankers (who know what firms are on a line of credit and expanding)

—any passenger you meet on an airplane

—listing of conference participants (an excellent way to approach the top people in a specific field)

—any Rolodex (listing of phone numbers) of someone you curiosity-interview

—all trade newspapers

Three days' intensive researching, photocopying, and collating should yield hundreds of organizations that deserve your résumé. Remember, the *white* business pages of your phone directory are your best source. Take a letter, using a ruler and flashlight (have you ever tried reading ten columns of phone numbers without a ruler and a bright light and you're wearing bifocals?!), read and record the addresses and phone numbers of a variety of organizations, write them up on 3" × 5" cards, phone and find out the name of their presidents, then send out your résumés with notes in your own hand: "I'll be phoning you Monday morning to determine when it would be convenient for us to meet." This strategy should double the number of interviews you receive. And remember, the better known, the bigger, and the older the institution, the more likelihood that your résumé will be minuted to the personnel department. The smaller, lesser-known, newer organizations (which are not likely to have a personnel department) are the least likely to receive any résumés.

"What specifically do you look for in the trade press?"

In addition to picking up the jargon of the industry, checking out the want ads (particularly how employers in this field describe jobs), and developing a feel for trade trends, you will find information on promotional reassignments and awards.

A nice letter of muted congratulations on your part and a shameless pitch to see the celebrated man or woman could pay off. None of us are thanked, congratulated, or praised enough. That includes people professedly making it. Recognition is important, particularly recognizing a person you would like to hire as your employer.

"I've heard that the best way to find a good job is to take the bull by the horns and simply drop in on the head of an organization and ask for a job. Is there any truth in this approach?"

That's the cold-turkey contact.

And whoever told you that gave excellent advice.

It's the most brazen and best way to find a job. Also the toughest and most discouraging.

How to do it?

Call the president of Sticky Wicket, Inc. or some junior officers. Say you want a job. Or drop in cold and, two to one, they will see you.

Cold-turkey contacts are direct and uncomplicated. People either say, "No, you can't see Mr. Fourflusher, he's in conference" (everyone you will find in job searching is in conference, at a meeting, or traveling) or, "Yes, will you give me your name, please?"

The president or other chiefs inside an organization carry weight down through the hierarchy. Seeing them first sets you up favorably with anyone else you see in the company; hiring authorities are predisposed to like you because you sail through a power channel. Don't cold-turkey personnel directors—their job is to tell you there are no jobs.

Learning the cold-turkey approach is tough; it takes brass. So appear effective. And by acquiring this skill, you will be set up for life in making valuable contacts. Hardly anybody likes to sell himself, which is the essence of job finding. If you cold-turkey a job, good grief, you can do a lot for your organization—because you've shown you can do a lot for yourself.

"Are there any advantages to looking for judgment jobs in organizations that are failing?"

Job searchers are wrong about layoffs and troubled industries. Yesterday's layoffs may be today's recruitment opportunities. Organizational tailspins mean problems to be solved.

When you find a job in a failing firm, it's smart to assume responsibility, learning much where mistakes have been made. Struggling firms need talent and brainpower. This strategy is particularly recommended for those crisis managers who like to turn organizations around. Layoffs don't solve problems. Intelligent job seekers know that employers want solutions, and proposing how to solve problems is a key to finding judgment jobs.

"What about taking short-term employment while looking for a full-time job?"

Remember in college when you waited on tables, worked in a national park or on a construction crew? You earned money and gained experience and met some fine people. So while looking for a judgment job, don't sneeze at taking a grunt or a stop-loss gig. It solves the money problem while you take your time finding the right job. Better to find a job you want (and take a year doing it) than to take a job you don't want but *must* accept.

Try finding jobs with variable hours: hacking, bartending, and hotel clerking, working nights and weekends, liberating you for workdays to pursue the job campaign. And don't fret about quitting a grunt job to accept a judgment job. For stopgap jobs, employers expect high turnover and plan for it. Besides, if hard times hit *him,* do you think he's going to feel responsible for you?

"What's the difference between looking for stop-loss, summertime, and short-term work and looking for that so-called judgment job?"

Almost everyone is successful at finding squat work. Don't knock it: It provides a steady income to finance a college education, for example, and gives young people a taste for coping with authority, dealing with frustration, and following directions. We find these jobs through our friends, personnel offices, job finding the traditional way.

What you've learned looking for and finding summer jobs is applicable in the judgment-job search: Showing up on a Monday morning at a construction worksite with your hard hat and toolbox is bound to yield a job offer when a hungover backhoe operator fails to show for roll call. The cold-turkey approach, which worked for our grandfathers and mothers, will work for you, too.

The major difference between the traditional and the self-managed job search is that you're being considered for a lot more than just your labor in a judgment job. Therefore, give up thinking that you're still just a busboy, bartender, or bushwacker, those jobs classically filled by personnel departments.

For important judgment jobs, for which there is an advertised demand, the personnel department can be a conduit rather than an obstacle. But for jobs where competition is intense, where many are called and few are chosen, go to the operating people who screen you *into* the system, not to those who screen you *out*.

"Is it fair to call back employers and ask why you didn't land a job?"

Most employers won't level; some will, and that kind of constructive feedback is too rare. It could sharpen your sales pitch at the next job interview. In fact, welcome criticism on your job search. But carefully weigh it, too. Some people like to intimidate the unemployed and give them poor advice. Judge the advisers wisely, and don't hesitate to stick to your convictions. That's what I mean by job finders having a mind of their own.

"What about recontacting firms that have already rejected you?"

Why not?

Organizations don't file a 3″ × 5″ index card on your candidacy. You're looking for a job, not election to the College of Cardinals. Last month, sure, the personnel department sent its form reject. Chances are, this time around, your résumé will surface on the desk of a division manager whose budget has just been increased.

And don't hesitate to send résumés to more than one person in large organizations. (Do you sincerely believe your résumé will be read by everyone at XYZ, Inc., who has need to see it? Yes? I'll bet you believe in the Tooth Fairy, too.) Remember, résumés are junk mail; some are shredded. The few effective résumés are at least *read,* if only by a secretary. And, as we now know, secretaries control paper flow, and your résumé could be the first thing the boss reads tomorrow after *The Wall Street Journal.*

"What about responding to want ads?"

Study the want ads.

While the job advertised isn't your cup of Sanka, maybe the organization is. In addition, study dated want ads; chances are the job hasn't been filled the first time around, or all the candidates were lacking, or money wasn't found for it three months ago and is available today. In all events, want-ad reading is a part of every job seekers' breakfast routine. Studying how an employer describes a job assists you in the vocabulary of describing yourself. In a word, appropriate key words and jargon written to portray a job and use the same words to describe yourself. It's scary how effective you appear, but it's what employers mean when they say, "Susan, you talk our language. When can you come aboard?"

"How can replying to a three-month-old ad find me a job?"

Employers often don't know what they want; like most job seekers, they fish. And the fish they hook help define what's wanted. Moreover, the politics of filling a job are often so involuted, organizations often blow their credibility with effective job candidates, who in the meantime accept other jobs. So back-read the Los Angeles *Times.* Local libraries stock newspapers from all over the nation, and an afternoon of ad reading nicely breaks the routine of job seeking.

"Should I respond to blind ads?"

Which employers use to conceal their identity, taking themselves off the hook; employers needn't respond to a sackful of résumés sent to a box number. Advertising with a blind ad is another way that organizations do market research on the labor supply before making important decisions about new plant sites or whether or where to relocate the home office. Finally, blind ads cover up a plethora of illegal, unethical, or shaky wheeler-dealer schemes. Religiously following up on blind ads is like kicking over a rock and watching the bugs scurry.

Never waste a cover letter on a blind ad. A functional format with a note scrawled on the top in your hand—"Give me a call if we can do business"—is sufficient. Watch out, however. Ten to one you'll receive a phone call for the "Mgt. exec's job, fine future, great pay" inviting you to sell aluminum siding in the greater Pittsburgh area.

"Any thoughts on giving employers a deadline?"

Why not?

After all, employers frequently demand a decision from you by Labor Day, or a month after graduation, and so forth.

Establish a deadline, therefore, if you must make other plans in case the job doesn't materialize. For example, if an investment banking firm is delaying making a decision about your employment, and it's either that or a two-year stint in graduate school in Geneva, let them know your need to know a week before your jet takes off from Kennedy. Pressing employers puts pressure on hiring authorities. Operating people will make calls during vacation to straighten out the personnel department, which is sitting on the paper. And any decision, yes or no, is better than no decision when your time (which is valuable) and your future are at stake.

"Any special hints on how to cope with frustration during the job search?"

The toughest talent of all, on the job or off, is patience. Particularly in the proposal-development approach, patience is a virtue. Like a child waiting for Christmas in July, many job seekers can't wait out their luck. The anxiety of joblessness compels them to accept the first job offer rather than patiently build a job campaign aimed at the job they want. Probably these men and women are disqualified for judgment jobs, because judgment jobs require people with unusual capacities to cope with frustration. Job hunting is frustrating.

"How would you rate the various strategies for finding a judgment job?"

B   Cold-turkey interviews of important strangers in key jobs

A+   Interviewing friends in key jobs

B	Functional résumés, widely and indiscriminately mailed within your field, with a telephone follow-up
F	Obit résumés with standard cover letter, indiscrimately mailed
F	Completing application blanks and interviewing personnel types
C	Using personnel agencies, executive search firms, and career counselors
C	Acquiring another advanced degree and interviewing through a college placement office
F	Curiosity interviewing in hopes that someone will like your looks and offer you a job
B+	Talking about your job campaign widely and collecting names of people to see
F	Hunkering down at a grunt job and stopping the judgment-job search
C+	Joining a job club like "Forty Plus"
A	Selling ideas and proposals
D	Registering at the U.S. Employment Service
C+	Mounting a blitz letter campaign to company presidents
A	Taking a stop-loss job and continuing your judgment-job search

"So dream jobs do exist, but you must make them come true on the job?"

Or sell an idea—i.e., the proposal-development approach—to fill the job you want.

The point is, job finders need a base: a job. After you're on a payroll, opportunities—given the right boss, organization, and your own talent and motivation—surface. That's when you truly hire yourself an employer. That's when people who feel good about themselves, folks who work for the pleasure it gives, design a future for themselves at XYZ, Inc. Detecting a real need at the firm, the intelligent person proposes how to fill that need. The trick is in meshing what needs to be done with what you *want* to do. Not easy, and the quality needed is good judgment.

Interview people who have jobs you want, "dream jobs." As sure as every monkey hangs by his own tail, a dream job is the product of a *single* person's initiative.

SIX

Face to Face

The intelligent job seeker ignores the many myths about interviewing before pounding the pavement. What follows is a list of these untruths and some helpful tips.

Myth 1: The aim of interviewing is to obtain a job offer.

Only half true. The real aim of an interview is to obtain the job *you want.* That often means rejecting job offers you don't want. Before you do backflips for an employer, be sure you want the job. Moreover, while interviewing, talk about yourself in terms of what you can *do,* rather than using the vocabulary of job titles ("I'm an operations analyst . . . ," "I'm a general manager . . . ," "I'm a commodity broker . . ."). Talk about yourself in terms of skills ("I'm a hell of an effective proposal writer . . . ," "I know how to *prospect* for new business . . . ," "I'm especially good at analyzing problems . . . ," and let your résumé backstop with *evidence* of your writing, marketing, and problem-solving skills.

Myth 2: Always please the interviewer.

Not true. Try to please yourself. Giving accommodating but not necessarily authentic answers, losing touch with your own feelings (in order to get in touch with some other person's feelings), and, in general, practicing an abject policy of appeasement get you nowhere. Of course, don't be hostile—nobody will hire someone disagreeable. But plainly a middle ground exists between being too ingratiating and being hostile. An effective interview (whether you are offered the job or not) is like an exciting conversational encounter with a seatmate on an airplane.

Myth 3: Try to control the interview.

Nobody controls an interview—neither you nor the interviewer —although one or both parties often try. Then it becomes a phony exchange between two human beings; no business is likely to be transacted. When somebody tries to control us, we resent it. When we try to control somebody, he resents us. Remember, you can't control what an employer thinks of you, just as she can't control what you think of her. So hang loose when interviewing. Never dominate the interview. Compulsive behavior turns off your authenticity.

Myth 4: Never interrupt the interviewer.

No dice. "Never talk when I'm interrupting," said McGeorge Bundy.

Good advice.

Study the style of an effective conversationalist: He both interrupts and is interrupted! A stimulating conversation makes us feel free—free to interrupt, to disagree, to agree enthusiastically. We feel comfortable with people who allow us to be natural. So, when interviewing, half the responsibility lies with you. Do you seem uptight? Try being yourself for a change. Employers either like or dislike you, but at least you'll make an *impression.* Leaving an employer indifferent is the worst impression you can make. The way to make an effective impression is feeling free, which frees your interviewer to be herself!

Myth 5: Don't disagree with the interviewer.

Another silly myth. If you don't disagree at times, you become, in effect, a "yes" person. Don't be afraid to disagree—in an agreeable way. And don't hesitate to change your mind. The worst that could happen would be that the interviewer says to himself, "There's a person with an open mind." The conventional wisdom says "be yourself." But how many people can be themselves if they don't feel free to disagree?

Myth 6: Never ask for a job; wait for it to be offered.

Another half-truth. Of course it's nicer to be asked than to ask for it. But it's also bad strategy to be an occupational wallflower. Asking for a job you want shows a healthy assertiveness and demonstrates a strong will and healthy ambition, excellent characteristics for important jobs. So don't crawfish: Be bold.

Once upon a time, like most fifteen-year-olds, I was compulsorily enrolled in my high school's dancing class. The drill was to line the girls up on one side of the gymnasium, the boys on the other, play a slow fox-trot and . . . dance. Boys were expected to stride across the floor and ask a girl.

There was only one girl I wanted—Dolores. Boy oh boy, did I want to dance with Dolores. But I thought, "What if Dolores doesn't want to dance with me? That would be a mistake, right? So I won't ask her to dance. I won't invite any girl to dance." It's understandable that I flunked dancing class.

Of course, the bold, effective approach means you'll have to cope with rejection and sometimes be turned down for a job you *do* want. But that's how you learn to be an effective job hunter: You bounce back from disappointment and persist in looking for work you want. Drive and stamina are the hallmarks of people who find judgment jobs.

Myth 7: Never reveal how much money you want.

Nonsense. "By the way, what's your ballpark figure?" is a frequent question during an interview. Most job seekers fail to tell the interviewer what they want. But savvy job hunters do just that (usually slightly more than the *maximum* of what's realistic). And then add, "Of course, I'm flexible." Translation: I'm ready to listen to any reasonable offer.

Having established your skills means going the final lap and finding somebody to pay you (and pay you very well) for the exercise of those skills. All of which means eliminating some employers and focusing on organizations that can foot your bill.

Putting a high price on your skills impresses next employers. How can you be worthwhile if you don't think so? Finding work you want and that pays well is a great confidence builder. But the basis of self-confidence is ability: Know thyself. People who don't know themselves think they have no abilities, no skills. They think they are worthless. Therefore, they accept scut wages for jobs they *don't* want.

Myth 8: Never interview after accepting a job.

Not true. You're never employed until on the payroll. Employers often make mistakes: They don't budget for jobs they offer, fail to convince their boss about the need for the job in the first place, don't clear it with Personnel, and so forth—horror stories. Therefore, protect your interests and don't cancel appointments to interview even after accepting a job offer you do want. Moreover, who is to say you won't be offered a better job?

Check the following list and weigh how well you interview.

(1) Do I always wait until an interviewer is seated before sitting down myself? (Answer: This is a business transaction, not a royal audience, but show some respect.)

(2) Do I always write a pleasantly short thank-you letter to those who took the time to interview me? (Super. Employers are bound to remember and like you.)

(3) Do I maintain good eye contact during an interview? (Swell. But a fixed stare is too much of a good thing.)

(4) Do I avoid being comic or cute when interviewing? (Good humor isn't forced; it's most effective when spontaneous and authentic.)

(5) Do I dress to please? (Yes, but also dress to fit your craft, talent, profession, field, and to please yourself. Obviously, dressing to interview as the business manager for a rock band isn't the same as facing a Procter & Gamble campus recruiter.)

(6) When an interviewer says, "Tell me about yourself," do I stress abilities and accomplishments? (Don't build on academic degrees or experience unless education and past jobs support the job you want. And practice a fifty-word background summary.)

(7) Do I show genuine curiosity about employers? (That is, do you ask the interviewer numerous questions? If an employer does most of the talking, it's clear he feels comfortable and you've made a favorable impression.)

(8) Do I ask for advice in the job hunt? (Most people love giving advice, and it's often useful.)

(9) Do I avoid a too casual interviewing manner? (Phony sophistication is a real turn-off to employers.)

(10) Do I have small talk ready to begin an interview? (Yesterday's Patriots-Redskins game, the devalued dollar, the wretched weather outside, all commonplace subjects, natural items of discourse between strangers.)

(11) Do I reveal strong feelings and values? (Smart *if* you persuasively backstop your opinions with conviction.)

(12) Do I buckle under stress questions? (All of which are meant to see if you can be intimidated: Do you freeze, babble like a child, self-destruct?)

(13) If I don't understand a question or why it's important, do I say so? ("Why is that question important, Ms. Employer?" An excellent way to find out what's really on the employer's mind.)

(14) Am I able to say "I don't know" without embarrassment? (Who knows the answers to everything?)

(15) Do I answer questions concisely? (Many long-winded job applicants answer questions that were never asked. Stick to "I don't know," or follow up with some questions to the employer to buy time to think out your answers.)

(16) Am I sensitive to an employer's being uninterested in my response? ("Am I giving you the information you want?" A good question to ask an interviewer when you note her eyes glazing over.)

(17) Am I being myself in a job interview? (Being yourself is tough. Anyplace. Some people, however, naturally interview better than others. These lucky people are in touch with themselves, know how to cope with authority, are self-assured, and self-confidently authentic. Moreover, they are excited about the prospect of finding a job.)

Most job seekers and all first-time job searchers are anxious about tricky questions. Many freeze when they sense a tough question has been asked and are certain—after the interview—that they blew it. Accordingly, some job searchers are convinced that accommodating and pleasing interviewers is the best policy. But the accommodating job candidate appears weak and indecisive, not exactly a stellar impression. To improve your interviewing skills, therefore, let's consider some tough questions an employer might ask and (a) how traditional job seekers might answer and (b) how someone hiring an employer might reply.

Question: *"What have you been doing since leaving your last job?"*

Answer (a) "Well, ah, I ah . . . have been seeking professional employment . . . and, ah, taking night courses in computer programming to, ah . . . enhance . . . my qualifications because, boy oh boy, do I need a job!"

Answer (b) "Mostly looking for work. It takes time, but I find it fun to talk to people—like yourself—doing interesting things. I'm giving myself four months to find a good job, and I think I'm going to come in under deadline. By the way, how much time are you giving yourself to fill this job?"

Question: *"So, how long have you been out of work?"*

Answer (a) "Well, let's see . . . about eight months . . . of course, I didn't seriously start looking until about two weeks ago. I mean, I had to work closely with my attorney, that is, the lawsuit had to be put together. . . . My former employer won't settle."

Answer (b) "Heck, I haven't been out of work; I just haven't been paid for it. I took a super vacation to Europe for two months and let me tell you, traveling is hard work. And looking for a job is hard work, too. But, as you can tell, my job goals are pretty focused and I'm sure I'm going to get close to what I want.

Question: *"Okay, why did you leave your last job?"*

Answer (a) "Well, I'm . . . ah . . . always on the lookout . . . for, ah, more money and it seemed the time to quit my dead-end job. . . . I mean, I wasn't going anyplace . . . and you can't believe how stupid the guy was I worked for."

Answer (b) "Gee, I liked my last job although the money wasn't all that good, but I took the bull by the horns and talked through my future with the boss (a hell of a nice woman) and she seemed to think, and I agree with her, that another working environment would offer more opportunity and responsibility. I helped find my replacement and decided that after five years without a real vacation, it was time to give myself that long trip. I'm sure glad I did because I'm ready to go to work now."

Question:	*"Are you considering other positions?"*
Answer (a)	"No, sir. I want work as a customer relations representative with XYZ Corp. I have no other plans.
Answer (b)	"As you can tell from my résumé, I've a series of different goals, any of which I would consider since they all relate to what I can contribute. I have two definite job leads with other employers and a third I'm pursuing. I sure would like to add XYZ to the list. How many candidates do you want to seriously consider before making a decision?"
Question:	*"Where do you see yourself in five years?"*
Answer (a)	"Five years closer to the grave . . . ha, ha, ha. . . ."
Answer (b)	"Liking my job, growing with it, and making a contribution. If I qualify for more responsibility, I would like to be paid for it. What are the chances, if your business prospers and I'm making a contribution, to climb the ladder?"
Question:	*"How do you feel about weekend work?"*
Answer (a)	"Do you pay overtime?"
Answer (b)	"I'm terribly active in Little League and a vestryperson at the church, but I'm prepared to give up these activities for the right job. Actually, I work best at odd hours. How many weekends did you work last year?"
Question:	*"What's your husband think about your traveling half-time?"*
Answer (a)	(long silence) "If you don't withdraw that question, I'll report you to the EEOC."
Answer (b)	"Fortunately, my husband is a self-employed architect and his office is in our home. I think he actually enjoys my being out from underfoot, especially

when he's on a big job. Does your wife object to your traveling?"

Question: *"What do you want from this job that you weren't getting from your last position?"*

Answer   "Actually . . . with the new house and everything I
(a)   really need more money. . . . And I like the idea of the company paying my country-club dues. Most of my friends would envy me if I got the job."

Answer   "More responsibility. Frankly, there is a bigger bud-
(b)   get to work with here and more resources, and I like the idea of being paid on the basis of what I produce rather than the time I'm in the job. That's why a lot of my friends want to work here."

Question: *"Why do you want to go into (government contracting, production management, project evaluation, et al.)?"*

Answer   "I have the experience and training to do the job."
(a)

Answer   "I have the ability and motivation. If you find a bet-
(b)   ter person, hire him or her."

Question: *"If you had your druthers, what would you really like to do?"*

Answer   (anxious silence) Well, I'm not really sure. . . . I
(a)   never thought about what I wanted. . . . I'm look-ing for work where I'm needed."

Answer   "Even if I didn't need the money, I'm fairly sure I
(b)   would like to work in marine insurance. I have my own boat, like to be close to the water, and selling people what they need is my idea of the way I like to spend my life. Most people here seem to like what they are doing."

Question: *"Whom would you choose for this job?"*

Answer   "Well, I'm not sure. . . . Well, I would hire the
(a)   most qualified person."

Answer   "Whomever you choose should have a high energy
(b)   level and know how to analyze problems and dele-gate authority. I need only six hours of sleep a night, have spent my life solving thorny problems, and

have a hunch I'm able to pick the people to solve problems I've diagnosed. Do you think these qualities are what's needed?"

Question:	*"How can you help our organization in the long run?"*
Answer (a)	"In the long run, we're all dead . . . ha, ha.
Answer (b)	"If I can't, I hope I'm not here for the long run or even for the hundred-yard dash."
Question:	*"Why do you want to work here?"*
Answer (a)	"Because there's a job I think I can do."
Answer (b)	"I'm not sure I do until I know more about it. Tell me, what do you want this person to accomplish in this position?"
Question:	*"Are you able to relocate?"*
Answer (a)	"Well, would you pay my moving expenses?"
Answer (b)	"What I do is more important than where I live. Let's talk about what you want me to do."
Question:	*"Are you a leader?"*
Answer (a)	"Oh, yeah."
Answer (b)	"That's for you and my references to judge. I know I'm a good follower."
Question:	*"What are your pet peeves on the job?"*
Answer (a)	"Oh, I don't know. . . . Nothing much makes any difference."
Answer (b)	"I don't much care to work around people who don't like their work; I hate endless meetings; people who are afraid to confront other people; a lack of pride in what's being done."
Question:	*"What are the adjectives that best describe your weaknesses?"*
Answer (a)	(long silence) Uh . . . ah . . .

Answer (b)	"I've never thought about it. I'm impatient with downtimers and clock-watchers. Impatience, I suppose. And I'm glad this job doesn't require a lot of budget planning. If I can't do something, I know how to find someone who can."
Question:	*"What else can you tell me about yourself?"*
Answer (a)	"I, uh, that is . . . have you read my résumé?"
Answer (b)	"Well, I'm a compulsive Celtics fan, can recite six passages from Shakespeare, and my friends tell me I'm a good person in the clutch. What more do I need to know about the job?"
Question:	*"What does your spouse do?"*
Answer (a)	"He's a pharmacist."
Answer (b)	"Can you tell me why that question is important?"
Question:	*"Why haven't you made more progress in your career?"*
Answer (a)	"I had some awfully bad breaks. First, I . . . (ten minutes later) . . . and then on my last job, they wiped out my division with only two weeks' notice, and me with a second mortgage. . . ."
Answer (b)	"That's why I want to work *here.*"
Question:	*"What can we do to help you function better on the job?"*
Answer (a)	"Well, I sure could use a company car and a full-time assistant."
Answer (b)	"Establish clear lines of accountability, give me the tools and the authority, and let me do the job.
Question:	*"Have you ever made a suggestion to top management?"*
Answer (a)	"I once made a suggestion that they include peanut butter sandwiches in the cafeteria . . . but nothing happened."
Answer (b)	"I showed management how to overhaul the whole food-service scheme where I worked and was offered the job of managing our industrial cafeteria system

nationwide. I turned it down because I felt my real strengths were in designing systems, not managing them."

Question:	*"How did you solve a difficult problem on the job?"*
Answer (a)	"Well, I . . . ah . . . never like to make trouble . . . so I kind of learned to give with the punches."
Answer (b)	"I had to confront my boss with the fact that his best friend was milking the petty-cash fund. He blew his stack and asked me to prove it. I had written documentation in hand and he had to fire the man. A month later he thanked me—I've included his name on my references."

Question:	*"Are you a team player?"*
Answer (a)	"You bet. I was the captain of my college Frisbee team."
Answer (b)	"Yes and no: I like collaboration to achieve a common goal. And no, it's usually one man who must take the responsibility. I'd like to be that woman."

Question:	*"What was your greatest achievement on the last job?"*
Answer (a)	"I received regular in-step increases in pay."
Answer (b)	"I jumped up two levels in responsibility after reorganizing the company's distribution system."

Question:	*"What was your greatest disappointment on the job?"*
Answer (a)	"I guess . . . nobody has ever asked me that. . . . I'm, well . . . nothing disappoints me much."
Answer (b)	"I don't rake up past failures. I learn most from my accomplishments. I remember knocking myself out to improve organizational communications and didn't get the resources I needed. The company was having a bad year. It was the downturn in '81, so I don't feel bad about trying."

Some questions require answers prepared in advance. Typical of these are:

(1) "Tell me about yourself."
(2) "Isn't this a career switch?"

(3) "Do you think your education qualifies you for this position?" (When the job seeker does not have the appropriate degree.)

(4) "You don't have the experience/background for this position. How could you handle it?"

(5) "You're overqualified for this position, aren't you?"

Now, of course, there are no perfect answers, but with a little practice you'll improve, largely answering the same questions—over and over—through a whole series of interviews. At some point you might need to guard against glibness, appearing too smooth. So slow down the delivery, ponder the question for a few seconds, and relax.

For the record, here are some more questions you might be asked while interviewing. Try to think out loud how you would answer them.

"What was your rank in your college graduating class?"

"What four adjectives would best describe your strengths?"

"What have you read recently?"

"Tell me, why were you fired from your last job?"

"Do you like working with figures more than words?"

"Why did you major in canoe paddling at North Dakota State?"

"Why don't you go back to graduate school?" ("Why did you go to grad school?")

"Draw me a table of organization where you last worked and tell me where you fit."

"How many people did you supervise on your last job?"

"By the way, what are your salary requirements?"

"Name three people in public life you admire most."

"I'm going to describe four kinds of jobs. Which would you want?"

"How much money did you ever account for?"

"How many people have you fired, and how did you do it?"

"Show me some samples of your writing."

"Did you ever put your job on the line for something you believed in?"

"What men and women influenced your life most and why?"

"What do you want from a job: money, power, relevance, etc.?"

"Describe several problems you've had in your occupational life and how you've solved them."

"Would you rather do a job, design it, evaluate it, or manage others doing it?"

"When can you start work?"

A disclaimer:

Not all of these questions fit everybody. But the real hummer of a question, the one absolutely guaranteed to bring you to your knees and confess your incompetence, is, "What do you really *want?*"

Job interviews are not scientific (no matter what mumbo-jumbo schools of personnel administration say). Interviews are simply two people sizing each other up. That's why so much business goes on at cocktail parties, lunches, and even in locker rooms. The more informal both parties to an interview are, the better each judges the other.

Accordingly, conduct parity interviews with your employer. Remember, although the organization for which you might work pays you, you give it your life.

For openers, here are ten questions I would ask my next employer.

(1) "Why, exactly, do you want somebody for this job?"

(2) "Who is my boss and whom does he report to?"

(3) "Why don't you promote somebody within your organization?"

(4) "The job sounds interesting, but can you afford me?"

(5) "Can you draw me a table of organization? Where do I fit? And can you describe an average day's activities and the amount of time each task would require?"

(6) "I like coming to work late and working late—any problem?"

(7) "How many people did this job for your organization within the last five years? Can I talk to any of them?"

(8) "With whom do I relate on the job? Can I talk with them?"

(9) "You've been with this organization for five years. What have you liked *most* and *least* about it?"

(10) "How much money can I spend? How many people do I supervise? When would I start?"

Agreeably asking demanding questions of the interviewer protects your interests. Timely questions on important topics is another
way you hire yourself an employer. There's a collegial middle way
between sycophancy and hostility.

Again, you and the employer are doing each other a favor if you
accept a job he offers. It's a business deal, and, unlike so many
unproductive exchanges in life, a good business deal, renegotiated
from time to time and brought up to date, sometimes survives a
lifetime. When you look for a judgment job, avoid sounding like a
serf in the manor house. Don't be hostile to potential employers,
because you depend on them for a living. They depend on you for
the same thing.

Hostility is often found in the confused and unsuccessful job
applicant. It's the fruit of a bad job-hunting strategy, a lack of goals,
or an inability to empathize with employers.

It's contagious and obvious to everyone.

Antidotes: hard work, fun, and a good sense of humor. If you
look for a job, you can be almost anything—even flighty and silly—
but never sullen. All the more reason to list those qualities you
want from an organization. The idea is to check out your employer
before signing on for the long cruise. After all, Sticky Wicket, Inc.,
is checking you out!

Here's a list to help you decide whether an employer is worth
hiring.

—At your last interview, which concluded at 6:30 P.M., how
many people were still working at Sticky Wicket? (If none, start to
worry. Sticky Wicket, Inc., is either uncommonly efficient or the
hired hands stampede to hit the elevator at quitting time.)

—Does a secrecy syndrome pervade the organization? (It does?
Watch out! Sticky Wicket, Inc., is in real trouble. Maybe the boss
should be cashiered.)

—Do women, minorities, and young and old people occupy important, decision-making positions? (Yes. Then you know the organization is "fundamentally sound," as they say on Wall Street.)

—Does everyone in the organization dress and look alike? (No?
Fine! You'll feel right at home.)

—Did people you interviewed *laugh,* particularly at themselves?
(Great God, when do you start work?)

—Are people overworked at Sticky Wicket, Inc.? (No? What the hell do they need you for?)

—How long before you report to work? (Six weeks? Everything is true that I said about the personnel department.)

—Did the people you interviewed *like* one another? (Yes. Okay, *if* at the same time they seemed effective, competent, and potent. Otherwise, think twice about the Sunday Breakfast Club atmosphere.)

—Must you render periodic reports, attend scheduled meetings, make decisions based on published guidelines? (If so, you might chalk up employment at Sticky Wicket, Inc., as an unrewarding experience.)

Some final do's and don'ts:

If you're a woman, *do* extend your hand upon meeting your interviewer (male or female). Men still feel awkward about the protocol, so take the initiative! Shake hands firmly; no limpy, sensitive handclasps—this *is* a job interview.

Always address interviewers by their title: Ms., Mr., Dr., Colonel. If an interviewer, however, asks you to use his first name, don't back off, do so and ask him to do the same. The farther west you drift in North America, the more likely you are to swap first names. By the time you reach L.A., you're using nicknames.

Avoid a laid-back, play-it-cool, no-sweat psychology. This is the mark of bluffers and con men.

Don't trash your background or put down previous employers, colleagues, movements, schools, or experiences.

Admit mistakes; admitting an error of judgment ("making a mistake") and learning from it is qualifying for judgment jobs.

Now, for women, here are some questions savvy distaff types have asked *me* where I work. The questions are blunt but important. And reveal that she intends to make her way on merit as a professional while at the same time protecting her interests as a woman.

(1) "Why do all the men sit in offices and all the women in little cubicles?"

(2) "Could you describe to me the day-care facilities at Sticky Wicket, Inc.?"

(3) "Do I have to be especially tactful to men who work under me?"

(4) "What's your company policy on pregnancy?"

(5) "Why aren't there any women vice-presidents at Sticky Wicket, Inc.?"

(6) "Why is it, exactly, that only women are hired for the routine jobs?"

(7) "By the way, how many women sit on your board of directors?"

(8) "Would you mind describing similar positions you've filled here and tell me something about the qualifications of the candidates?"

(9) "As my boss, would you mind sharing some of the office duties, like Xeroxing, greeting visitors, making coffee, taking notes at important meetings, going to the deli, and arranging the department's Christmas party?"

(10) "Am I expected to engage in a lot of witless intramural flirtations on this job?"

If you're a woman, there are additional obstacles in the job search. While the fundamental approach to hiring yourself an employer remains the same regardless of race, sex, occupational status, and so forth, in the job market it is in the nature of things for you to be perceived differently. That will *never* change, unless unisex sweeps all before it.

Women have a positive duty to insist on egalitarian treatment in the marketplace. For no other reason than that economy necessitates a job. Women who don't *need* to work are rare exceptions these days; many women must work to keep their families economically afloat.

My contribution to the subject is that women are not *special.* That is, how they act as job seekers, on the job, and terminating from a job is in no wise different from their male counterparts.

For openers, women who seek important work, judgment jobs, a place in the organizational sun, should:

(1) Quit feeling sorry for themselves.

(2) Recognize that most younger and middle-aged men are stronger advocates of equity between the sexes on the job than are many women (according to a national poll).

(3) Know that—as a class—they are making enormous progress, far greater than any minority group, in the organizational world.

(4) Realize that bad luck on the job market (e.g., the promotion missed, the job that fell through, the contract not awarded) is not necessarily happening to you *because you're a woman.*

(5) Realize that taking on the shibboleths, dress, and manners of males is nonsense. (Women from the better business schools, for example, are interviewing in three-piece tailored suits.) Paying males the compliment of imitation is not building on your strengths.

(6) Guard against swapping the boredom of suburbia for the boredom of the boardroom. Boredom is inside every one of us, not a product of our environments.

(7) Face the fact that 10 percent of jobs in America are judgment jobs—tough to find, to qualify for, and to hold on to. Women who want them must be effective. No, not "nice" or "aggressive" or "cunning" . . .

(8) Realize that the balancing act of mother and wife with career is a difficult and tricky art. *No* woman succeeds at combining all three; men, particularly, fail. All the more reason to think through whether it's a judgment job you really want.

(9) Face it: 90 percent of jobs in America are not decisive inside organizations. Are you prepared to pay your dues in qualifying for a judgment job?

(10) Realize that economic independence, having a job, project, cottage industry—a talent you can exercise—is crucial to becoming happy with yourself. Also, it makes people (namely your husband, children, in-laws) happier with you.

Men shouldn't want women to be *dependent* on them. That's okay during the first stages of courtship, marriage, and procreation, but a drag as a marriage/relationship moves into its second stages (husbands should welcome a second income or a tax shelter). Whether it's a vocation or avocation, a special project or a regular job, a mad hobby or place in the corporate sun, an outside-the-home project (i.e., where a woman invests her emotions), a job helps the people around her, particularly her children, who see far too much of her anyway.

Children become more independent and self-reliant when

Mommy stops keeping them dependent on her. Many women deliberately tie husband and children to their apron strings. That way she needn't face up to personal (and job-search problems). Conversely, some wives work outside the home in order to *escape* family problems. At all events, women workaholics are as pitiful as domestic drudges who have no life outside the home.

Whether you are recycling into the job market (after a twenty-year stint bringing up baby) or a young woman new on the job market the walls of Jericho won't come tumbling down because you happen to be the new woman on the block. Most working women today must sweat out time on the line before employers pass out the plums.

Now that women are breaking down the doors of law, business, and other professional schools, it's worth repeating that many judgment jobs in America today are technical. In high technology, engineering, and applied-science organizations, women are as rare as a Swedish heat wave. If your daughter has a knack for math and likes science, give her a lot of love and encouragement.

SEVEN

Interviewing As If You Mattered

At this stage, you no longer investigate job leads and follow up on advice generated through curiosity interviewing. Now you're focused on two or three *real* objectives. That's because you are sure of what you want and where to look. Now you want to qualify for a real job.

"What do you mean by a 'real' job?"

A judgment job has a starting date, a salary range, definite purpose(s), specific people the hired candidate reports to and manages. Above all, there is a real commitment on the part of the employer to hire.

Genuine commitment is important. Many employers, to repeat, often can't make up their minds. They have a problem but can't define it and have trouble delineating the kind of person who *can* solve it.

"So employers are as confused as job applicants?"

Often.

Frequently they play games with job applicants. A confused employer, often without knowing it, schedules a series of interviews with a variety of people to educate himself. The process is not entirely invalid. By seeing a lot of people, the employer gradually defines a set of personal and job criteria he needs satisfied; he tests the manpower pool to discover if Mr. or Ms. Right really exists; he often accidentally falls upon *the* person with most of these characteristics.

All of this is time-consuming and frustrating for job seekers. But what employers are doing is *interviewing for information.* That is, they are trying to decide whether a job is worth filling (or creating) by comparing it against the available manpower. But watch out for game playing.

"Games employers play?"

(1) *"Now I have a job, now I don't."* Henry Hoax didn't line up his ducks. He has no approval from the controller, no idea what qualifications he seeks, and is vague about the specific purpose of the job.

He is incompetent.

You don't want to work for him (unless he's looking for someone to straighten out his atrocious hiring techniques).

(2) *"Would you mind—as part of your job as my special assistant—doing a few clerical chores?"* You are about to be hired as a secretary. If you've accepted, you've been had. Make crystal clear that you are a professional applicant. Let your résumé and person show it.

(3) *"I'm looking for a young person with a Ph.D. in statistics, with five years' progressively more responsible experience in a research organization, a fine publications history, a minority member, and someone who speaks fluent Finnish."* An employer of unreasonably utopian vision. In two months—when his own job is on the line—he'll take a second look at you.

(4) *"Say the job you want won't open up for about two months—would you mind terribly coming on as an administrative assistant until the urban-planning job becomes available?"*

"Certainly, but I want my *next* job defined and agreed to in writing."

"But don't employers have a responsibility to know what they want?"

Well, it would save them a lot of money (and time) if they did. Employers are often confused. A typical employer needs help, and the smart job seeker helps the employer *think through* the job. This is part of what I mean by hiring yourself an employer. And it means appealing to an employer's hidden agenda.

"What's an employer's 'hidden agenda'?"

A hidden agenda is what an employer hides from himself when looking for a person to fill a job. Employers won't admit it, but they are human. Thus, the personal factor, how you survive an interview as a human being, is as important as the qualifications and strengths you bring to a job.

"Isn't an employer's hidden agenda a formula to hire someone like himself?"

Often.

Effective employers, however, should hire personal, temperamental, and professional opposites—men and women who supplement their weaknesses rather than complement their strengths. Above all, employers should hire competent strangers, rather than just products of the old-boy/old-girl network.

The mark of a first-rate professional is the quality of his staff. If they are all, in certain respects, smarter than the boss, it's a mark of genius. Strong people surround themselves with a highly competent and disparate staff.

Again, hidden agendas are hidden even from employers themselves. Most people, including me, won't acknowledge that subconscious sympathies and antipathies often rule our thought processes. Accordingly, *this* employer won't hire you because you're over six feet tall, *that* employer won't hire you because you're not a lawyer, *this* woman likes you because you opposed the war in Vietnam, *that* man will hire you because you fought in Vietnam. It's obvious that no job searcher can control what employers might think any more than employers can control what you will think of them. Plainly, our being hired or not hired has more to do with hidden forces than employers are prepared to admit.

An unreported but vital factor in the whole interview process, something so obvious both employers and job seekers overlook it, is whether both parties to the interview *like* each other. Often this is the *only* factor that is important. But liking (and being liked) is often a matter of what we ate for breakfast that morning.

"Yes, but won't employers hire second-rate people so that they look good?"

And why work for them? That's what's meant by "First-rate people hire first-rate people, second-rate people hire third-rate people." (Rule #5) All the more reason to be discriminating in choosing an employer.

"What exactly, does an employer learn in an interview?"

Well, not much . . . and a great deal.

Sure, she can tell whether you're alert, intelligent, enthusiastic, "young," "old," etc. But what an employer really learns is whether she likes you, whether the signals are right, whether the *human* factors are working for both of you.

Remember, an organization is the sum of human beings who make it up. Two hours inside it and you know whether people working there are a class you want to work with for eight or more hours a day. So interview the employer. If the chemistry's good, chances are the job is for you. If the vibes are bad, chalk up those interviews to experience and let it help refine what's wanted in an employer you do hire.

During these hopeless interviews, switch your job pitch to a curiosity interview. Eventually you and some employer will light some fires. But remember, you can sometimes wade through fifty interviews before job lightning strikes.

"Is the climate of the interview important?"

The great factors in the interview are mood and atmosphere. You won't survive an interview if your interviewer:

—just fought with his spouse on the phone
—has five or more telephone interruptions
—hasn't lunched yet and it's 3 P.M.
—has seen five job applicants that day
—has four important decisions to make while he talks to you

What can you do?

Agreeably, tell your interviewer that it's a bad day and you'd be happy to come back at a less hectic time for another appointment.

"Will employers interview me on the phone?"

Don't let them.

Your job is to capture a face-to-face interview. Nobody is going to hire you—sight unseen—on the phone. But employers are "pre-qualifying" you.

Switch out the interviewer and press to see him *personally*. Tough with busy employers; but if you are interviewed by phone *without* a follow-up interview, no business will be transacted. Occasionally, it's okay to curiosity-interview by telephone. But the idea is to collect more phone numbers to call for face-to-face interviews.

"What do you wear?"

Knowing what you want to do is knowing what to wear.

Another reason to curiosity-interview is to observe the sartorial splendor of the working classes. This ranges in some places, like Cambridge, from proletarian drag to Beverly Hills décolleté.

An on-campus recruiter once hired a student dressed in a chemically soiled apron and another in his jogging pants. Both sprinted direct from lab and track to keep the interview!

Why not wing it and wear what you want? If your uniform fits the environment, maybe you've found a home. If it doesn't, why work there? Otherwise the conventional wisdom holds: conservative dress, shiny shoes, neat appearance, styled hairdo, and striped tie. *But knowing what you want to do is how you know what to wear.* And that's a product of curiosity interviewing. Note how engineers dress in the California's Silicon Valley; it isn't the same uniform as for investment bankers in New York City.

How does the royal family differ from thee and me? Well, note that royalty is trained never to touch themselves in public. Good advice for job candidates. Touching your nose, scratching hair, and all the rest are signs of stress. Composed interviewees use their hands animatedly and let them help in the interview. A poor job candidate uses his hands against himself. Mock interviews with friends will pick up this mannerism.

A personal bias on dressing for success: I simply can't hack the ubiquitous bows professional women are wearing. Yes, dress for success in the job interview, but on the job let the imagination in dress matters come into play. As for men, no man wearing a polyester leisure suit or sporting a diamond on his pinky was ever offered a job in my shop. And I'm not alone when I say that cheap shoes are a dead giveaway that a job searcher isn't a judgment-job candidate. And, please, unless you're interviewing in a recreational job, never, never wear *jogging* shoes to an interview. Otherwise, come as you are. Another tip to men: have two or three shirts custom-tailored. When the interview reaches the "let's get down to work" phase and the interviewer invites you to remove your jacket you'll come on like the Hathaway man.

Why is appearance so important? And so unimportant? In the mind's eye employers establish what a person should look like for a job, even though we know it's nonsense. How otherwise explain the uniform looks of advertising executives, industrial consultants, Marine Corps drill sergeants?

To test this theory out, I conducted an experiment. My company was simultaneously hiring for four different contracts. All of them differed in scope of work, objectives, and types of manpower. Of more than a hundred people I talked with over a four-week period, I could spot, by quickly glancing across the waiting room, which person was a candidate for what contract. The four kinds of jobs included (a) academics, (b) inner-city community-action types, (c) system analysts, and (d) political-action people.

There was no particular prescience on my part; anyone could have done at least as well. After twenty years in the people business, I feel like a casting director. Sure, appearance is important in up-front jobs. But I've hired plenty of effectives who needed hosing down, too. Of course, we keep them in the back room with the lawyers.

"Is there any way I can overcome feeling awkward in an interview?"

One reason you feel ill at ease is that you're trying to please someone besides yourself. You are not putting yourself first. And the result is an uptight, false, and unproductive exchange.

Employers are no different. I've seen them change from genial, put-together individuals into positive Manchurian mandarins. Or conversely, I've seen job seekers reduce normally tough and productive employers to gibbering eunuchs.

What accounts for this?

Each party starts playing a role completely outside his real character. The job applicant—deferential, petitionary, hat in hand; the employer—gruff, no-nonsense, business-is-*my*-business attitude.

But you can block out this kind of situation by simple authenticity, asking unexpected questions, interviewing the interviewer (asking him about *his* job)—in a word, treating your employer as an *equal*. And if he doesn't respond, why work for him anyway? He's flunked the interview—*with you*.

"What happens when interviewers say I'm too young for a job?"

—Ask your interviewer how old she was when she obtained her first job.

—Dress up in age: Style your hair, wear tasteful business apparel, adopt a restrained but not undemonstrative demeanor, all of which adds five years to your chronological age. But only if you feel comfortable.

—*Agree* with an interviewer that "the older you get, the better."

—Laugh slyly and indicate that youth is why you're so successful with older men/women!

"How do I evade embarrassing questions?"

Questions about your recent divorce, for example; or your five jobs in the past three years; or why you quit your last job.

Evading questions of a sensitive nature (why is it that so-called delicate matters are so indelicate?) is an invitation to a beheading. Your cover-up (as if recent American history weren't an example) is a greater problem than what's concealed; it causes interviewers to suspect *much* worse.

At the same time, there are questions that are downright rude and unnecessary. The best way to handle this kind of knuckle ball is to *ask* a question: "Mr. Employer, can you tell me why that question is important?" That puts the ball back in his court. And chances are, the question is important. I'm required as an employer to ask tough, indelicate questions. But I admire job candidates who make me give reasons for them.

Don't be disagreeable when you go up to bat. The employer is entitled to ask questions; in fact, it's *her* job. By finding out her reasons, too, you find out more about an employer's hidden agenda, and that information is golden.

"What about future-oriented questions?"

You mean like:

"Do you intend to go back to law school, marry, have children, follow your spouse to his next assignment, resume your artistic career, take a year off to travel in the Orient, become self-employed . . . ?"

Nobody reads the future. Don't let employers mousetrap you into thinking about future plans that don't include XYZ, Inc. And that's *not lying.* We don't know, in fact, what *may* happen; yes, we may marry, inherit money, start our own business. Don't read tea leaves in a job interview.

Answer this kind of question honestly. "I don't know. Obviously what I want to happen I've spelled out in my job objectives, and that's why I'm here talking to you. And so long as I'm effective and willing, you can count on me."

And that *is* the truth. Plenty of job finders, however, suffer from hoof-and-mouth disease. As soon as a soothsaying interviewer probes the future, our self-destructive candidate starts babbling like a running brook. Who is to say you won't turn on to Sticky Wicket and retire as its executive V.P. in thirty years?

"Isn't some communication in interviews nonverbal?"

The silent language. Yes indeed.

Raising your eyebrows, looking at your watch, staring distractedly into the middle distance, the light in your eyes, the twitch in his left earlobe—these often convey more than words. In all events, a few mock interviews with friends constructively bring some mannerisms to the surface that could put employers off.

Everyone knows the vocabulary of the silent language. Focus on what *you* do that subtracts from an otherwise excellent impression.

Smokers, take note: Smoking anything is a no-no these days. You'll cripple your chances of a job offer by lighting up. If it's difficult, get a prescription for nicotine gum and chew between interviews to relieve the craving. Of course, if the employer lights up and invites you to have a smoke, okay. But the no-smoking revolution is sweeping all before it. In five years the smoking prohibition will be uniform everywhere except at R. J. Reynolds.

"What about stress interviewers?"

Professional bullies; it's why they are in the interviewing business. Ten to one they were bullied on the playground and are paying society back. But bullies they are, nonetheless.

If someone deliberately:

—stands up in an interview and walks around you, *stand up* and follow him.

—plays games on the phone (while you wait biting your nails), open your briefcase and read *Rolling Stone.*

—interviews *across* his desk, stand up, pick up your chair, and place it *beside* his desk.

Stress interviews are favored by hard-nosed and boneheaded managers. Like the hypothetical problem-solving interview, it fosters gamesmanship and role playing. But job interviews never correspond to on-the-job situations. Inducing phony stress factors violates the essential condition of a business relationship: trust.

Employers who win through intimidation are slobs, losers, power trippers. Game players never win with unintimidatable people—i.e., people who know who they are, what they want, and what they can do. If you sense game playing in an interview, where how you play the boss is more important than what you do, make fast tracks. The folks who people this place are *insecure;* they feel that power is outside themselves and existence itself simply a *reflection* of their organizational identity. Another example of the frightful leading the frightened.

"What's the toughest stress question you ever asked?"

Occasionally I'll karate-chop an otherwise appealing job candidate with a question like "By the way, what makes you think *you're* so important?"

Now, of course, you *are* important! But often defenses crumble under the weight of someone who asks why. And people who love the pits quickly agree they are unimportant, ineffective, unemployable. Remember, it's your *manner* (as much as the *matter* of your answers) that is being evaluated. All the more reason to keep your eye on the bouncing ball. Put-down questions are asked to find out if employers can make you put yourself down.

"What about hypothetical problem-solving questions?"

A favorite pastime of many employers. Of course, it doesn't work.

Hypothetical casework is ivory-towerism; it certifies model builders, theoreticians, and business intellectuals—which is okay if an employer is hiring for a think tank, a college faculty, or the *Harvard Business Review*. Such tactics do reveal intelligence and logical intellectual processes. But for most jobs, be prepared to talk about past accomplishments and future contributions to employers.

"Any hints on starting the interview?"

The weather is still the best conversation starter, whether you're interviewing for a job, or sizing up a company president for a takeover bid. Name dropping is okay, if that's how you won the interview. Avoid a snappy opening gag; humor that seems forced isn't authentic.

Most employers are not practiced interviewers; they may feel more awkward than you. They fumble your name, lose your résumé, can't ask simple, direct questions—in other words, just like you and me. First names? Well, to repeat, in California you're safe in using first names; elsewhere ask, "May I call you Tom?" The point is to address each other *mutually* either by first names or as Mr. or Ms. But if I call you Tom and you call me Mister, suddenly you're subordinate and I'm superior and not much business is going to be transacted.

The exception is probably the young looking for that entry job. Sure, it's okay for Joe and Jane College to call an employer Mr. or Ms. even though they might be saying Joe and Jane. Again, use good judgment. In the South, the young still refer to their elders as "sir" and "ma'am," and it's both correct and attractive.

Don't let the interviewer use the résumé to guide the interview. This is a confession of the employer's inexperience. The résumé got you the interview, but only you can take the interview. Do bring extra copies to give the interviewer to pass around.

If interrupted, try refocusing on the subject to refresh the interviewer's memory. If the subject is boring, bring up another topic congenial to your showing off your strengths. And no fussbudgeting: ballpoint-pen clicking, rubber-band snapping, finger thumping, foot tapping—all anxiety symptoms.

A few hints on preparation: Schedule no more than three interviews a day (multiple interviews or overscheduling can cause embarassing conflicts and reflect on your time-management skills). Try arriving early for the interview to size up the turf, learn the secretaries' nicknames, and skim the company propaganda. If possible, have a long phone conversation with a colleague *inside* the company before the interview. Carry a small notebook or pad to take down telephone numbers and referrals, and some kind of carrying case for résumés, references, and writing samples. Not to mention aspirin tablets.

"How do you identify the decision makers inside an organization?"

Whether curiosity or job interviewing, make a habit of asking who the effective people are. In any firm or department composed of one hundred people or fewer, no more than ten people are important enough to interview. Power doesn't always match titles or a box on the organization chart. And power goes up (as well as down) the vertical chain of command. Trust the political judgment of *insiders* to reveal the key players.

"What happens when you've found a desirable hidden job and are about to interview the person who can make the offer?"

Well, what you *don't* do is:

—act casual and indifferent

—gush enthusiasm and become accommodating

—sit back and let the interviewer show his/her hand, answering questions when you don't know the answers

The best strategy is to describe what you want, what he needs, show the identity of objectives and ask for the job. This means saying "I don't know" when you don't know, asking him his opinion, and—above all—stressing that you *want* the job. Remember the salesman's creed: "Always *ask* for the sale!" Surprise: Many otherwise qualified candidates never ask for *the* job. Good jobs go to the *able and willing.* Therefore, follow up with a letter or a phone call repeating your theme song in a different octave.

"Is honesty the best policy?"

Exactly.

Next to courage, honesty is the most precious virtue. Your honesty might be the most memorable part of any successful job interview and what wins you the job.

Even if it doesn't, an employer is likely to remember you. Because of your candor, you'll be the first to hear about another opening at the XYZ organization. Honesty will, as Mark Twain once said, "please most people and astonish everyone."

Honesty gives you an instant name and organizational visibility. In an interview, honesty can be charming and memorable, and your job is to make an impression—even if you don't get the job. (The guy who remembers you is going to call about a job you *do* fit.)

So don't bluff.

Bluffing is especially obnoxious in the young. (Intergenerational conflict is no joke. Most employers over forty envy the young because they *are* young.) To add bluff to your natural—and desirable —enthusiasm is to rub out chances of finding a good job.

Bluff is not related to gumption—the tough art of hiring yourself an employer. Gumption means you don't give up, no matter how discouraged. Gumption is the main asset of a job seeker, new to a strange city, unconnected, but *not* powerless in the face of adversity.

Bluffers seem strangely serene when jobless. They know their only chance of landing a job is to fool an employer. Underneath the polish and glitter, however, they lack self-confidence. Because bluffers don't know who they are, what they want, or what they can do.

Plenty of people looking for work don't tell the truth. In a recent study, one of four job applicants lied in their résumés. For those who lie or can't tell the truth, the prospects are bleak.

To discover the truth, many employers ask the same question in different ways. Much like a trial lawyer who questions a witness. Be prepared to tell about a spotty work record, five relocations in three years, and a patchy education. Most job-search problems are attitudinal: We believe our work record is spotty when, in fact, it's in the nature of our work; our relocations might be necessary to our jobs or personal life; and our education (or lack of it) might have nothing to do with our work.

"Do employers lie in interviews, too?"

More downright mendacity is exchanged between employer and potential employee than in any other social situation known to mankind, save sexual seduction. When people go job hunting, the downright, doggone, deep bayou country lying that goes on is truly mind-bending.

And not all the lying is found on the part of the job candidate, hat in hand, best foot forward, the world-is-my-oyster profile. No, whether they represent the go-go semiconductor industry, a hotshot new government alphabetic agency, or a new and swingin' progressive institution of higher learning, employers start swapping lies with their interlocutors to the point the air is blue with the B.S. factor.

Whether you hire or want to hire yourself an employer, with a few important exceptions, always tell the truth.

"How can an employer tell when a job candidate is telling the truth?"

When there is no inconsistency among her (a) résumé, (b) interview, and (c) reference checkout.

A lot of answers flow from the candidate's referees, information that affirms, differs from or plays no role in what the candidate tells the employer. Reference checkouts complete an authentic profile of a job candidate: How well did she know herself in comparison with those who know her and her work best?

"But won't candor tick some employers off?"

So what?

If you know who you are, what you can do, and the kind of contribution you'll make to an employer, don't feel modest about revealing it. But trying to please, without pleasing yourself, won't work, sure as shootin'.

"Why do I always think about what I'm going to say next rather than listening to what's being said?"

Self-consciousness.

The opposite of self-awareness.

Self-conscious people are not active listeners; they don't listen to themselves. And thus don't listen to what employers are saying, thus eliminating themselves.

Active listening isn't passive any more than close reading is. But if we aren't listening to what's being said (i.e., we aren't listening to our feelings about what is being said), it's exactly like reading without understanding.

"Why do I self-efface in an interview?"

To efface something means to rub it out.

The self-effacing in an interview, therefore, cancel out.

An anxious interviewee sometimes thinks self-effacement is a form of respect to others. But showing respect to others isn't the same as self-effacement. Showing respect to others is a measure of self-respect. Moreover, a person who self-effaces with superiors often demonstrates contempt for inferiors. And that's not a particularly effective strategy in winning people's hearts and minds.

"But isn't there such a thing as coming on too strong?"

For starters, a person who comes on too strong often reveals information altogether unnecessary for an employer to know. Coming on too strong, being glib or long-winded, displeases employers and causes an employer to suspect a job searcher can't promote and protect his own interests. And if he can't defend his own interests, what self-respecting employer believes he could protect his?

Another kind of person who self-destructs is the small talker, so folksy he can't talk about important matters, being a Dutch Master at small matters. Thus, the focus is never on him or the job. The interview never takes off. True, small talk is what an interview begins and ends with, but it's often a crutch for the job seeker frightened of being stage center. Small talk is the way we evade feeling important. And small talk makes employers think we are unimportant. But small talkers are small fry compared to the too talky.

Remember, an exciting interview is simply two people exchanging and revealing feelings in a timely and appropriate manner. Feelings are real; employers listen to authentic people. A bad interview is when someone conceals what he feels or is unaware of what he is feeling and fills the void with talk. Such talk is anxious and unreal. The too talky are also poor listeners, since they evade real feelings (especially their own) and discourage an authentic exchange with an employer.

"Why do I start sweating in job interviews?"

Sweaty palms are a result of acute anxiety. The body is sending signals and the message is that we are about to eliminate ourselves. Anyone would sweat who was about to cancel out!

Why are we so worried?

Are we frightened of being evaluated? Do we think employers are more important than we are? Do we think employers are in control? Anxiety is a form of magic: We think that if we worry enough, the gods will intercede and obtain us the job. Unreal. The way to quash worry is self-awareness. Anxiety about measuring up defeats us from standing tall.

"How can people become less self-defeating in job interviews?"

By building on what's *real* in themselves: reciting accomplishments with conviction (not humbly), being demonstratively agreeable (never appeasing), strong-willed (not willful), conscious of self-interests (not dumbly accommodating), and being truly open and free with an interviewer (never disagreeable and hostile). Appeasers back off from confrontational situations and solve problems by evasion. Willful people are spiteful and self-destructive. And hostile folk communicate self-hatred and are unemployable (except maybe as prison guards, Mafia hit men, or art critics).

"How about note taking during an interview?"

That's okay for student interns, Gallup pollsters, and gumshoes, but bad form for judgment-job seekers. Keeping a handy pocket-size notebook to jot down addresses and phone numbers is useful, but never carry a steno pad to a job interview.

"Is it true that the first five minutes of an interview are most important?"

Half true.

That first five minutes transmits an impression that is hard to shake. Still, I've interviewed plenty of people (slow starters with good judgment) who don't reveal themselves so quickly that interviewers perceive that nothing is there. Keep in mind, when interviewing, to psych up before crossing the employer's threshold.

Warming up means some healthy anxiety. And some manageable anxiety is better than indifference or a slack demeanor. Tension, at the outset of an interview, is natural and desirable; it causes adrenaline to flow and brain cells to function. It's part of the fun in finding a job—and the challenge.

"How important are first appearances?"

Very, for some jobs. Airline flight attendants, front-office secretaries, customer-relations types, et al.

But for most judgment jobs a good first appearance gets you a free pass to first base, and that's all. From then on you've gotta circle the bases on talent. And that's what you've got plenty of. How you handle yourself in the interview, especially after it passes the uptight stage, is most important.

That's the body language of an interview.

"Body language?"

Eyes are important in hitting a baseball, lovemaking, and finding a job. Always—in an interview situation—from time to time look your interlocutor directly in the eyes.

Never wear dark glasses.

Body language is the *lingua franca* of the interview: Don't sit with arms akimbo or downturned face before the interviewer.

Open yourself physically in the interview.

Pay attention.

Help the interviewer. Ask the questions!

If humor comes, let it. The sooner you two become human beings the better.

And don't become infatuated with your own voice. Long-winded job searchers and employers deserve each other.

The economy of your speech, résumé, and person tells a good employer about your on-the-job EFFECTIVENESS.

Cultivate a passion for conscious concision. If asked a question, answer it, or say, "I don't know." In interviewing over ten thousand people in twenty years, I've found that the incredible inability of many job seekers to answer fairly simple analytical questions is astonishing. This goes for Ph.D.s, cabinet-level officials, and university presidents. Paying attention, responding frankly, honestly, and briefly makes a far better impression than *what* you say. Convey *sincerity* in what you say (and write), and employers listen.

Answer questions, therefore, *briefly* and stick to the point.

Let the long-winded stand in unemployment lines: many big talkers there.

"How can you tell whether a job is worth doing in the first place?"

—Ask to interview anyone who has held the job in the past five years.

—Ask what would happen if the job can't be filled.

—How many people does the job holder report to? Plenty of people in the world of work have more than one boss. Be sure you're not the fall guy for three supervisors who aren't communicating.

—Figure out if the job is *line* or *staff;* most jobs are an interesting mixture.

—Query the criteria used to screen out candidates for the job; pressing employers about a job's definition wins you high marks in the "taking a long, hard look" department.

"What are some of the questions I'm likely to face in a standard employment test?"

There's a slew of questions (repeated in various forms throughout the quiz) on:

—how well you loved Mommy and Daddy (you liked Daddy slightly better).

—your energy level (you never need more than five hours' sleep a night).

—your spouse (you love him/her to distraction, but you love your job *more).*

—your spare-time activities (you have none, loving work above all else).

—how you get along (people are never a problem, you love everybody).

Two generations of Americans have been raised on these tests, and everyone lies. The test givers know the test takers lie. The test takers know that they lie. Employers know the tests are worthless. So yes, sometimes it's okay to lie.

For plenty of sensitive jobs employers are increasingly insisting on lie- and drug-detection tests. Thus, the price we pay for some judgment jobs is an invasive violation of our civil rights. It is for each judgment-job seeker to weigh whether the price is too steep to pay. Examine every job as an employer must and ask yourself whether the comprehensive testing is necessary. And for plenty of jobs where the nation's security or people's lives are at issue, the answer is bound to be yes.

Other candidates for key jobs should expect a thorough medical checkout. A doctor's statement that you can present to a potential employer establishing an ability to work without restriction despite your double bypass helps lubricate the interviewing process. That goes for any other disability that won't play a significant role in your on-the-job effectiveness. Volunteering the information and documenting a clean bill of health when you sense an employer's unease makes a lot of sense.

"Aren't these tests designed to screen in the team players?"

That's my point. The last person who admitted he wasn't a team player died in 1938. It is reported that his was a full and happy life!

The real reason large employers still rely on tests is to get their personnel department off the hook. "Well, Mr. President, his Minnesota Multiphasic was high and our Urban Affairs people wanted to take a chance on the guy."

And test scores are great alibis for the personnel department. Scores mean nobody confronts a job applicant as a human being, says no, or rejects him. But, of course, saying no is an employer's right *and* responsibility—if he can't bear it, he's not doing his job.

"One of my big problems is being told repeatedly I'm not qualified for a job. What should I do?"

Do you have a set of realistic job goals?

Does your résumé support these goals on the basis of your real skills?

Do you know how to disagree pleasantly with an employer when he tells you that you are underqualified?

Again, most jobs are filled by people who meet only *some* of a job's specifications.

Job specs are written by personnel people who can't know the truth about any job unless it's in the personnel department. That's why job descriptions are to employment what political science is to politics.

Are you an educator? And somebody wants an educational technologist? List the reading you've done in the field, your familiarity with programmed instruction, and how you've used teaching machines in the past. So you don't have a Ph.D.; but if you are keenly interested in the field, you'll learn *on the job.*

In job hunting, make sure you put your best foot forward in an area where you seem less than qualified. Some tips:

(1) Show you can learn a job on the job. That's one of your chief skills, remember? Give examples.

(2) Analyze strengths. Show your skills to be substantially what the employer wants. Does a job require a demonstrated record in technical illustration? Point out that you got an A in draftsmanship in high school, helped illustrate a college manual, and taught elementary graph development in the Army.

(3) Be curious and interview your prospective employer. If you ask the *right* questions (i.e., questions she can't answer), that's leverage to qualify for the job.

(4) Show that your salary expectations are *lower* than those of other professionals in the field. Doesn't it make sense to hire an upward-bound person and pay him less?

(5) Convey a hard-charging, enthusiastic interest in the job. That's a quality for which you are never underqualified.

"Yes, but I've even been told I'm overqualified for a job!"

I bet it wasn't a judgment job, and what you were looking for was stop-loss employment to earn income. Because of a graduate degree, your fluent Urdu, or an excellent earnings record, you'll threaten stop-loss employers. You need a job—any job—because you're broke and "overqualified."

My advice, if it's a stop-loss or grunt job, is *not* to lie. Study what's in your background that precludes your being seriously considered for a stop-loss position. Eliminate these factors from your résumé and consciously avoid them during interviews. In fact, don't use a résumé at all.

You're home free.

Employers, quite properly, hedge at hiring those who might bore easily on a job. And since stop-loss jobs can be mind-blowing, hiring a tiger in a fast-food outlet is not the best way to discourage turnover on the job.

But that's the employer's problem.

"What about the middle managers who don't hire you but for whom you must work?"

Ah yes, the middle managers, the vestal virgins with brass knuckles.

Every job seeker knows them. Fifty years ago they wore cuff guards and green eyeshades. Today you can spot them by their white socks, shiny pants, and cheap shoes. A solemn demeanor is a middle manager's certain hallmark.

You'll have the bad luck many times during your job search to feel their brass knuckles. And if you're so unlucky as to work for one, there are no words to express my condolences.

That's why you should be certain before accepting a job that you'll be working for the person who hires you.

But in larger organizational complexes, often you are hired at the top and work at the bottom. Between you and your patron there is a gulf swarming with middle managers ready to zap the bright and spirited. Therefore, before accepting a job ask to interview (or even reinterview) the person you'll work under.

"What about jobs where you pass through a whole series of interviews or face a panel?"

Murder, Incorporated.

Surviving this barrage means to be in physical shape.

It's like oral comprehensives in college, or the Inquisition.

Ten interviews in one day (which was my record) left me limp and mentally lame. My mouth dried up. My cheeks hurt, I'd been so goddamned agreeable. My advice is to eat regular meals, no alcohol, and read the New York *Times.* You'd be surprised how many questions are likely to be culled from your interlocutor's breakfast reading.

Groups develop a dynamic hostile to effective recruitment. Nobody can work for a group. That's why the mortality rate among the few chief executive officers reporting to a *working* board of

directors is so high. Boards that set and execute policy are by definition racked with contradictions, rivalries, hidden agendas, and suppressed policy conflicts. A judgment-job candidate faced with this
kind of collective taffy pull might opt out of a job altogether, or win
the support of a bare majority of the board and spend the next two
years fending off those who never wanted to hire him in the first
place. And, of course, group decisions invariably imply compromise. Which is fatal to good health within organizations.

The trouble with compromise solutions—not only in choosing
people but on a whole range of management choices—is that ac-
countability for decision making is blurred; no one takes the blame
or wins the kudos. Management by committee is the triumph of
group-think over individual conviction.

And don't worry too much about stress questions. There's a long-
legged beastie who is not going to like you because his bile duct
was plugged that morning. His comments will be dismissed if everyone else thought you were St. Peter.

Be sure to *take your time* answering questions. A profound ten-
second lapse before you reply to somebody's soft curve across the
plate guarantees high marks in the "still waters run deep" department.

You have this advantage: You're practiced in the niceties of personal self-expression, thanks to half a hundred interviews you've
had lately. Something you might do to prep for this obstacle course
is to run through some mock interviews with a group of friends. Let
the group be the panel; you, the job candidate.

"How can I tell my rank where I might accept a job?"

In healthy organizations, the status symbols so treasured by dying
organizations are invisible. This is tough on ex-military, ministers,
and academics who come from a world where rank, title, and status
are notorious.

In free-form institutions hierarchical authority is deliberately
amorphous. But it still exists.

A mark of your sensitivity on a judgment job within a vital organization is to sort out where the power is, who exercises it, when
and whether you should buck it. Hierarchy—even in the free-form
institution—is necessary; the great thing about authority in free-

form institutions is its constant change. There's simply no time or place for status back tickling. Or executive grab-ass.

"Will employers ever tell me the real reasons for not hiring me?"

Employers, like all human beings, loathe saying no. In rejecting you for a job, therefore, the runaround begins:

—"We normally hire only full-time professionals with five years' line experience."

—"An M.B.A. is usually your ticket of admission to our organization."

—"We like going with younger people who have the time to invest twenty years in our organization."

—"Our organization, whenever possible, promotes from within."

And so forth. Now, none of these statements is necessarily *false*. But are they necessarily true? Chances are better than even that the organization (a) has eliminated the job, (b) still hasn't settled on a person to fill it, (c) can't decide what the person does in the job, (d) has decided on someone else for the job. All of which means that the other competitors for the job must be told the score. Unfortunately, employers at this point, hating to say no, but unable to say yes, start talking Chinese. Most won't level and come out with the truth, which generally is "You were a fine candidate but we chose the best. I'm sure you'll qualify for a similar job elsewhere."

Don't self-destruct when you finish number two, number three, number four in the judgment-job sweepstakes. This is constructive feedback at its best: It means you are on the right track (i.e., have realistic objectives), interview well, and are only five yards from the goal line. Therefore, ignore 99 percent of what employers say; it's an employer's clumsy way of avoiding the pain of saying no.

"How can I tell I'm about to be offered a job?"

Lunching together, discussing non-work-related subjects, swapping ideas with an employer, are all signs. The personalizing of the encounter is a clue. Meeting the boss's boss or being invited to see the organization's wage and salary administrators, or an invitation for a final interview the following Monday, all testify to your being seriously considered.

The signs you will discern might be the lights going on in the employer's eyes, an enthusiasm and warmth never sensed in previous encounters, a hitherto undetected ambience of camaraderie, the use of the editorial "we."

Salespeople sense a customer's mood and know when to close. You are the salesperson, and the signs to look for in an employer's behavior are no different from customer psychology. So close on the employer and ask for the job.

"Suppose the job for which I'm interviewing has been filled?"

Disappointing, but it happens all the time. All the more reason to switch to a curiosity interview. Ask for advice, secure names of other department heads, request an assessment of your employability. "Don't curse the darkness; light a candle," as Confucius said. And, for my sake, don't apologize for taking an employer's time, thank her profusely for being considered, go into a funk and try to make her feel guilty, or interview (as if the job hadn't been filled) in the hopes she will change her mind.

"How do you reject a job offer graciously?"

—Back off and ask for the weekend to think over the offer. Then a nice letter in your own hand *thanking* employers you turn down and giving reasons. If you *like* the firm, and the people who work there and what they do, enlist their assistance in looking for a job elsewhere at Sticky Wicket, Inc.

—And above all, don't apologize for your decision.

"Okay. But do people back off from job offers—really good ones—to choose something better?"

I remember the names, faces, and background of about seven people in as many years whom I've recruited and offered excellent judgment jobs.

The reasons I remember them so well is that all of them *turned down* the jobs, rejected what I thought were really good offers.

I remember them because I admired their decision and what went into making a tough decision like that. And three or four of them I've since called for other reasons because I know them even better for their conveying *why* they decided as they did.

If you're going to turn your back on a job, level with your recruiter, tell him *why,* and thank him for his time. If you make sense, he'll remember you the next time another first-rate job surfaces, and phone you.

At the same time, I bet there are two hundred people I've hired who didn't have the guts (i.e., self-knowledge) to turn me down when they should have.

Why?

Because I sensed they wanted to *please me* rather than themselves. My loss and theirs. Another triumph of hope over experience. Being strong enough to resist organizational blandishments is not of inconsiderable merit.

"What about using third parties to recommend you for a job?"

It depends on the clout of the third party, the timing of his call, and the relationship between the third party and the employer. Using a key person to call on your behalf *at the right time* sways people's judgment.

If you are qualifying for a special assistant's job with a firm's president (and his chief stockholder happens to be your next-door neighbor), call your neighbor, outline the situation, and let him godfather your candidacy.

The big problem, of course, is how much these people respect each other. Again, it's a question of good judgment, and the risk is small compared to the potential gain.

"Will an organization always do a reference check on me before we negotiate a salary?"

Some do, some don't.

Many will actually negotiate, sign you up, and put you to work *before* the reference check is complete.

Not terribly efficient.

But employers usually protect themselves with a three-month probationary clause that permits them to discharge you without cause while the checkout's being made. That's why it's important not to fudge on any vital facts in your background and to make sure you've leveled with your employer on all matters that might have derogatory implications.

In a word, your employer should do a pretty complete reference check on you. I am astonished, however, at how many employers *don't* check out new employees. Years ago I fired eight people in the firm where I worked. Seven went on to higher-paying positions. No one at the successor institutions thought it worthwhile to discover why these chaps left our employ. That's what I mean when I say that employers don't always know what they are doing.

Therefore, if you hire an employer worthy of you, he's going to check you out.

Now, nobody by nature likes to snoop. But don't blame an organization (which is about to invest thousands of dollars on your ability to produce) if it makes some perfectly normal inquiries about your background, previous earnings, personal honesty, and on-the-job efficiency. You wouldn't buy a house without some rudimentary checking, would you?

Would you?

"Should I let people know I'm using their names as references?"
Indubitably, Dr. Watson!

A nice note in your own hand (including a résumé) to those who know you best is very much in order. And if your referees happen to be on assignment in Bangkok, ask for a general letter of reference which, photocopied, you can use if an employer requests letters of reference.

"What does an interviewer mean when he says, 'Stay in touch'?"
It telegraphs that you passed muster. At the same time he's saying, "There's no job *now* at ABC, Inc., so stay in touch." And the same goes for replies that conclude, "Although there is no current position at Greater Consolidated Manufactories, do drop by if you are ever in the Cincinnati area." A nice way of saying, "We *are* interested and would like to look you over." All the more reason to generate three or four interviews in the Ohio Valley to justify a swing through the Midwest.

"In a buyer's market shouldn't you hedge and accept the first tolerable job that's offered?"
There's no final answer, of course; it depends on various circumstances surrounding the job search, your financial means, objectives, how *this* job compares with *that* . . . and how long you've tested your background against the job market.

But the theme of this book is that judgment jobs are discovered, that it's nonsense to accept a job because you *must,* and that it's better to work loose (at a stop-loss or grunt job) than to accept so-called professional employment because it's a social necessity. Hanging in and looking for *your* job is a far better way to spend a year than punching a time clock in an indifferent job. Because by disbelieving that you can find the job, you'll be postponing, perhaps forever, the possibility that a job can be more than a meal ticket.

Job hunting is a lottery. Make sure Lady Luck is your companion. Which means treating your job search as if it could change your life.

EIGHT

How to Chase Those Unemployment Blahs

Yes, the blahs, really the four phases of unemployment, character-ized by the following symptoms (listed in the order in which they occur):

(1) "After I lost my job, I felt a strange sense of relief."

(2) "When someone asked, 'How's the job search going?' I went into a funk."

(3) "I can't sleep, worry a lot, and feel sorry for myself."

(4) "I'm excited about finding a job."

Each of these statements represents one of the distinct, predict-able, but not necessarily inevitable stages of being out of a job. Let's examine one at a time.

"After I lost my job, I felt a strange sense of relief."

The first stage of unemployment is usually marked by relief and even pleasure. The worst has already happened; we've lost our job. Thinking about a job loss is often worse than becoming unem-ployed. It's like a pain in the neck: We postpone seeing a doctor, hoping the pain will disappear. But after you've checked it out, a diagnosis is made, the pain is given a name, a cure is prescribed. Anybody would feel relief.

The same with unemployment. The dread of unemployment is worse than the fact. Once the worst has happened—losing a job—the relief of not going to work at a disappointing job is compensa-tion for being unemployed. It's fun having time to do things for ourselves. The first stage of unemployment is often a lark, especially if the worst was expected to happen: We lunch with friends, tinker with the résumé, do odd jobs about the house, even take a short vacation.

"When someone asked, 'How's the job search going?' I went into a funk."
The second stage begins when we write out the rent or mortgage check, a good friend says, "It's a terrible time to look for work," and family members eye us significantly. The phone isn't ringing off the hook from friends contacted in Stage One. The *invisible* symptoms of Stage Two unemployment are, first, worry, then anxiety, finally panic.

The *visible* signs are feverish activity: We answer want ads compulsively, whether the job fits or not, chase job leads that evaporate, and check out personnel agencies in the Yellow Pages. We hear about "career advisory" services, fly-blown firms that clip us for a harrowing chunk of now dwindling cash reserves in exchange for holding hands and writing our résumé. We're confused and fair prey for those who live off the desperation of the unemployed.

But the overriding problem of the desperately unemployed is the sudden sense that we do not so much want a job as need one. This makes a world of difference.

"I can't sleep, worry a lot, and feel sorry for myself."
The unemployed in this stage stop looking for work: Time is something we don't so much use as kill. Immense self-pity often overwhelms us. The anxiety of Stage Two yields to the apathy of Stage Three: We become the discouraged unemployed. Minor physical disabilities surface: back pain, frequent colds, and migraines. Stage-three people compulsively *suffer* unemployment.

To suffer is a form of penance. The unemployed do penance in order to propitiate the gods. But the gods don't punish the unemployed; the jobless punish themselves. The worst of the suffering is the shame of feeling useless. The jobless feel responsible for their uselessness; guilty as charged.

Fortunately, nobody can abide the charge of guilt for long. Eventually, the unemployed in Stage Three grow tired of being tired, bored with being bored, and angry at being depressed. They snap out of it. These unemployed have suffered enough, paid their penance, served their sentences.

The unemployed who can't get up to look for work are sunk in apathy. Apathy vaccinates the unemployed against *feeling*. And in feelings are rooted desire, goals, and . . . action. Worrying doesn't solve problems. Suffering doesn't help. Both make unemployment worse. Doing something about a problem reduces anxiety; doing nothing increases it.

"I'm excited about finding a job."

The unemployed in Stage Four evince *desire*. The idea of going back to work seems *fun*. We focus on new objectives, stop suffering unemployment and start doing something about it. Stage Three unemployed have an interesting past; Stage Four unemployed have an interesting future. Action banishes anxiety and apathy.

Attitude helps the unemployed hurdle Stages Two and Three. It's not inevitable to experience all four stages. But there's a problem: thinking that the unemployed have no *right* to enjoy unemployment. People expect the jobless to feel depressed; being excited is considered odd. Thus, effective job searchers go against the grain and take pleasure in looking for work. Doing so astonishes friends, raises self-esteem, and pleases next employers.

Now for some practical advice on jumping from Stage One to Stage Four:

(1) Expanding a job search to include almost any kind of employer is defective job-hunting strategy. Far better to restrict, narrow, and focus on employers who provide the job you want (there are far more of them than you think). That way you're less likely to quit a job you don't like only to begin the dreary search again.

Targeting.

(2) Personnel, career guidance, and executive-search specialists, with some noteworthy exceptions, are the last people you want to talk to in looking for the job you require. Personnel agencies work for employers, not you. Avoid agencies where *you* pay the fee. And don't sign your name—it might mean the agency has an exclusive.

Career-advisory services?

Most of them should be investigated by the Federal Trade Commission. And Ralph Nader should eviscerate them. No career service is going to find you the job you want. Don't waste time with those that prominently advertise services in the want ads or business sections of the local paper. One such advisory service charges $5,000! As H. L. Mencken once said, "No one ever went broke underestimating the intelligence of the American public."

Executive-placement services?

Okay for $50,000-plus jobs. But like employment agencies, executive-placement firms peddle flesh for a profit. Don't let anyone slot you into a job that you haven't carefully investigated. Executive-search specialists, by definition, recruit only people who are doing jobs *now* the headhunters want to fill. It's a waste of time, postage, and patience to mail out hundreds of résumés to as many headhunters. If you're truly effective on the job, someday a headhunter will call and you won't even need a résumé.

What if a headhunter does call?

Compare his job against what you want. One warning: Beware of the blitz! You could be hustled; it's nice knowing you're wanted, all the more reason to review what *you want* (where, for whom, and how it connects with your abilities).

(3) Judgment jobs are only occasionally advertised; if they are, it's either affirmative action in action or a rare combination of skills that requires employers to advertise.

(4) There are far more judgment jobs available than effective job searchers to fill them. Finding proven, effective people is the employer's greatest problem; focusing on ability and goals is the job seeker's greatest difficulty.

(5) Avoid fee-paid computerized job banks. It was only a question of time (after we had computerized everything from dating services to bomb strikes on Vietnam) before some scientific bureaucrats met in a smoke-filled room in Chicago and mapped out how to match job seekers with jobs by using computers.

Well, fellow Americans, the whistle hasn't been blown on the personnel programmer—yet. We will probably waste another few million on this kind of electronic exorbitancy before the scientific approach to computer personnel placement is blown from here to the Harvard School of Business Administration.

It doesn't work.

To repeat: Finding a job is whimsical, capricious, irrational, and human. A person—not a machine—is going to hire you. Computers simply can't be programmed to include the hidden requirements of every job, and the hidden agendas of employers and job seekers alike. And the good vibes that take place between the job seeker and the employer are not mechanical exchanges of information.

(6) Buy, rent, or steal a word processor. The greatest boon to job seekers these past ten years hasn't been the job-market revolution, falling interest rates, an expanding business economy; it's the word processor. It's now possible to do to employers what junk-mailers have been doing to you: a personalized letter in their mail-bag at the start of every business day. Adapt the first and last paragraphs of a cover letter to fit a targeted group of employers, and enclose a résumé. Many job seekers have word processors or access to them; the rest can rent these services. As with a résumé, put a cover letter through three or four drafts. Be sure one or more people who read English without moving their lips scan it for typos, misspelling, and other gremlins. Make it a picture of your personal *style*.

(7) Check out new business start-ups. Especially in hard times, the best sources of jobs are small to medium-size firms and new start-up ventures. City Hall can provide listings of new incorporations.

(8) Join a job club. The worst feeling in the job search is isolation. Therefore, conduct a search in the company of other effective job seekers who meet periodically to swap leads and give encouragement. Forty Plus is a job club. Your local church or community college might manage a job club. The business section in the local paper routinely publishes job-search information.

(9) About half the Fortune 500 companies now offer outplacement services to some or all of their separating professional staff. If involuntarily terminated, ask your employer about exit-management assistance.

The cure for unemployment is a job. Attitude is everything. The following suggestions should help.

For starters:

(1) **Stop blaming yourself.** Losing a job these days is due to the times, not necessarily the person.

A lot of job seekers take unemployment personally—they feel somehow responsible and helpless. But feeling responsible for being unemployed and helpless to gain new employment isn't cooperating with reality. Chasing the unemployment blahs means changing these destructive attitudes. A major problem is attitudinal: If you think there's no work, you won't find it.

(2) **While it's difficult, avoid the gloom-and-doom talk.** It's as unrealistic to think times will grow worse as to think that times will grow better. Nobody knows, least of all the experts. Besides, for the unemployed, the worst has happened; the only direction is up.

Therefore, except for the want ads, skip reading the papers and watching the TV. The unemployed spend so much time reading about bad times, they don't seize the time to find a job. The media thrive on calamity; everybody feels better off if some people (e.g., the unemployed) are shown to be worse off. Besides, TV is a known depressant!

(3) **Don't associate with the desperate unemployed.** They will *insist* there are no jobs. Besides, you make them look bad if you find work.

(4) **Avoid the U.S. Employment Service.** It's nothing but a big, dumb computer that prints unemployment checks. It's responsible for filling less than 1 percent of the available jobs. Moreover, the long gray lines of the unemployed depress the spirits.

(5) **Get physical.** Jogging, racquetball, long walks, all reduce worry and raise the spirits. Most working people complain of having no time to exercise. The unemployed no longer have that excuse. Exercise increases vitality. And vitality is what employers notice first in an interview.

Physical activity works out aggressions otherwise turned on the self. Self-pity, for example, is an attack on the self. No other state of mind is so destructive. The antidote is self-awareness. Whenever you feel sorry for yourself, jog ten times around the block, paint the hallway, or work out on barbells. Otherwise a bad dose of the blahs results.

(6) **Share feelings** about unemployment with those nearest and dearest. Covering up is certain to cause mental ill health. Unemployment is like an automobile accident; the victims go into deep shock and need time to recover their senses. Like a lot of people in deep shock, they often don't make sense. The knack is getting friends and family to help. That means ideas, introductions, and information. It's lonely looking for work. Friends are for helping you through the isolation of unemployment.

(7) **Spend money.** Savings are for emergencies; unemployment is an emergency. Therefore, spend savings on *yourself*. A new suit of clothes, shuttle tickets to Boston, taxi rides to interviews, all raise self-esteem. Nothing so characterizes a poor job search than someone who wears a hairshirt. Spending money causes us to feel important. Feeling important is a precondition to being important in a job interview. Employers make job offers to those who feel good about themselves; remember, they back off from people who seem desperate. Spending money on the job search routs resentment and vanquishes self-pity.

(8) **No excuses.** Thinking you are too young or too old, too inexperienced or too specialized, too uneducated or too educated to get a job offer is evidence of the worm eating its own tail. The unemployed have a thousand reasons—all wrong—why there are no job offers. Usually it isn't the person; it's the times. Scarce jobs and keen competition are not your fault, but no excuse for not looking for a job.

(9) **Be self-disciplined.** Scary. Nobody likes discipline. Self-discipline means going against the grain. When it doesn't work, the unemployed are without inner resources. That's why employment agencies and career-advisory services are in business.

Self-discipline means focusing on the self. That's the problem. Many job seekers are focused on employers and blind to themselves; thus the unemployment blahs.

Why?

Successful job searchers do it for *themselves*. Feeling responsible in order to please other people—employers, friends, family—means not being responsible to yourself. In other words, you're without *self*-discipline. It isn't human nature to please others and not the self. As soon as job seekers look for work—which pleases them—they are self-disciplined.

(10) **See a therapist.** If you can't muster the pleasure of self-discipline, consider professional help. If you're single, alone in a strange city, and without connections, hire a therapist. A weekly meeting reduces anxiety, and banishing anxiety, remember, is crucial to chasing the jobless blahs. Looking for self-fulfilling work, putting yourself first for a change, taking pleasure in the job search, all this rich stuff is intimidating. A therapist or an effective career counselor may help you:

—change (in desire begins responsibility).

—find courage (nobody can find a job *alone).*

—cope with the pleasure of changing jobs (remember, feeling free causes pleasure . . . and guilt).

—redefine responsibility (to yourself, not to others).

—cooperate with reality (therapy establishes reality and demonstrates how you can shape it).

—recognize that part of reality is inside your own head (attitude is everything).

—establish that you're a free person, that you needn't accept any job because you feel you must, that unfree people rarely qualify for judgment jobs, that freedom in the job search is likely to be more self-fulfilling, with a consequent increase in personal self-esteem and happiness, that nobody controls the future but you can plan for that next job, that people are "lucky" who plan for it, that you do have *choices* and that choosing the third-best job (because the first two weren't offered) doesn't mean you are "locked in for life," that you're not a *victim* powerless to control your environment, that you act as much on your environment as it acts on you, that good jobs go to those who want them, and that "the size of a dog in a fight is less important than the size of the fight in the dog," as Woody Hayes put it.

Ambition is important in the job search (and on the job). Without it, there is no engine to drive to your goals or there are no goals toward which you have the drive. What follows is a list of statements made by people who rationalized why they couldn't find the wherewithal to get up in the job search or on the job. If you find yourself nodding agreement with five or more, take two steps back

and examine whether attitude isn't the problem. Attitude is everything and a simple thing. But not an easy thing.

(1) "I can't compete with better-educated people for judgment
jobs."

(2) "I'd lose friends if I made a lot of money."

(3) "I often fantasize I could get a better job."

(4) "It's sinful to earn more money than you need."

(5) "Most wealthy people are miserable. I'd rather stay where I
am."

(6) "Some people are just meant to be successful."

(7) "It's usually the brown-nosers that get ahead."

(8) "Jobs are bought, not earned."

(9) "Those high-paid pencil pushers don't know what hard work
is."

(10) "Somebody has to do this work; it might as well be me."

(11) "I like the simple life. I don't want to earn a lot of money."

(12) "I'm happy as long as I can pay my bills."

(13) "To want more than you need is greed."

(14) "I'm no gambler—so I'll just stay put."

(15) "What do you mean, 'ask for a raise'? I'll get one if I deserve it."

(16) "People who jump from one job to the next are irresponsible."

(17) "I've got more important things to worry about than getting ahead."

(18) "It's worth keeping a disagreeable job as long as the family
is happy."

(19) "As long as I'm putting food on the table, I'm satisfied."

(20) "A woman has to be pretty attractive to be well paid."

(21) "I know how to get a good job. I just don't want the headaches."

(22) "This job is okay. I get off at five o'clock and forget about it
until the next day."

(23) "All I want is a job that supports my hobbies."

(24) "I want a job because I deserve it, not because I 'know
somebody.' You'll never catch me pulling strings."

(25) "I often find myself wishing that I could have his/her opportunities."

Effective job searchers are *ambitious*. But the desperate unemployed, caught in the jobless blahs, sense every tomorrow is just like all their graying yesterdays.

Take a playful attitude in the job search. Find time to take in a ball game, see a movie, go to the beach. Money, time, and imagination spent on the self are an investment.

It's not easy being unemployed, but it's made easier if the unemployed don't make it harder.

Let's recap.

(1) Get exercise and have fun.

(2) Use a friend, career counselor, coach, or psychiatrist.

(3) Acquire a stop-loss job.

(4) Focus on the desire for, not the need of, a job.

(5) Create a first-rate functional résumé.

(6) Interview three or four times a day. Plenty of people think two interviews a week and five or ten employer contacts a month is putting that old shoulder to the wheel. But a minimum of twenty-five contacts *per week* (if you're unemployed) and *ten* (if you're working full-time) is more like an effective job search. Nobody gives you that judgment job because you're deserving.

(7) Reject jobs you don't want. This increases self-esteem, although it could trigger guilt. It's tough to turn down a job when you sense your strengths don't match. And be sure it's not because you can't stand the heat *in* the kitchen, increased competition, augmented visibility; after all, what we mean, really, by a judgment job is being *pushed,* tested, asked to perform at peak proficiency.

(8) Show, from time to time, at home and away from the job search, *real* anger. The frustrations of job hunting are real, and not showing them causes attitudinal damage.

(9) Do the most disagreeable task first thing in the morning. If that's mailing your alimony check, do it; if it's calling back on a job you wanted and are certain not to get, do it; if it's touching base with twenty employers who received résumés from you last week, do it.

Everything *else* the rest of the day seems easy; but avoiding painful responsibilities leads to declining self-esteem. And remember, appearing effective is central in looking for a judgment job.

(10) Take some risks. Don't quit a job until offered another one (Rule #1). If, however, you're a born risk taker, hold a $23,000 job and are looking for $35,000, chances are good you'll find it. Borrowing two to three thousand dollars and finding *the* job is cost-effective.

(11) Indulge thyself! Take cabs to interviews, buy a job-search wardrobe, go into debt. People are debtors in order to buy an education, take a vacation, or do something enjoyable. Finding a good job is fun. Enjoy!

If you think cheap, you're poor. Employers are impressed by a touch of class. Think rich. Only one out of a hundred job seekers will, and that makes you stand out. If you can't stand going into debt, then start saving; accumulate capital for your job search.

Pay yourself first.

Regularly—once a month—write a check to yourself. The check may be for savings, insurance, stock, whatever causes an increase in capital. Pay yourself before paying the butcher, baker, or candlestick maker. This is your capital.

What remains (after paying your bills) is your walk-around money, and that's surely less than you want, but is the price you pay —the terms and conditions—if you're to find the capital base for a productive job search.

Sure, finding money to find *the* job is a problem—and an opportunity. The savings habit, once acquired, however, reduces anxiety (which paralyzes free behavior) and makes the *means* available. We dun our rich maiden aunts to put us through law school; our friendly savings and loan lends us a ransom to restore our parents' brownstone; but we hesitate to go into hock to look for a better-paying job. If you make $31,000 per annum, find a job paying $38,000, and spend $2,800 doing it, who's ahead?

(12) Avoid destructive hindsighting. Creative hindsighting, getting yourself together, is great. But be sure to stop thinking too much about yourself when you step out on the sidewalk and start to cold-turkey employers. Too much introspection is a bad thing.

Hindsighting.

"Oh, if I'd only gone to law school, I wouldn't be in this job fix today!"

"Good grief, I should never have quit my last job without another job to go to."

"Europe was great, but two years off the job market leaves me right where I was when I left."

Etcetera, etcetera, etcetera . . .

Quarterbacking your past on a gloomy, jobless Monday morning is my definition of purgatory. Suddenly everything right about life seems wrong.

It's tough not to, but in finding a job, raking up past disappointments downright debilitates attitudes necessary to impress employers.

(13) Learn to be self-accepting.

If it's okay to ask for a job an employer doesn't have, it's also okay to seek a job for which you are not entirely qualified. Think about it: How many people would be working today if every job required someone with three to five years' experience?

Not all employers (or even most) are necessarily going to like you, any more than you're going to like equally all employers. Unrealistic. Remember, cooperating with reality is essential in conducting a self-managed job search. So, even though likable, you'll be rejected for jobs because you're unqualified and if you're qualified you might be rejected because you aren't as likeable as another candidate. Job offers go to qualified candidates employers *like*. That's why we need to contact many employers before a judgment job offer is made. Give Lady Luck her chance.

For example, years ago I required a research assistant who could speak and read French, do library research, write and edit information in an easily retrievable fashion. I interviewed four qualified candidates. The woman who got the job was indeed qualified, but the reason I hired her (and "rejected" the others) was that her father once pitched for the Chicago White Sox. She is the only woman I know who can define the infield fly rule. Of course, as a frustrated relief pitcher, I offered her the job.

We might be rejected for a job (despite our qualifications and likability) because we don't fit an employer's personnel mix. We are either too young, too old, too educated, too uneducated, too experienced, not experienced enough, too expensive, too . . . *something*. Whatever the reason, we feel disappointment. That's appropriate. But diving into a deep depression is self-destructive. Being rejected causes pain (as it should). The cop-out is avoiding the pain by refusing to look for a job at all.

(14) Pay your discouragement dues, the terms and conditions of finding judgment jobs. And if you're not prepared to be discouraged, take my advice: Stay in graduate school or belt the commonweal in your current job and quit bitching.

You can't be rejected for a job that isn't available. Any more than you're rejected by a woman who is affianced to someone else. But it's no more a "mistake" to ask an employer for a job (who doesn't have one) than it's mistaken to ask a woman for a date who, unknown to you, is engaged to someone else. When we are rejected, it's usually due to some characteristic we possess or don't have. Employers are usually rejecting the characteristic, not the person.

Sure, *this* otherwise qualified, able, and likable job candidate is rejected because he's a smoker, while that qualified, able, and likable nonsmoker gets the offer. But what the employer is rejecting is your habit, *not you.*

Athletes handle rejection and know how to win . . . and lose. Swinging a bat to hit the ball means we often miss. The same in the job search: You'll be disappointed but never destroyed by rejection. Disappointment is commonplace, in school and on the playing field. Overcoming failures, disappointments, and misfires is how we know we're growing up. To be destroyed by rejection is knowing we have a lot of growing up to do.

Being rejected for a job we really want helps us know we really want it. It causes many job seekers to become more determined. A person with spirit is challenged by rejection. Overcoming the rejection, redoubling our efforts, and pushing on despite other people's no is another way we say yes to ourselves. It's called character.

People rejected for jobs often believe something is wrong with them (asking for a job they want and don't get). But what *is* wrong is *not* asking, and then accepting an unwanted job offer just because it's offered. That's always a mistake. Being Irish, I know that hearts are meant to be broken and that nobody ever died of a broken heart who has heart.

Many of us want to be offered jobs we expect and don't especially want, like the girl who doesn't want to go to the prom but wants to be *asked*. An even worse obstacle is knowing what you want, being offered it, accepting and—after three months—saying to yourself, "This isn't what I want at all." Oh boy, will your ego toughen if this happens!

Another characteristic of a tough ego is being able to manage mistakes. Sure, you could accept a job and discover it's not what you wanted. That's a mistake; but tough egos do not so much blame themselves for the mistake as learn from it. The least effective job searchers are those who can't allow themselves to be wrong. Perfectionists. Allow yourself some mistakes, an imperfect job search being a beautiful thing to behold.

(15) Finally, on the job search, don't get between a dog and a lamppost.

PART THREE

We cannot live in the afternoon of life according to the program of life's morning.

CARL JUNG

NINE

Coming to Terms

For now, let's assume you've been offered a job. Still, there's one last hurdle: Coming to Terms. Now's the time to be particularly tough and able.

You are now in the catbird seat.

For those of you new to the game or who need a refresher course in haggling for more pay, this book is a guide to techniques long known to the wicked and the worldly but never before found in print except in a plain brown wrapper. Before reading further, therefore, one caveat: Don't feel guilty if you want more money. That's okay in Kiev in a People's Republic, where things money can buy are scarce. But elsewhere, hustling a high salary is sustaining a life-support system. Whether you work in the steno pool or are a $100,000 stem-winder for a growth industry, money is the second most important thing.

Unless you clip coupons for a living or happen to hold the highest winning ticket from last week's off-track betting, your salary is usually all that stands between you and the high cost of living. Here in the financial seat of the Western world, a person without money is stateless, an atavistic relic of the extended-family system, a throwback to the barter economy and the Neolithic garden culture. You either join the moneychangers in the temple or are paid extravagantly for chasing them out.

When you go out on the job market, you're the seller—you're up for sale forty hours a week (or maybe longer). As a live candidate you always ask for somewhat more than you're worth (i.e., more than some employer is likely to pay).

So ask for more than you expect the employer to offer. Then the final "price"—your salary—will be more than the minimum and near the maximum the employer expects to pay. This makes sense to your employer (who thinks he's found a bargain) and at the same time raises your real price to what the market allows.

You have, customarily, more leverage with an employer *before* accepting the job. Once you've said yes, Mr. Employer drives a harder bargain. So *don't* say yes until the salary (plus cash fringes) is agreed upon verbally and then clearly written out in an employment agreement. That's what we capitalists mean by the sanctity of contract.

A few facts:

(1) Nobody knows what someone else is worth.

(2) What an organization pays top management automatically predetermines professional pay for *all* people down the line.

(3) What counts is "what the other fellow makes." In other words, pay scales are subtle badges of rank; "Y is paid more than X. Therefore, Y is more important than X." All is subsumed under the term "comparability."

(4) Compensation isn't usually rationally negotiated on the basis of productivity. Prevailing industrial rates, previous earnings, and future expectations—plus hard bargaining on both parties' parts—determine the compensation package.

(5) Because pay rates are negotiated more and more on the basis of equity, not on performance, you're paid *relative* to someone else. In elephantine organizations, increasingly, the problem of equity among comparable executives is delegated to computer-science types.

Automatic pay adjustments are a product of human-relations ("Let's not hurt anyone's feelings") or organizational-development administration (a data-processing clerk in Division A must be paid what a clerk in Division B is), even though the missions, means, and results of the two divisions are as different from each other as the Swiss Confederacy from Imperial France.

(6) Organizations wrongly continue to believe that money is what makes their people run.

Peace Corps volunteers are paid nothing but subsistence; otherwise they would be ineffective.

The chairman of the executive committee at Procter & Gamble makes over $500,000. Would he be any less effective if he were paid $50,000 per annum?

The point is, there isn't necessarily a correspondence between what we are paid and how effective/happy we are on the job.

This flies in the face of executive-compensation experts, replete in the institutional life of our country, hell bent on overpaying the white-collar classes. I'm with Bob Townsend and others who believe no chief executive officer should be paid more than $50,000 straight salary; additional earnings should be based on a percentage of profits. Which could mean a helluva lot *more* than $50,000 per year! Pay should be based on production. No, *not* effort or good intentions, but on present performance.

Chief executive officers negotiate, like ball players, fixed contracts: two-, five-, seven-year agreements with an organization. This is a poor policy. If the new president doesn't work out, the organization buys out his contract. People with contracts have no incentive to *change* and needn't take risks.

If a lawyer advises you to lock up your senior job with a written contract (charging his usual fee of $100 per hour), he will happily offer to accompany you to the negotiations to protect your interests. Lawyers, however, are often deal breakers (rather than deal makers). Pushing for a contract and using your lawyer to thrash out its details invites an organization to use *its* lawyer to haggle with yours. And using third parties aborts an otherwise astute negotiation strategy. So if you use a lawyer, be sure he's your legal adviser *behind the scenes*. Don't let him negotiate directly with the employer; use him only as a counselor, not as a negotiator, on tap, not on top. And don't let your lawyer rewrite the employment agreement; if a legal agreement is replete with legalistic bafflegab, it's a dead giveaway to employers you're excessively interested in your compensation, not in what you will contribute.

Don't hesitate to negotiate important fringes, which are a significant part of the total compensation package: a signing bonus, deferred compensation, stock options, profit sharing, moving expenses, an annual renegotiation clause (which means that performance will be reviewed with an eye toward a significant promotion and salary raise one year after you're hired.)

Here are three examples of how you come to terms based on productivity.

"My job for the next three months is to abstract every article written in the last ten years on population trends in Latin America. My staff includes three researchers, three writers, a demographer, and a secretary. Fifty thousand dollars is the limit of my nondirect spending authority. My report will be delivered no later than May 1. Progress reports will be verbal. If I finish by April 1, I receive a $3,500 bonus. If my work is so good as to generate add-on business for the firm, the organization and I will discuss a significant raise in base pay."

"I have one year to add $500,000 of new business in our West Coast operation. Spending limits are subject to negotiation with the West Coast regional manager, but in no case will be less than $100,000. Staff, marketing strategy, and product lines are at my discretion. Should I add more than $250,000 I will receive a 5 percent bonus of the difference between the first and the second figures. Should I not meet the quota I will suffer a 10 percent reduction in base salary, terminate the position or negotiate reassignment, if any, within the firm."

"Of the sixteen students, three fourths will have been admitted into colleges by July 1. My staff includes four teachers, all of whom will be hired at my discretion. I have one year to complete the task. Should I meet my goal, I will be seriously considered for a promotion to rank of 'senior teacher' with no less than a 20 percent increase in pay. All texts, curricula, and tests are subject to review by the headmaster."

Simplistic?

Maybe. But every salary negotiation in a free-formed organization should conclude with productivity indexes and rewards. Constant attention to individual performance on the job (which is real equity) is far superior to plausible but impractical schemes to establish organization-wide wage uniformity. It used to be called a day's pay for a day's work.

What happens if you forget, as so many job searchers do, to put your maximum salary requirements out on the table before the employer announces what you'll be paid? What works some to most of the time is simply to hear out the employer's offer and then lapse into a profound silence. Count slowly, under your breath,

"One . . . two . . . three . . . four" (all the way to ten). Usually by "five" the employer, uncomfortable with his offer, will escalate: "Well, as a matter of fact, I think the company could probably swing three thousand more, but, of course, I'll have to clear this with . . ."

But let's suppose salary is non-negotiable (fixed), which often happens if:

—a number of people are hired to do the same job.
—entrance-level inductees are all paid equally.
—industry-wide averages are used to establish threshold salaries.
—fixed compensation, based on industry-wide labor agreements, is negotiated on behalf of professional engineers, professors, computer-science types by union officials.

Normally, you'll know this information *before* a job offer. If not, press employers for the reason salaries are fixed. More often than not, the reasoning is sound; often, however, you'll negotiate substantially more by bargaining before coming to terms.

Fixed salaries are usually negotiated with experts, technicians, craftspeople; negotiable salaries are associated with judgment jobs that are difficult to define, evaluate, and quantify. That's your latitude of negotiability where good judgment is the most important qualification. Check out the reasons for the employer's frozen position, and if justified, be reasonable and yield. There are limits in coming to terms. An employer is signaling that this is his final offer. Don't be mulish.

Another caveat: In the unhappy event you negotiate more money than someone on the payroll who has similar responsibilities (and has been with the firm five years), expect the night of the long knives. Many will make it a point to see that you fail on the job. So use good judgment and wait until you're on the job before taking that big stride *up* the salary ladder.

In curiosity interviewing about the hidden job market, a legitimate line of inquiry is the salary structure of the firm and the profession. Remember, salaries are established inside organizations through a complex series of human interactions that are subsumed under the title "comparability." Whiz kids recruited from the outside at higher pay for similar responsibilities jeopardize organizational equilibrium. Ask about salary ranges of the men and women working at your expected level in the hierarchy and in the job search ask for slightly more. Plainly, *your clout is greater with an employer before accepting a job offer you feel sure he will make.*

Why?

Because the employer *wants* to hire you. No, not candidates two, three, and four—she wants you, Numero Uno. Attitudinally, the boss has already hired you. And that's why you do yourself no favor when taking second place, putting feelings on the back burner, accommodating her wishes and supinely accepting what's offered.

Unfortunately, some job seekers don't know what they want (what they are worth), fail to put that amount (and slightly more) out on the table where both can discuss it, and gratefully accept what employers are apparently prepared to pay. But every judgment job is negotiable; there's a salary *range:* Asking for slightly more than the high figure guarantees a salary greater than either party expected.

Clearly the job seeker must initiate the negotiation. If the employer is on his own side and you're on his side, then who's on *your* side? Job seekers, however, from a malignant sense of gratitude, often forget what they want (and deserve) at the critical time in an employment negotiation—i.e., when they sense the offer of a job.

Recall, you're negotiating a *judgment* job. Higher salary demands, far from putting off an employer, could put him on to you. I've filled lots of judgment jobs (and been a candidate for a few), and salary was secondarily important in the negotiations.

The most important fact in coming to terms is your highest previous earnings. In jumping fields, taking ten years off to raise a couple of kids, or pursuing an expensive graduate education, you can't build on previous earnings to negotiate. That's building on a weakness. Your strength, however, is precisely that you're better educated, ten years additionally experienced, or transferring your expertise from one field to another.

So it's okay to admit previous highest earnings. But it's more effective to reveal why you *deserve* what's asked. If you've been poorly paid or were a volunteer, all the more reason—for the first time in your life—to establish real worth based on ability. Give reasons: education, experience, acquired knowledge, accomplishments, talent, and motivation—all ammunition to justify demands.

In brief, it's a question of *timing, conviction, good judgment,* and *follow-through.* And knowing when to ice the cake is another qualifying factor in being chosen for a judgment job. For now, let's recap the important points.

(1) Never accept a job before you know and agree to the salary; play one employer off against another. Compare salary, job responsibility, personal growth, and job interest of one job against the other. Keep in mind those two jobs that *might* develop. Do you have the means and patience to wait them out?

A bird in hand is worth two in the bush, to coin a phrase; don't be so clever that you reject all your job offers.

Let it be known that you are being wooed by another organization. If it's a competitor, your value on the marketplace escalates. By skillful negotiation you raise your starting salary. Don't be shy in keeping one employer a secret from the other.

Negotiating compensation finally depends on whether the prospective organization has the money available. Don't take less than the best because you're grateful for the job in the first place or to make a good first impression on the boss. Ask and it *might* be given.

(2) Don't hesitate to sleep on a salary offer—two or three days' reflection and a few phone calls to knowledgeable friends should convince you whether you're being euchred and raise some employer's opinion of you.

(3) If you have no previous earnings, invent hypothetical salaries you might have been paid had you not gone to graduate school. And—on top of those salaries—cost-of-living increments and merit increases.

(4) Always say, "It's not just the money that's important, Mr. Employer. I'd hardly be a good representative for Sticky Wicket, Inc., and represent its best interests if I can't represent *my own.*"

(5) Try, delicately, to find out the salaries of people doing equivalent work. If your salary is lower, ask for a review and an upgrade to their level after a three-month probationary hitch.

(6) In hard-nosed business organizations, push hard for equity in compensation. In nonprofit organizations, don't push so much that anyone doubts your commitment to the purposes of the organization. Nobody working there will admit it's the money that keeps

him; the organization has a hammerlock on "commitment" greater than Corning's on glass.

(7) Be tough on federal, state, and city employers. They are point-conscious: 10 points for being a veteran, 5 points for being an ex–Peace Corps volunteer, 10 for being blind or a hunchback, 15 for having a master's degree. "Equivalent experience" is the big buzzword here. Demonstrate that your experience is equal, as it is, to two years in grad school. And you've got 'em by the short hairs.

(8) Ask employers for an employment letter spelling out details of employment. Be sure a provision exists to review your salary after three months or (at least) after the first year.

Most employers will spell out terms for both parties to sign. So long as the organization is free to fire you and you're free to quit, the letter serves an important purpose. It says what you do, when, for how long, at how much pay, and enumerates the conditions of employment.

A healthy organization never hires until employer and employee share the same bed for three months. "Jack, I want to hire you, but quite frankly you might not be the guy for the job. I want to make you an offer contingent on your ability to perform and our ability to plug you in to the right situation. We'll make you an offer of three months' employment, and—if everything else is equal—you're on board after that time, subject to your performance and business activity. Now, this is what we would like you to do. . . ."

Make sure your final agreement is in black and white, thus avoiding misunderstanding six months hence. Offer to do the first draft, let your employer edit, and agree on the third and final draft.

(9) If hired as a consultant on a daily basis, be sure to calculate your daily worth (divide 261 days into your annualized highest salary) and then add 25 to 50 percent. Consultants are often unemployed, and the added amount finances finding your next assignment and pays your overhead (i.e., health and disability insurance and so forth.)

(10) If a contract-hire (hired for a specific length of time for a certain task), ask to see your organization's budget to manage that contract. Some employers might be miffed at this brazenness, but

it's a simple fact that the employer put a price on your head before seeing you. You've a right to know what that price is and to get it.

(11) On your résumé, establish a salary range, for example, $80,000 to 100,000 (negotiable). This means you are prepared to talk about anything—or nothing.

(12) Remember, focus on meaningful cash fringes—free travel privileges, paid health insurance, rent-free housing, board. Compute the cost in cash for these items, add to the salary offered, and calculate real take-home pay.

(13) Women, since the law is on your side, need to press to be paid at the appropriate level of responsibility. Avoid falling into the "What are your previous earnings?" trap.

(14) Search out what other organizations in the same field pay for a comparable job. Be certain that your salary requirements *match dollars* paid to people with equal responsibilities and functions. Back off and negotiate *downward* if your salary demands *exceed* compensation paid to key players performing at an *equal* level.

(15) Establish your highest previous earnings—whether hourly, daily, weekly, monthly, or annually—and focus on the figure that works out to the highest annualized earnings. If you have none, hypothesize, but don't lie about previous earnings. Effective employers always check out a person's past employment *and* earnings. And what if you've lied about salaries and gotten tremendous raises?

Sure, it works.

So you lie again, and again, and then gotcha. And shaking a history of lies is the hardest job of all in looking for a job. Smart employers, headhunters—yes, even personnel departments—check up on you. Lying will get you to second base, but you'll be picked off going to third and the story will follow you your whole life.

(16) Consider leaving a *margin* between what you're paid and what you expect as a negotiating point at your first performance-review session. This means the possibility of a meaningful jump in pay after your probationary period. Employers like rewarding performance on the job, not potential to fill a job.

(17) Does your Ph.D. in mining engineering support this job? Give yourself an additional $5,000 to $7,000.

(18) Schedule regular performance-review sessions to provide for regular merit increases based on *productivity.*

(19) Focus on the special abilities, talent, or flair you bring to the job (because you are you) in order to support salary demands.

(20) Don't stress a need for money. If you bought a house you can't afford, are still paying on last year's winter vacation to Catalina Island, and bought season tickets to the Bruins—that's *your* problem, not the employer's. Don't talk about needs (school debts to repay, a down payment on a vacation cottage, your $3,000 music system). Bargaining from weakness is incompetent and reflects questionable personal judgment, hardly a winning strategy in qualifying for a judgment job.

If money is the object in the job search, say so. Don't talk about "a challenging career with a new firm" or "wanting to be where the action is." Bushwa! Flat out, say you want more money, deserve it, and can show any employer why.

If you want to make a lot of money, it's for sure that you're going to make money for the organization that has the good sense to hire you. Why not advertise yourself as a marketing person, the man or woman who can bring in the business and fulfill the objectives of the organization? Without people out front selling whatever it is your organization does, nobody else has a job. So back up ten steps and rethink your prejudices about salespeople.

Effective salespeople know how to be rejected; they don't slash their wrists and bleed all over you when they blow a sale. They are not so much aggressive as they are persistent; they never give up if they believe what they are selling *helps* a customer. Effective salespeople are *trustworthy;* people trust them. Which is the essence, remember, of the business relationship. Effective salespeople are, like everyone else, hard to find. In business, they are shock troops on the front lines deserving your firm's highest medals of honor.

A low-paying but interesting job might be okay if it's relevant and encourages personal growth. But are you making a mere $35,000 per annum as a CPA in Pottsville, Pennsylvania? And your employer wants you in the accounting division in the White Plains plant? Then you need a bare $75,000 to maintain your high standard of living out there in O'Hara country. So, the next lesson is to double your price if you are New York City–bound.

Money, in the abstract, is meaningless; it's how you intend to spend it that counts. What are your objectives? The man or woman who says, "I won't accept less than forty-five thousand," is not necessarily rating quality of work *second* to compensation. The nub of the problem is that money alone is never satisfactory. Nor is self-fulfillment an end in itself (poets must eat). Reconciling these twin objectives, making compensation and career congruent, while a tough balancing act, is not impossible. Moreover, most natural money-makers are not materialists. Means, not ends, are central to those who are beneficiaries of great wealth (i.e., earned wealth).

Finally, a simple formula for mid-career job changers: Multiply your age times $1,000. Are you forty-nine years old and a candidate to manage the southern region of your organization's marketing department? Well, according to this formula, you're now making $49,000 (salary including meaningful fringes, or profit sharing) with prospects of making (in constant dollars) $65,000 when you slink off to your sunset years.

For many men and women hooked on this formula, however, the anxiety caused by being $10,000 or $15,000 shy of this hypothetical figure forces us to play catch-up ball in a line of work we no longer love. And ignores what should be the goal of every man and woman: self-fulfillment. Many people who switch fields, change careers, pioneer new endeavors, face a medium to drastic reduction in pay. My strong feeling is that those who find fulfillment in new careers recover earning power rapidly and often exceed their highest previous salary.

And if you're an entry-level professional, starting salary is important—not for the now, but for what you're paid ten years hence. Not your salary, but your *salary base* is what's important.

Some rules of thumb: If you have no experience and have just graduated from college, you should receive no less than $18,000—anyplace. Add another $3,000 if you have a master's and $5,000 if you're a Ph.D. without previous appropriate work experience.

Don't clutch if you don't have degrees. Equivalent experience is worth $4,000 to $8,000 in most work. And every year you work adds a grand or two to your worth. The money awards follow as an inevitable concomitant of ability. Toby Tyler ran away to the circus and worked for *nothing,* and he did the right thing. But if Toby took a job with IBM tomorrow, as its assistant publications chief, he should bargain for $42,000 minimum, meaningful fringes, and a corner office.

My observations support the following generalizations:

—Glamour jobs pay either nothing or everything.

—Public-service positions pay more than the public suspects.

—Technical jobs pay well to start, but tend to sag in salary later on.

—Grunt employment often finances finding judgment jobs.

—Industrial jobs often pay well, but it's the profit sharing, stock options, and incentive bonuses that count.

—International employment pays well to good, but it's the travel and the benefits that hook us in the end.

—Subsistence or expenses-only employment for a cause is a wacky life and usually a full one for a younger, single, or retired person.

Finally, as Samuel Johnson once remarked, "No one is more harmlessly employed than in the making of money." So, first of all, don't be ashamed of it, and make damned sure your interest in money is conveyed to potential employers. If you want to make a lot of money, it's for sure that you're going to make money for the organization that has the good sense to hire you.

TEN

Management by Subjectives

"What happens if I'm fired?"

"Yes, Virginia, there are people who are fired, but who don't necessarily fail."

If it happens, make tracks and find another berth. But be careful of accepting any job; plenty of reputations fade in rebounding from a bad job situation.

If we are fired, our propensity to rationalize comes into play. We make up a thousand reasons why we haven't worked out on the job, nine hundred and ninety-nine of them untrue. Do yourself and your boss a favor: If you're not working out, confront her with this fact. A long discussion follows and often clears the air.

The best test of a manager is how she fires people.

The best test, if you're fired, is how you handle it (which says a lot about you): management by subjectives.

Let's face it, people lose jobs for a variety of reasons: a political reshuffling, a departmental merger, a clash of principles versus pragmatics . . . and on and on and on. The best thing to do is set aside an hour, write out the reasons you think you should leave, and ask for an appointment with the boss.

When you take the initiative (making sense in a tough situation), a frank exchange takes place and clears the air. You took your boss off the hook and showed some mettle. That's why he'll think twice before firing you from Sticky Wicket, Inc.

But if you've been fired for outrageous reasons and nobody levels with you, dip your quill in the nearest pen pot and write the boss (or his board) a nice, pointed little note. It won't help any-thing but the ego, but that's the most important thing you've got.

"So you can't hire until you learn how to fire?"

The art of firing key people is essential to a manager's develop-ment. A favorite question headhunters query of job candidates is "By the way, how many people in the course of your work have you fired . . . and how?" A rule is never to hire a manager who hasn't learned to fire. This lack in supervisory makeup could be a built-in booby trap and blow up in the face of whoever hired her. Remember, hiring and firing are the *central responsibility of manage-ment.* Organizations that abandon this principle are managed thenceforth by executive committees, collectivized soviets, or by appeals to personnel manuals—all of which signal stagnating orga-nizations.

"So you don't think being fired or doing the firing is the worst part of going to work each day?"

Not if people stop being afraid of each other. Being fired or doing the firing is vital to organizations. There is a right way to do it. And if it's done right, ten to one both parties salvage what's best in the relationship.

Hiring yourself an employer, after all, is establishing a business relationship—not a fraternal bond. There is no way it can be. And business relationships are among the most satisfying established in a lifetime. But such relationships need constant renewal and renova-tion. Who's to say a severed relationship can't be reestablished in another environment on different terms at a later date?

Most people are fired for political reasons. Once the weather vane is blowing in the wrong direction, it's time to job-jump. If you're not moving up, then think . . . maybe some other organi-zation needs your talents.

Job-jumping is okay—if you jump up.

Job-hopping, however, is a no-no. When you job-hop, you don't jump up, you jump sideways.

What you do *today* for your organization is what counts. That's why I deplore the downplaying of the grading system in college. Fairly or unfairly, somebody is keeping score in school and the workplace. "What have you done for us lately?" is management's toughest question. And the one they should be asking everyone, from the executive vice-president dining on the expense-account circuit down to the squaw people working in administration.

Work is an honorable estate.

Those who feel forced to work because it's their duty, who feel grateful to employers "for keeping them on" while others pull their weight, secretly die a cubit every working day. Employers do no one a favor by making someone labor against his real wishes. That is truly hard-hearted and cynical. To keep a man or woman in bondage because of an organization's retirement program is cynical and self-destructive.

There's both bribery and blackmail at work here and a sickness unto death.

And it's bad for organizations and people.

"What are some other reasons for which people are fired?"

"Rigid" . . . "poor team player" . . . "aloof" . . . "unable to change" . . . "can't get along to go along"—these are a few. The bottom line: Employers and colleagues don't *like* them. The typical fired executive is generally in his or her forties, earns over $45,000 a year, and has been ten or more years with a firm. The person is achievement-oriented, well educated, often a perfectionist, and possesses a technical skill that earned an entrance-level professional job.

So far so good. But the typical terminated professional is happiest working alone and is impatient with other people. Blunt and vainglorious, these people often give individualism a bad name. Respected, often; liked, no.

When this person is fired, nobody is surprised except the person. "Why not evaluate me on the basis of results," he cries. Promoted to a position in general management where the right stuff is how well he manages other people, the perfectionist of the world usually folds.

"I thought individualism was a quality employers always searched out."

Individualism.

Losing its sheen as this century wears on . . . its history, like that of classical free enterprise, a glorious one, but its future these days is dim.

Rugged. Free-spirited. Swashbuckling. Arrogant.

Great qualities still, recruiting entrepreneurs, CIA spooks, literary critics.

Rugged individualists are gunners, mavericks, and eccentrics. Even a genius here and there. In organizational environments, aloof from and noninvolved with people, as most individualists are, they lack the kind of engagement with the environment required in judgment jobs where people are central.

"So industry puts a high premium on 'getting along'?"

It was truer in the fifties than now.

The Organization Man is still with us, however, complete with button-down brain, gray-flannel mouth, and lockstep locomotion.

It's not all his fault.

Most people hate working in mega-organizations. But since many employment opportunities are found, obviously, among huge organizations, the price we pay is a diminution in personality development—hence, the Organization Man.

Studies of people who work in these industrial/corporate/governmental/academic octopi suggest that the great problem is smooth interpersonal relationships—in a word, getting along. The motto of the Organization Man is "Don't spit in the soup; we all have to eat."

Countless manpower studies bear out this truth. Thus, when you look for a job, your people skills, management by subjectives, are carefully evaluated. This doesn't mean you become part of a homogeneous mass, the specific gravity of most organizations. Just the opposite. It's your job to become a visible, productive, and vital part of the organization, and *at the same time* make it with the people you work with, over, and for. Not an easy art; nobody bats 100 percent in the Smooth Interpersonal Relationship department. But by becoming effective on the job, winning the loyalty of staff, the admiration of peers, and the gratitude of superiors—yours is a great future.

You think you have the potential?

Think again. Repeatedly, in many types of organizations, organizational heroes (ranging from the tiger in the bullpen to the executive chairman) unravel during people crises. People crises are a thousand things.

(1) A secretary suddenly feels oppressed working for you.

(2) The boss doesn't have lunch with you anymore.

(3) You're dead wrong on some issue and can't admit it.

(4) The job is dissolved, your ego liquidated.

(5) You do a good job and somebody else gets the credit.

(6) You suddenly lose your sense of humor and find titles, job descriptions, and status in an organization important. You are in grave trouble and about to quit.

As with the person who can't make a marriage work, a divorce seems called for. Solution by elimination. Until, of course, you're reemployed and the same difficulty surfaces again. I'd wager my Keogh Plan that most chronic job hoppers quit every organization for the same reason.

Time and time again in my job, which is acting both as participant and observer to these inevitable subjective management problems, the *act* of confrontation often *solves* the problem. A new work environment, a new relationship, in fact, two new people emerge. Sensational. Practically occult.

What happens is that one party to a bad relationship, either an unhappy and increasingly counterproductive job holder or his noncommunicating and withdrawing boss, takes the bull by the horns and set the stage for a showdown. Both parties now confront a real problem, namely whether it's worthwhile to continue such a half-assed relationship.

More often than most people think, the result is salubrious from both parties' point of view; a new relationship flames from the ashes. If termination is not the result, the employer in plain fact has hired himself a new employee. And the job holder has herself a new boss.

"How soon can you tell whether someone is going to work out in a judgment job?"

Nine months is the old ball game: a period of gestation when either something of real issue is brought to birth or the job and its holder abort. During the honeymoon, the marriage is given a chance to coalesce; expectations on the part of both parties are in suspense.

It's both the best and sometimes the worst of times. It doesn't necessarily take nine months to tell if this marriage can be saved. But in nine months a manager is certain of the rightness of his choice in filling a job.

"So everyone, according to you, is a candidate for the pink slip?"
Many times. Although most of us don't know it. After nine months, these are the invariable signs of time's passage, blips picked up on the radarscope.

(1) "When does a deserving person like me get a raise?"
(2) "Why does my most elementary work require this nitpicking supervision?"
(3) "Does the boss know his purchasing director is a chump?"
(4) "Why, with what I've learned here, I could easily double my income and responsibility elsewhere."
(5) "Good God, do I want to work with Anaconda Consolidated the rest of my life?"
(6) "Thank God it's Friday."

All of these signal foul weather ahead. At this point managers—and the managed alike—switch off their earphones. Instead of talking out problems, people begin talking to themselves. That's why you say it's *bedlam* where you work. Crazy.

"You mean people send signals when they want to be fired?"
People start unconsciously signaling the boss.
A secretary recently can't seem to finish important assignments.
A project director in Buffalo doesn't return phone calls.
The project's budget analyst is taking three-hour lunches and caught flu four times last winter.
A special assistant is turning out sloppy work and spends a good hour a week photocopying her résumé.

It's a confusing situation.
On the one hand, we tell ourselves we want to *quit*. On the other hand, we're sending a message to the executive suite: "Please fire me, I can't cope."
And the boss suffers the same confusion. On the one hand, she's saying to herself, "I really ought to fire this guy." On the other hand, she starts sending signals: "Please quit, I can't cope."

The message is sent in a thousand codes, but the meaning is the same: "Please quit and get off my back."

Here is an example of how employers think.

> "I'll temporarily detail Brown to work for Green—they hate each other's guts."

> "Sure, I've sent Brown every year to our annual conference; let's send Blue this year."

> "At our next staff meeting, I'll ask Brown's opinion—*last.*"

> "I'll tell Brown to fire Gray—they play golf together every Saturday."

That way Brown will quit and solve the boss's problem.

A working woman denied a promotion, for example, will go into a deep funk. Her depression is a result of unexpressed anger (her best friend gets the job, the job was promised as a reward for work well done, an outsider is brought in to fill the position). It does no good if she doesn't say what she feels to the people who need to know it.

The problem with letting feelings all hang out is that it's unprofessional. Uncool. And it wrecks relationships on the job. While she still feels the shock, it's appropriate to disguise her own feelings. But it does her mental health no good, once she's collected her thoughts, not to confront the need-to-know person or persons and show real anger.

Personal confrontation is something most working people avoid, at great personal damage to themselves. That's why people suffer acute depression on the job. Anger that should go outward goes inward.

Feelings of failure are another symptom. Working people often feel something in their makeup is responsible. When it could be something outside themselves, such as a budget cutback over which there was no control. Feeling out of control and in someone else's control is bound to cause plenty of working people the deep bends. But nobody, finally, controls his environment. Compulsive people have a mistaken view of reality. Reality is that we propose but other people dispose even if we are the boss. Nothing so characterizes a person on the job as the ability to quit it gracefully. Accordingly, how you manage the boss, her boss, and working colleagues says a lot about you. The point is to exit gracefully in manner that bespeaks professionalism and high self-esteem. Above all, it means taking yourself into consideration before considering other people —the boss, for example.

Many people remain at jobs they no longer like out of a displaced sense of loyalty, often for target groups of the organization: customers, students, stockholders, yes, even our staff. Being considerate to them often means eliminating responsibility to ourselves. And our work and relationships begin to reflect the resentment we feel remaining on the job.

Some working people forgo job jumping for fear of being labeled a job hopper. There is a danger, of course, in constantly switching positions. Employers suspect you're never long enough in any one job to become expert. But if you can demonstrate an upward spiral of earnings and responsibilities in every new job you take, employers won't question why you left.

Job hoppers are often called ticket punchers or grasshoppers. They move in and out of jobs and organizations with the sinuosity a snake would envy. Different from job jumpers who always move up in terms of responsibility or quality of job (even though they might move *down* in pay): ticket punchers are main-chance operators. Ambitious for the quick score, ticket punchers are to the world of work what social climbers are to society.

Ticket punchers are easily spotted. Name dropping, glibness, bluff, shallow charm mark them for life. Ticket punchers are not expert at anything; never long enough at a job to learn, the one chance at occupational survival is to glide so quickly across the surface of the pond that nobody knows whether they made a ripple.

There is also a case for taking a cut in pay, assuming lesser responsibilities, and jumping *down* into a job you're certain (almost) to love. Friends might think you're crazy, your current employer questions your judgment, and spouses and loved ones might think it risky, but that's the price of fulfillment.

Another factor in changing jobs is our need to impress other people. "Are you still working as a buyer at Bloomie's?" an old girlfriend asks. As if this friend had somehow missed the bus in staying put doing a job year after year. Feeling change—any kind of change—is necessary is to be a captive of other people's expectations.

"I really want a job, but I don't like the politics on the job. Am I being unrealistic?"

Unless you want to be a stack librarian. And I'm not so sure about librarians anymore.

Politics is as much a part of life as sport, sex, illness, or in-laws. Found anywhere two or more people gather. Where you work, there you find it. Don't fight it; go with it.

Politics is compromise, trading one idea for another, acting out responsibilities and dreams and revealing convictions. In any organization, the politics of the place can be ruthless and claustrophobic. But politics also enlivens and changes the work environment overnight. If you care about yourself, your job on the job is to find allies, people who think like you. Conflict, the drama of politics, results as opposing forces collide. Nothing wrong with conflict: It causes sparks and lights fires, and with light an organization sees its way.

Whether you have a judgment job, want one, or are hiring people for judgment jobs, an important quality to look for in yourself or in others is this capacity to play politics. Leaders in every organization, from IBM to the Roman Catholic Church, are politicians. Avoiding politics is to select yourself out of a shot at top management.

A central reason people leave jobs is bad politics. That is, people squabbling over other people. Most people call the problem a "personality conflict" or a "breakdown in communications," but these are the consequences, not the causes, of a failure in on-the-job relationships.

Whenever a job candidate says he isn't interested in such-and-such a position because it's too political, it's the tip-off that he is easily intimidated, that he doesn't want a judgment job.

Most people say they want work with people, and every judgment job is *that*—squared. But what these selfsame people can't face is that people and politics are like a horse and carriage. You can't separate the two if you want movement.

"I want work with an institution that I can change. Is this necessarily a naïve notion?"

And you want to change it into a more democratic, just, and humane working environment. If you succeed, you'll be doing the institution for which you work a good turn.

For those who want a career of changing institutions, working in the Establishment—anyplace—offers a fertile field for socially constructive change. Making the organization work so that there is a little more distributive justice is not an ignoble calling.

Many people are fired on principle from their first job. Before you quit, or are fired, give the organization a chance to change. Quitting is often the easy way out. Find allies within the organization and present your demands collectively and with dignity. Ill-mannered demonstrations provoke irrational response and do little except massage the egos of those challenging the organization. If you change the system some (and are not cashiered), you live another day when you can change it more. Don't wear a whistle around your neck. But carry it on every job—and blow it for the country's sake.

Be an effective politician; if you believe in the organization, put it and yourself *first.* By doing so, you steal a march on everyone else who puts only *himself* first. And if the organization's not worth it (and you and your allies can't change it), start another job campaign. Hire yourself an employer for whom you can be effective. In other words, where you can play politics.

Your politics.

"But suppose I like it where I am and just want more responsibility and money?"

You're saying that you like your current job and employer. But you're going broke on your current salary, right? All the more reason to hustle up other employment and then confront the boss with the sad story of your "not being able to afford XYZ, Inc." Of course, you confess, in your gut XYZ is your kind of firm. Nine times out of ten the boss will waste no time upgrading the job and giving you a healthy raise equal to what you found in the hidden job market if you've been especially effective on the job.

"What about job jumping before you're fired?"

Not a bad idea.

After nine months on a job, if you're not moving up, then think . . . maybe some other organization needs your talents.

Job jumping is okay—if you jump up!

Job hopping, however, is bad. When you job-hop, you don't jump up—you jump sideways.

Beware. Most job hoppers don't leave one job *for* another: they flee one job and take any other.

Job hoppers move sideways all their occupational lives, usually at the same salary level, and always with an appropriate story of woe.

Before you change jobs (although not necessarily careers), be sure it's a step up in salary, responsibility, and relevance. Otherwise ten years hence you'll have a lot of explaining to do in hundreds of awkward interviews.

"What about quitting—how do I do it?"

There are three ways to face the problem: (1) Let the situation grow worse; (2) circumvent the problem, go around it (the non-job is a product of circumvential problem solving); (3) face the problem head-on.

Ask for an appointment first thing tomorrow morning. Tell the boss why you feel ineffective on the job. Suddenly you feel free.

There are three outcomes of such a confrontation: (1) you're fired forthwith, (2) you're allowed to stay on for, say, three months to find another job, at which time you must leave, and surprisingly, (3) the terms and conditions of your current job change now that both you and the boss know the true state of each other's feelings. Result (1) happens much more rarely than you think; result (2) is the usual outcome; result (3) happens much more often than you think.

"Why do two people dislike each other less after this kind of exchange?"

Both parties feel free. And feeling free and *acting* freely, for a change, is better than a Dr Pepper on the rocks.

That's why people who are fired or who do the firing feel so strangely elated once the task is done. But it's not so strange, because human elation is caused by acting freely. Both parties are going to feel so good about themselves, chances are the employment relationship won't terminate at all.

"Are you saying we only function well in jobs we feel free to quit?"
Management by subjectives.

And if we manage people, we only feel effective when we are free to fire them.

The key, of course, is personal freedom. The person who feels dependent on his employer is never as effective as the individual who can turn his back on the employer, drop the gate, and find another job. That's why job-search skills are important; they give us the confidence to put our jobs on the line time and time again.

"So there are no dream jobs? I've known and heard of people who really seem to have terrific opportunities."
Far be it from me, humble reader, to destroy your dreams. That's the point of writing your obituary, remember—to ignite that old dream mechanism.

Yes indeed. Dream jobs *do* exist. But you make them happen. How good a job you do is the leverage you need to expand your current job into something with greater scope. You do this by changing the attitudes of your peers, staff, and superiors, defining another objective for your department, taking on new responsibilities, asking for more work and making your humdrum, pedestrian job into the dream job you've always wanted.

That's because you know yourself so well and know how to put yourself first, showing your boss how this helps him and the organization, and presto!—you've worked yourself out of the common rut and staked out a new job, the kind of job everyone always wants and never finds. It's the job you truly make yourself.

"So you can learn from the job search and apply it on the job?"
Let's face it: You learn more about business by negotiating one contract, more about personnel by hiring ten people, more about sales by making five sales than from all the textbooks ever written.

Make your job hunt an experience in sales, learning your field, ideamongering, management by subjectives. The carryover on the job is astounding.

"What's a real job search like?"

It's an adventure.

It means feeling free.

But most people fear freedom. They take a job, any job, based on its availability instead of as a positive choice. Competent job seekers have no such problem. Taking a job they want, they stay as long as it satisfies. Once this feeling is gone, they grapple with what they want to do *next*—either inside or outside the organization. Job seekers are free to live adventurously, free to go hire an employer. That's what looking for work means.

It does take time—the way a shopper cost-compares items to determine value. A purchase is made when one chooses a job that comes closest to what one *wants.*

"Yes, but job searchers are dependent on job offers."

That's the trouble.

Employers are equally dependent on employees.

And that's the trouble, too.

Any kind of a dependency relationship—whether between mother and child, wife and husband, or employee and employer—may breed resentment and hostility. How many people do you know who hate their employer? Why? Because they need that paycheck. They feel forced to work. They call it their duty, and they say it's for the spouse and kids, but in truth they despise their employers. Now, nobody desiring a reasonably healthy mental life wants that. To hate what you do and for whom you do it eight hours a day breeds psychosomatic diseases and kinky neuroses.

The cause of the curse is that people think jobs are property, a piece of real estate to be bought and sold on an exchange. "This job belongs to me because I fill it; until I leave it, it is mine alone."

Of course, the property analogy is not a bad one; talent, skill, achievements, experience, and education, the accumulation of a lifetime, are a person's qualifications or property. We do not lose our talent when we lose a job. Rather, our property is what's carried from one job to another, what a judgment-job candidate carries in his head. This can never be taken away.

But jobs are eliminated and created every day depending on the changing objectives of an organization, the business climate, and the job candidates themselves. If a job is eliminated, chances are that events and outside forces governed the decision. Essentially the employment relationship, while at best tentative, mutually beneficial, often more social than we think (how many of our best friends happen to be also our working companions?), is based on a reciprocity of dues and services.

"So your point is that organizational loyalty is largely outdated?"
Not entirely.

If the purposes of the organization for which you freely labor suit your craft, talents, and beliefs, then the relationship is healthy, although still tentative. Tentative because organizations and the individuals who constitute them are constantly changing. We continually renew, readjust, or terminate employment because changing conditions no longer make it healthy. Learning how to find a new job, switching fields, job jumping are skills that should be taught—even at business schools. Repeated morale surveys support this proposition: People are really loyal to those they feel most free with; any other kind of employee behavior is largely dependent in nature.

"What do you mean, 'management by subjectives'?"
Everyone is familiar with the concept of MBO (management by objectives). It means that the foremost responsibility of a manager is to establish organizational objectives and persuade his staff to achieve them. What's not so well known is that everyone has personal objectives that might or might not be congruent with those of the organization.

So management by subjectives is (1) knowing your personal objectives, (2) sharing them with the boss, (3) establishing the common denominator between the two, (4) taking responsibility for yourself before fulfilling responsibilities to other people, (5) cultivating the fine art of self-awareness (not self-consciousness), and (6) taking responsibility for your own life and persuading your staff to do the same.

The aim of an organization is not to "take care of Freddie." Freddie's job is to take care of himself by becoming a self-manager: management by subjectives.

ELEVEN

The Flair Factor

Hire people's strengths, not their weaknesses. It sounds easy, but is it?

Peter Drucker, in his excellent book *The Effective Executive,* retells a story I've repeated a dozen times around the country. About Abraham Lincoln's management problems during the Civil War—his search for a general.

Lincoln churned practically the whole Union Army General Staff before finding his right man. There were Pope and Meade and Burnside and McClellan and others. All his generals checked out: graduates of West Point, excellent performance ratings, combat experience (the Mexican War). All passed muster. But none turned around the Army of the Potomac and marched south.

A sad tale, repeated many times in hundreds of institutions from universities to corporations to government organizations each year. The right person eludes.

And modern-day institutions—like the Union Army—whip through a succession of superstar commanders (directors, presidents, CEOs), making headhunters rich and the public sorry. What's the message, as my sixth-grade teacher was wont to say, of this tale? Well, the message is that management doesn't usually know what it wants.

Abe Lincoln initially picked his generals on the basis of credentials, qualifications. The problem with all these carefully hand-picked generals was that they lacked that flair necessary in a war-time commander: aggressiveness. All were interested in protecting the Army of the Potomac (and their own reputations) rather than engaging Lee. Finally, in desperation, Lincoln turned to the one commander with the "X" factor. Lincoln named Ulysses S. Grant to command the Army of the Potomac.

And who was Grant?

An undistinguished graduate of West Point, a lackluster quartermaster captain in the Mexican War voluntarily retired at an early age to return to Illinois to indifferently manage a country store, and then recruited by the state militia in Illinois (not the Regular Army) at the outbreak of the War Between the States.

As a battlefield commander, Grant was a success in the sideshow war with Lee's army in the West. Grant liked his brandy, possessed none of the social graces, and wasn't well connected in the corridors of power. In short, Grant wasn't a qualified job candidate except in one crucial sense: He had a habit of fighting.

So Grant became commander of the Army of the Potomac, mobilized the superior armaments, materials, and manpower of the North, and marched his army toward Richmond. Defeated by Lee and defeated again, through the sheer weight of material superiority, Grant broke Lee's forces and ended the war a year later at Appomattox Court House.

A grand story.

A grateful nation made him President, the electorate being more miserably endowed with prescience in the people-picking business than was Lincoln. Grant was the worst President in American history (although a couple of recent examples are competing for this dubious-achievement award). The Peter Principle, unknown a hundred years ago, found its application in Grant's election: He was promoted to his level of incompetence. Everything that made him a great general conspired to ruin him and his administration as President.

Sic transit gloria mundi.

But we were talking about the message of this tale. And at the risk of simplifying the whole story, let me sum up and say that nobody, neither the mailroom attendant nor the Supreme Allied Commander, should be chosen for a job based on nonessentials: the so-called fail factors.

So the message to management is to hire on the basis of ability;

the message for job seekers is to know (and reveal) your abilities. Employers confuse a job's real definition by augmenting it with altogether too many nonessential redundancies, sometimes completely obscuring the essence of what needs to be done. Job applicants, doing an inventory of their backgrounds, include a host of detail that rarely wholly supports the job they want. The result is a blurred photograph of what is needed in a job *and* a job seeker.

Thus, employers confuse the issue by specifying a whole series of irrelevant (but desirable) characteristics that make people picking harder than it should be. Often an employer is unconsciously more interested in who a person is rather than what he does, or rationalizes a host of insignificant and non-germane factors into a candidate profile that fits the admissions standards of a country club but is woefully inadequate for a job.

Hiring on the basis of character traits, personality inventories, value systems, doesn't work. It's the reason two out of three important hiring decisions abort.

Far better for employers to treat each employment decision separately—using candidates from any source, specialty, way of life, age bracket, sex, or nationality category. Effective men and women are hard to find. Looking for the all-purpose candidate dooms employers to disappointment.

Now, in Grant's case the main quality Lincoln wanted in a general was aggressiveness. Nothing else really mattered. The same is true for every job. One characteristic, sometimes two, never more than three are absolutely vital in satisfying the real demands of a judgment job. Job descriptions, with their hopeless muddle of peripheral and nonessential requirements, never highlight the supremely important factor without which no candidate should be considered. The job of management, and the job of job seekers, is to identify this factor. For purposes of exegesis, let's call it the flair factor. That vital "X" element, skill, capacity, orientation, or ineffable intangible without which no candidate—no matter how well recommended or otherwise qualified—succeeds on the job.

Let me list two columns, the job title on the left, the quintessential flair factor on the right.

THE JOB	FLAIR FACTOR
College president	Accomplished fund-raiser and grantsman
Confidential secretary	150-word-per-minute whiz
Investigative reporter	Persistent, nosy, nattering nabob
Lobbyist	Intelligence-gathering gossip
Salesman	All alone with nothing but my silver voice and sample box

I jest?

Not a whit. Every institution has a classification and assignment clerk, a cosmetician paid to conceal the real essence of any job. The first function of someone who hires is to ignore the job description and, like a laser beam, focus on *what must be done*. That means a gloves-off, sometimes unflattering distillation of a judgment job.

In real life, because management doesn't focus or is confused about what it wants, a slew of inappropriate candidates are passed through a series of lugubrious interviews, with no one precisely sure (least of all the candidates themselves) about what's wanted. Because management (read search committee, the production chief, the chairman of the board—the hiring authority) did not face up to what's really wanted. The result is a failure of imagination and the continued stagnation of the organization.

Let's go back and look at these same jobs. Without the flair factor, the so-called fail factors. Read the list of qualifications for the job as a classification officer would phrase it.

THE JOB	QUALIFICATIONS
College president	A Ph.D. with five years' educational administration experience and an equal number of years' university teaching within accredited institutions of higher learning. Demonstrated publications record. Successful candidates must be married. It is also desirable that . . .

Confidential secretary	Five years' experience as a steno typist, written recommendations of proficiency, be of attractive appearance and cheerful disposition. Graduation from an approved secretarial school essential. It is desirable but not mandatory that the candidate have a bachelor's degree and . . .
Investigative reporter	All candidates must be *cum laude* graduates of recognized schools of journalism, have five years' major metropolitan newspaper experience, possess writing samples reflecting an urban-studies orientation. It is desirable that . . .
Lobbyist	Advanced degree in political science, five years' experience representing trade, manufacturing, or industrial concern in Washington, D.C. Desirable that candidates have worked in legislative/executive branches for no less than three years and . . .
Salesman	No less than five years' experience as purchasing officer in the Mid-Atlantic region. Must demonstrate sales leadership potential, prove an annual commission income of no less than $75,000, and possess an M.B.A. degree or its equivalent from an accredited business school. Desirable that . . .

Does anyone twenty-one or over believe that any of the above organizations has a snowball's chance in hell of recruiting the *right* person for the jobs they have open? If so, I reserve the right to interview the candidates, before finally passing judgment on their classification function.

Okay. Let's take the same list and let me substitute the fail factor, the irrelevant characteristic for which a person was hired.

THE JOB	FAIL FACTOR
College president	Leading authority on the photosynthesis process
Confidential secretary	Cute, and laugh a minute
Investigative reporter	*Cum laude* graduate of the Columbia School of Journalism
Lobbyist	Ph.D. in political science
Salesman	Five years' successful purchasing-officer experience

All of these factors *seem* to fit. But in point of fact, not one of these characteristics is vital. What happened to these mismatches?

I've heard a few thousand explanations about why the last man or woman didn't work out. Educators call it a "learning experience," but many employers never learn. They go on repeating their mistakes the rest of their lives—like the many job seekers who habitually follow career paths they hate.

Message: Employers don't know what they want.

Identifying job objectives.

Defining goals.

This is the chief responsibility of organizations and individuals. Every day a CEO where you work should ask himself, "What the hell do we *do* around here?" Every day people who work for this man should be saying, "What is my job—what am I here for?"

Managers should:

(1) Analyze what a job really requires.

(2) Hire someone who has the talent.

(3) Don't hire anyone simply for the additional niceties; these are desirable attributes, never essential.

Finding talent to fill judgment jobs is hard enough without asking candidates to be all things to all people. Hired for the fail factors. Degrees, pedigree, and previous experience are fine, but they don't necessarily fit what's wanted.

Like Lincoln, employers are mesmerized by nonessentials; superb general recommendations, credentials fit for royalty, educational credits galore, but not answering the question "What is to be *done*, and can she do it?"

Think about it. How many jobs have you had where you lacked strict fail-factor qualifications, but for which you were hired? How did your work compare with that of experienced hands? Think harder. Who would be working today at *any* task if the experience edict applied universally? Nobody.

Now let's go back to Chapter Two. The way to discover the flair factor is to study accomplishments and, if you're an employer, the way to choose effective people is to analyze their accomplishments and match them up against a job's requirements. Look over the partial lists of three job candidates.

CANDIDATE # 1	CANDIDATE # 2	CANDIDATE # 3
Finished term-paper assignment in three days without sleep.	Conducted open-ended business survey for employer that was used as basis for new marketing campaign.	Failed every subject in prep school except art. Was cited as the outstanding art student in the history of the school.
Beat out three more qualified applicants for a key job in XYZ programming division.	Developed most successful profit center within XYZ, Inc., on my own initiative with no encouragement from top management.	Landed three industrial clients for my consultant services: leasing antique furniture to cash-rich firms.
Nominated by board chairman to attend prestigious mid-career-level business course from among twenty candidates selected by top management.	Started own self-service laundry scheme in college and financed college education on profits.	At University of Nancy, where I learned French, I completed four years of work in three semesters.
Chosen by fraternity as the brother most likely to succeed.	Broke my own record as high-jump champion at college.	Wrought first industrial sculpture ever displayed in Europe from Army-surplus material.
Cited by commander general Eighth Army for being "Soldier of the Month" four times in succession.	Refused invitation to turn pro in order to enter law school full time.	Declined full professorship in art history at college that flunked me out ten years before.
One of twenty young men selected by Junior Jaycees	Refused Junior Jaycee offer to become member despite	Published original work of art criticism that was criti-

CANDIDATE # 2
strong organizational pressure to "mix" in commu-
nity.

CANDIDATE # 3
cally well received, but
sold only two thousand
copies.

Well, the lists go on and on. But we know enough about these fellows to make an educated judgment about the flair factors. If you're looking for a museum director, candidate three is your woman; want someone to start up a new component in your industry? Number two seems to fit. A regional manager for your firm's northwestern office? Number one looks as if he fits the bill.

ITEM: Of eight speechwriters I hired, four journalists, two novelists, a college dropout, and a drunk, the last two were least qualified. Guess which two were most effective?

ITEM: I once hired ten schoolteachers for an important contract —the three most effective had *never* taught school before.

ITEM: Of the five truly great entrepreneurs I know, none went to business schools.

ITEM: Of eight great college presidents I know, one has no college degree and five others lack a Ph.D., and none had been a college president before.

ITEM: The best top sergeant I knew in the army never went to NCO school, my best college professor never published a book, the best economist I know is a lawyer.

This is not to knock economists, or the Ph.D., or the NCO Academy, or the value of publishing or the importance of experience. My point is simple: People are either *effective* or *ineffective* on the job. There are plenty of effective college presidents with Ph.D.s, first-rate NCOs who attended the NCO Academy, excellent professors who publish, top-flight speechwriters who are journalists, and effective economists who attended the Wharton School. But their badges are not proof of *effectiveness*.

Reducing the job down to its basic elements frees an employer to find the most *effective* people, not necessarily the most *qualified*. The difference between the two groups is the distinction between growing and failing organizations. In good times and bad, there is always a need for effective people. Contrary to convention, the hardest jobs to fill are judgment jobs. What is scarce in the employment mart is not judgment jobs but people to fill them.

This is no idle observation.

People, effective people at every level, are what's hard to find.

Drawing from a rich manpower pool, employers choose people who make a habit of success in one field and transfer that success to another, the flair factor. The wise manager goes with proven success, competence, and drive—no matter what field—rather than lamely falling back on the experiential, educational, and fail-factor qualifications.

Who says an M.B.A. won't make a fine infantry platoon commander; that a theologian won't work out as a diplomat; that a circus barker can't audition for the "Today" show? Nobody. And everybody. All of us have been trained since infancy to believe there is an organic connection between employment and education, forgetting that people who make a habit of success know what they want and go after it. Judgment jobs are too much in flux to commit to paper; except for what's to be accomplished, managers are no more able to freeze people in neat little boxes with solid and dotted lines running every which way than they are able to control events.

Poor jobs are notoriously protected by a thicket of qualifications. Hard to qualify for, these jobs are often stupefyingly secure once all the hurdles are jumped. Security, not only of income, but security of *place*. Status in our society is often established by *what we do*, until, of course, the organization itself finally fails.

Remember, we fill a job in much the same way as we find a job. We begin the whole process by asking advice. We make a list of other employers at the peak of their business, profession, or skill and call them. Flattered by being asked for their advice, employers give four more leads on where to look. Pretty soon we have five candidates (all of whom, if they're not interested, recommend others).

In like manner, the job searcher carries out the same process.

Interviewing the interviewer means evaluating employers, checking out the boss.

Does the employer:

—have his control problem (every manager *has* this problem) under control?

—seem easily intimidated by brains, drive, and talent?

—admit mistakes and learn from them? (Managers make the *right* decision about one out of three decisions.)

—welcome problems? (That's why she's so well paid.)

—think long and hard about decisions she makes and feel unafraid to make and take responsibility for them when they backfire?

—lavish praise on the deserving for outstanding work and feel unafraid to chastise drones and downtimers?

—give up the tiller to people who know what they are doing? (One of her jobs is to hire people who know what they are doing.)

—crave results that count, never ignoring the means to these ends, which means constant attention to matters of equity, ethics, and justice?

—hire people for their flair?

—know how to cut her losses?

—know how to fire someone she likes very much?

—solve problems face to face?

You ask, "If a manager can't control people, how can he assign them work?"

No problem.

At 2 A.M. an editor tells a newsman to cover a downtown fire.

A company commander orders a platoon sergeant to take hill #609.

The CEO mandates a market-research project on the feasibility of selling fridges to Eskimos.

Nobody is trying to control anybody; newspapers print the news, armies fight battles, businesses sell products and services.

The lazy newsman who's resentful at being dragged from the sack, the platoon sergeant angry for having to move on the enemy, and the researcher who prefers building a market model in greater L.A.—all suffer from control problems of their own. They don't accept the terms of their employment or the objectives of the organizations. They can't control their environment any more than the boss can. What they can do is change environments—find another job.

But nothing in Scripture prevents us from discussing *how* to do the job. For example, the newsman suggests a photo story, the sergeant advises a dawn attack, the researcher counsels aiming at the urban Aleut market. In a word, all would discuss and participate in the decision and agree or disagree with leadership, if they felt real *conviction*. In fact, that's what judgment-job holders are paid to do.

Managers' control problems often stem from a congenital inability to brook participation, conflict, and resolution. Managers frequently want to see people jump. Not think. Or feel. Or fight.

No way.

Now, still another list. Let's see if you have what it takes to be the boss.

(1) Am I willing to be called a bitch/bastard behind my back once I'm in the top job?

(2) Will I work weekends to get on top of my job?

(3) Am I prepared to take a chance on my rich relationship with my husband/wife, boyfriend/girlfriend, friends, children, professional colleagues?

(4) Do I have it in me to fire an ineffective person (late forties, three kids in college)?

(5) Am I prepared to be judged by organizational results—quotas met, sales made, people hired/fired? In short, am I a bottom-line person?

(6) Am I willing to give up my reputation as a nice person?

(7) Can I admit I'm wrong, hire a staff all of whom are smarter than I am in certain respects, and make crisis decisions based on insufficient information?

(8) Am I ready to go no faster than my slowest organizational runner? In other words, do I have the patience, sheer grit, and capacity for frustration and painstakingness that is the common lot of organizational leaders?

(9) Am I equipped to put organizational goals before personal feelings?

(10) Do I have my own control problems under control; that is, can I resist manipulating people when what's needed is leadership?

Especially able managers are those who cope with their compulsion problems. Leadership is understanding, no matter what power we wield inside an organization, regardless of our skill, experience, seniority, status, and title, that *we cannot control other people*. All we do is negotiate, bargain, discuss, disagree, and agree—there is never complete consonant agreement on every issue in the vast area of human relationships. Management's responsibility is to establish organizational objectives, on which all members of an organization focus. These objectives are independent of people's own subjective goals. That's why defining and redefining organizational objectives is so terribly important for institutions and setting goals so essential for people.

Because so much of our work environment is other people and our need to accommodate to this environment at any cost, it follows that people at every level spend a good deal of time and emotional energy trying to *control other people or fighting being controlled by others.* Then the people problems begin.

Organizational development is predetermined by goals. It is an organic and growing thing not lightly tampered with because it expresses institutional personality and purposes. Once managers define organizational goals and win over their people, they free themselves from their own control problems. Growth in an organization —like a flaming hibiscus—takes place.

Conflict *precedes* an orderly environment. Chaos follows when conflict is *suppressed.* Goldbricking, industrial sabotage, competitive brownie pointing, executive backbiting, and all the rest are usually the result of corporate benignity.

Because nobody likes to be controlled, free expression being natural, conflict that is the result of a free expression is as necessary as the water we drink. A test is how free people are with themselves and within institutions to express both dissent and agreement.

Let's say that you scored 100 percent, that you're prepared to pay your dues, that you really know the personal and professional consequences of being an Exceptional Person. Do you still want that top job? Well, if you do, that's a great qualification. Really wanting any job is half the battle in qualifying for it.

TWELVE

Special Situations

So far we've treated the job search without any special situational bias. That is, a secretary who hopes to be an office manager feels much the same way about the job search as the executive vice-president who wants to be a chief executive officer. But now let's focus on special problems and opportunities you face because you're married to a working spouse, a Ph.D., someone looking to work in government, and so forth. In other words, looking for a job is mostly the same for everyone, but we do represent different classes, races, and income and age levels, which causes us to put a special spin on our employment pitch.

First let's look at those seeking public-service employment. The time is long overdue for some plain talk on how to survive, nay prosper, while in the service of our government. What follows, therefore, is my modest contribution to the science of public administration. And don't blame me if your college placement counselor never breathed a word about it or it wasn't taught in Poli Sci 3A.

"What about 'freezes' on federal employment?"
There has been more or less a freeze on employment since the second term of Grover Cleveland. It's meaningless. But, as President Kennedy once quipped about the bureaucracy, it's worth seeing if the American government "intends to cooperate."

"You mean, the President, by himself, can't stop the government from hiring people?"

The President might order a 5 percent reduction in work force, but his bureaucracy really decides.

In other words, business as usual.

The hiring policies of most government agencies are the same as a generation ago, because the actual business of hiring, promoting, reassigning, and retiring bureaucrats goes on unabated. The President proposes, but the agencies themselves dispose. In fact, no public servant can remember a time when some sort of spending or employment crisis wasn't racking government. The favorite personnel put off is rejecting job applicants on the basis of such high-level policies, which are, at best, unevenly applied.

"Isn't there a personnel ceiling?"

There is.

It's a simple reporting device for the convenience of the Office of Management and Budget. As far as the job seeker or the effective bureaucrat is concerned, it bears about as much resemblance to reality as the deficit ceiling.

Why?

Because underneath the personnel ceiling is concealed the teeming activity, the sheer Machiavellian scheming, that transpires under its cover. There simply can't be a freeze on employment. Too many civil servants are retiring from government service, job jumping from one agency to another, dropping out from the job scene altogether, returning to school, being reassigned—*all of which means open slots for enterprising public servants or those who want to be.*

"Why does the President announce a freeze on employment if, in reality, it means so little?"

It means *something.*

It means the government is holding the line on the budget. And the policy reflects changing, but often unadmitted, new national priorities. For example, the Economic Development Administration might be reducing its staff, but the Defense Department is hiring more procurement specialists. And it does cripple job-jumping psychology.

Whether you work in the military/industrial complex or the peace/poverty axis, the Ping-Ponging between the public and private sectors is notorious. So, if you move out of government, you're likely to land on both feet with (a) a congressional committee monitoring the agency for which you worked, (b) a management-consulting firm that exploits your friendships, connections, and knowledge of the agency's politics, (c) a law firm, or (d) a legitimate interest group lobbying the government.

"Is there any one place to look for government jobs?"

Tracking down government jobs is being at the right place at the right time with ostensibly the right qualifications. Ask yourself: (a) Who are my friends and what jobs do they know of? (b) What are the nation's priorities and what agencies and contractors are working on them? (c) Is that where the money is? We can find out about judgment jobs in government service much the same way we do in the private sector: curiosity interviewing.

"Should a job seeker use his congresswoman for agency employment?"

Hundreds do.

This kind of political clout is largely overrated. But don't overlook the congressional connection if you come to Washington or go to your state capital.

"Well, if political connections are not as important as one supposes, what element is decisive?"

The decisive element is the character and quality of the comments of the public servants, past and present, who recommend you, and their political connections.

Choose your referees wisely. Select people in government who can take a profile of your strengths and back up what you say about yourself. One phone call from a respected bureaucrat to another civil servant is worth fifty job interviews.

And since none of us walks on water, be sure to include referees who can speak to your next employer about the kind of things you don't do well. Surprisingly, a balanced view of any job applicant is worth a hundred times more and is twice as effective as a blurb recommendation.

"Is it necessary to fill out a Form 171 (Government Application for Employment)?"

Yes.

The Form 171 was designed by a Soviet agent during the height of the cold war to throw confusion into our bureaucracy. Next to the fine print in *Robert's Rules of Order,* the works of R. D. Laing, and the later novels of Gertrude Stein, it ranks high in the obscurantist department.

In addition to a Form 171, prepare a functional résumé that is *so* good it opens up doors in the bureaucracy. The Form 171 has about as much sales appeal as an income-tax form. And it tells the feds nothing worth knowing. Slap your résumé on top of your Form 171 as a sales device.

"What's the best time of year to find a job with the government or one of its contractors?"

October 1.

That's the end of the fiscal year, when agencies often spend wildly so as to justify next year's fiscal request.

The result is that wholesale hiring goes on inside and outside the government; the rest of the year, government employment is sometimes a backwater.

"I've heard that government employment is badly paid."

Don't believe it.

The plain facts are that, except for grunt laborers at the General Service Administration, scientists, key medical personnel, clerks and secretaries, and foreign-service officers, federal employment is —relative to industry—more than holding its own, and at many levels often exceeds pay standards in the private sector.

"How do you avoid bureaucrats who tell you that you're underqualified?"

Don't try to get around this objection. Meet it head-on and prove you *are* qualified.

Sure, you need to type to qualify for the steno pool. College degrees for some obscure reason are required for most entry-level professional jobs. But the government usually provides a convenient loophole through which you could drive a Mack truck. The buzz expression is "or equivalent experience."

In nine out of ten judgment jobs filled, the hired bureaucrat does not meet all (or even most) of the necessary qualifications outlined. So if you hear of government jobs in the hidden job market and meet half the qualifications, chances are good that your application will carry the day.

"How serious are bureaucrats about their jobs?"
Deadly.

Sure, you can laugh at anything in Washington: the devalued dollar, prospects for a thermonuclear exchange—but *never* a person's job. You'll earn a lifetime enemy.

In the nation's capital every bureaucrat thinks his work is in the powerhouse. I knew a fellow who, while working on a task force to manage the war on poverty, burst out laughing when a high-level bureaucrat predicted the elimination of "poverty, disease, illiteracy, and injustice." My friend now works in Des Moines selling an interesting line of casualty insurance.

"Everyone says government employment is secure."
Another glittering half-truth.

It's nearly impossible to be fired from government service. Boozing, lechery, and high treason are about the only charges that can be made to stick if the government wants to fire you. (The last man fired for inefficiency was sacked during the administration of Chester Arthur.) However, for entirely different reasons, government employment is far more insecure than you would think.

The reasons: Winds of change blow in many directions in Washington, D.C., depending on the country's mood. A new administration with new plans takes power, intra-agency competition undermines your agency, the country's priorities are whipped about by political fashion to the consequent discomfort of those public servants who are working on *this* problem and not on *that*. Between Gramm-Rudman, freezes, rollbacks, and reductions in force, the fast-moving public servant must continually job-jump to stay even with where the judgment jobs are.

In a word, you can't be fired, but your job can be eliminated. Since your boss can't fire you, he'll probably promote you to a non-job, eliminate your job, or take away your responsibility so that you'll quit.

"But surely there are some imaginative men and women in government service."

Yes, there are.

Among government people you will find some truly fine public servants. Men and women who are flexible, imaginative, purposeful, and hardworking. You will find such people in about the same proportion in a government agency as teachers with the same characteristics in a public educational system. Nobody in government or outside it has figured out a way to give them the recognition they need and deserve except through grade creep.

"What is 'grade creep'?

The federal job you have is redefined and you move up one, two, or three grades.

Since 1963, there has been a noticeable, progressively deteriorating standard of work in the government. Many mid-level jobs have been upgraded far beyond comparable positions in private industry, making the cost of government prohibitive. It's not the *number* of federal employees that's shocking, but the middle-level bulge, which is costing the taxpayers.

"Is anything being done to reform the terms of tenure in government service?"

It's been done before. President Garfield presided over a thoroughgoing reform of the federal service late in the last century and eliminated the spoils system. But, of course, in its place we introduced into the government bloodstream the fatal bacillus of tenure and protected employment.

Why not try to reform once more the terms of government service? Now that civil servants are well paid, isn't it time to let the bracing winds of change blow through the government's rabbit warrens? Giving government executives the right to "fire" would help enormously.

A movement to reform the terms of government employment would be best, however, for those who now work for, or want to work in, the public interest. The insecurity of employment would attract the self-secure, and appeal to public-service-oriented Americans, and the substance of government would at last be in the hands of those who are truly the people's servants.

"Any special tips for the military retiree?"

Most military men and women cashing in on twenty years working for Uncle Sugar experience a mild to moderate form of panic. Being honorably discharged from the service seems a retirement from life as much as from the Air Force. And the idea of living on half your income—without a job—makes the old soldier apprehensive.

"Are civilian managers prejudiced against military retirees?"

Employers generally have preconceived notions about all job seekers, whether military or not. Some ideas derive from their own unhappy experiences while soldiering, some from unhappy experiences hiring ex-military. A frequent prejudice is that ex-military lack a bottom-line orientation. Still another bias is that they are goldbricks—a generation of comic strips and sitcoms have done nothing to defuse this myth. Still another hang-up is that ex-military aren't self-starters—won't initiate projects or assume more responsibility, and are inflexible in dealing with people. Finally, empire building often doesn't wash on the outside, except, of course, in other government service.

"Do officers have an easier time finding work than enlisted personnel?"

Actual studies show that enlisted personnel find jobs faster than officers. The latter are frequently less skilled in the job search, less adaptable, and accustomed to a higher social rank in the world of work. Often enlisted personnel moonlight while in the service and are accustomed to working for younger men and women. Officers didn't start at the top in the military and shouldn't expect to in the civilian economy; enlisted personnel knew that all along.

"Isn't the military/industrial complex the place to find the best jobs?"

Many flag-rank officers are recruited away from the military in order to tap their expertise and exploit Pentagon contacts. When the expertise becomes obsolete and the contacts dry up, they are politely shown the door: not good for the ego. The message is to beware of defense contractors who come calling. Try to sign on with that company that values you for more than whom you "do lunch" with.

"What about overlapping on important jobs?"

The new person on the block doesn't want his predecessor looking over his shoulder for the next three months ("while he learns the ropes"). Overlapping never works. Both parties suffer from enormous control problems, each inhibits the other, and both bend over backward to please. Result: surefire displeasure for both persons.

The Navy does the job right: A new captain is piped on board, there is a touching ceremony on the rear deck commemorating the change in command. Then the old skipper, with a jaunty salute to Old Glory, marches down the gangplank and off to his next post.

"Are inexperienced Ph.D.s a good bet for business?"

A client of mine likes to hire Ph.D.s for the following reason: "They learn quicker, promote faster, and stay longer." My work with Ph.D.s suggests that those who have written a lengthy and complex dissertation know how to grub; they know how to start, sustain, and finish a project. No assignment in the workplace will ever be as difficult as winning that Ph.D. That's a terrific recommendation for those of you with advanced degrees who want to venture into the world of applied learning.

A lot of confusion exists in the minds of newly minted doctoral types embarking on nonacademic professional careers. All want to know "what's out there." Well, there's a great deal out there if you learn to call yourself something besides a Ph.D.

What follows is a random list of job titles people with advanced degrees have obtained as a result of reading this book and/or attending one of my workshops:

> demographer, statistician, analyst, specialist, research scientist, editor, consultant, project manager, senior social scientist, social worker, health-services administrator, associate investigator, special assistant, test and measurement specialist, political analyst, alcoholism counselor, community organizer, archivist, and so forth

One trick is substituting a nonacademic title for an academic skill. And remember, too, experts say ours is the Information Age. Well, if so, highly trained academics should be on the cutting edge of the job-market revolution. Information is now a *commodity*, something institutions pay a lot of money to obtain.

Defrocked academics are able to make it on the outside. But believing they are unskilled at *doing* something (rather than *teaching* something) is a setup for failure. Languishing in disappointing teaching jobs or pursuing yet another advanced degree avoids the self-confrontation needed to gain purchase in the "real world." The free-form nature of many organizations, particularly smaller business organizations where more than half the professional labor force finds work, means that power runs *down* and *up*, rank is often ambiguous, and status is what someone did for the organization yesterday.

For example, unless the Ph.D. is seeking work in think tanks, foundations or educational publishing houses, it's not a bad idea for her to drop her title. That would be true, too, of the retired lieutenant-colonel looking for work in, say, hotel management. All of which is reminiscent of a friend of mine, a management consultant, who enjoyed a short-term consulting assignment in a university. Memos addressed to him were signed "John Doe, Ph.D." His replies were signed "James Smith, B.A." His assignment was, well, short.

The knack is to forget "fields of study," "disciplines," "bodies of knowledge," and focus instead on what was accomplished in the course of earning a Ph.D. What a job applicant can do, not what's been studied, is what's important to employers. The focus is on *function*. And what can Ph.D.s do? Well, they can research, analyze, instruct, organize, write, and a hundred other skills. Backing up each skill with a series of concrete accomplishments drawn both from academia and outside of it makes the ex-academic believable.

"Must an exiting Ph.D. change his values to make it in the 'real world'?"
No indeed.

Many Ph.D.s selectively misperceive what they call the real world. It's an expression often bandied about in the groves of academe. The implication, of course, is that within those walls a happy few pursue what is ideal, while outside those walls the harried masses spend their time getting and spending. Attitude is everything: If defrocked academics feel forced to leave the ideal for the real, their transition seems their downfall.

Trained to believe academia is ideal, and indoctrinated with the view that the real world is inimical to the life of the mind, many scholars dread the job search. But it's surprising to find how pleased they are to find men and women on the outside who are vital, bright, and effective. To be sure, the real world is crass, vulgar, and unattractive, too. All the more reason why Ph.D.s with another value system, besides the Babylonian, stand out. And why the life of the mind becomes even more important.

Another problem is the self-promotion syndrome. Developing a functional résumé, conducting a self-managed job campaign, managing by subjectives, all suggest that ex-academics must market their skills like toothpaste. Anathema. Some, above the hurly-burly of the real world, drop out of the job search entirely, postponing a confrontation with the self that a truly *self*-managed job search implies.

The good news reported by Ph.Ds is the relative ease in working in the real world as opposed to academia. Schedules are more flexible, decision making faster, and collaborating with other colleagues easier. In many ways, competition outside academia is much different from and healthier than inside it. And the pleasure of cooperating in a task-force environment is a bonus for those accustomed to the publish or perish atmosphere of the academy.

Another characteristic often noteworthy in defrocked academics is their seeming lack of ambition. True, this is often a pose and represents a repressed passion. But somehow to be openly ambitious is *gauche*. Successful people are often equated with jackals or jackasses. And there are many of them in the worlds of work and academia. But there are many more people who do an honest day's work, charge a fair price, and feel good about taking care of themselves and their families.

Ex-academics who are successful in making the career transition evince desire, goals . . . ambition. Their will is liberated. And freeing up the human will to do something is the essence of effective career transition.

"What are the strong and weak points about consultancy work?"

PRO	CON
Varied assignments with many clients	Frequent periods of unemployment
Excellent pay for short-term assignments	Cash-flow problems
Chance for quickie vacations and stimulating downtime	Unwholesome boredom
No boss overseeing every nit-picking detail	Lack of structure: no boss to tell you how well/how badly you are doing
No political hassles	No real involvement over a long period of time
A feeling of freedom, independence	Enormous anxiety, guilt, unhappiness
No "career" progression	No "career" progression
No operational authority	No operational authority

Clearly, being a consultant depends primarily on what a person *wants*. Understandably, many consultants yearn to stay put on longer-term jobs. And many operational types yearn for the freedom of the consultant. Without wanting to make too strong a case, those newly on the job market should eschew consultancy; what young people want *fast* are responsibility and power. Middle-aging and senior types, however, should give thought to consulting.

An effective consultant is always landing assignments in a wide variety of fields. One of his qualifications is finding work. A busy consultant never grows stagnant. The crossruff of his experiences gradually qualifies him for a whole host of special assignments.

One qualification is being available. A consultant must have the confidence to face unemployment. Being a consultant is often a euphemism for being unemployed. But the work is bracing and gives exposure needed to learn where the hidden jobs are.

The best consultants work alone. And besides, one-man bands don't have to answer to a lot of porked-up pardners back at headquarters who spend their time thinking about profit maximization and forgetting client needs.

(1) Most big-ten consulting firms are too expensive; organizations that call on Booz, Allen are firms *that can afford the fee.* Therefore, managers often hire consultants consonant with Parkinson's law, which says that *expenses rise to meet income.*

(2) Every idea a consultant shares with his client, which he mostly pulls out of the boilerplate back at headquarters, has been thought of by some sharpie deep in the bowels of an organization. The idea, however, never reached a high level because communications are so bad (which is to say that people confrontations are cleverly discouraged by elaborate administrative procedure) that no one with clout can transform the idea through from conceptualization to execution. Just what an organization wants, isn't it?

Unhappily, it isn't. Many managers like to keep their people docile, dull, and safe. Most prefer spending thousands of precious overhead dollars rather than act on their own people's advice. "Stansberry, Case, & Funk's people told us this is what we gotta do and we paid them $175,000 for the advice and by God, we're going to do it."

(3) A poor consultant is as worthless as the *size, weight,* and *slickness* quotient of his final report. The best advice is verbal, trenchant, given with conviction and able to be understood by the brightest student intern. That's why the best consultants, the ones who really know their business, need only a day or two to give employers the advice they need. Their "data base" is often in their head.

(4) Effective consultants give employers their home phone number and are on the spot when needed. Above all, they talk in plain Anglo-Saxon and eschew business-school jargon.

(5) Finally and most important, a consultant *cares.* He is not competing against anyone except himself; he makes so much money he has time to do what he *wants;* he can look at employer programs objectively; he genuinely likes employers, although he often thinks their heads need shrinking, and consequently he tells *painful and disturbing* things to them. The rare, great consultant is probably one of three people in America most effective chief executive officers feel truly comfortable with, all the time. Effective consultants, like

rare vintage wines, are hard to find, terribly expensive, sparingly used, and always blessedly antibureaucratic. People hired as consultants don't develop a hammerlock on a job, never think of it as *permanent,* and stop working the day the task is finished. And are not reemployed until other *tasks* are undertaken.

"Any thoughts on job sharing?"

Some employers are discovering if you hire a job-sharer, you lock her in full-time. People don't stop thinking about work when they walk onto the employee parking lot. Hiring a working couple to do one job is securing a 300 percent effort. The difficulty is convincing an employer.

Message to employers: Job sharing often works better than filling the job full-time with one person; it depends on the quality of the people and how well they work together. Message to job sharers: It's your job to convince employers job sharing works. Message to both: Job sharing works *least* well with people unequal in ability, motivation, and dependability or those infected with control problems. Control problems are difficult enough to resolve in marriage without compounding them on the same job.

"Why do people burn out at work?"

How often have you said to yourself, "I want a job where I'm needed"? And the love-starved say, "I want some one to need me." Well, our dreams come true and we enter into a life of service. And marry someone, no doubt, who needs us. Then we have no free time. Focusing ten hours a day on other people's needs and another eight on our family's—working wives are the worst victims—is setting yourself up for a case of burnout. Being pleasing, accommodating, and nice to everyone but yourself eliminates the self. Nice going. No wonder you pop greenies.

Burnout is especially obvious in the "helping professions": social workers, clergymen, nurses, teachers, and counselors. But everyone suffers mildly from the disease to please. Stop fighting everyone's battles but your own.

Being able to say no to potential clients, sick patients, impatient customers, eager students, and dependent employees means feeling free. If we can't say no to them, we say no to ourselves. And burnout. Guess who isn't effective on the job anymore? And guess who senses we don't care? Well, it's clients, patients, customers, students, and employees.

The antidote to burnout is saying no to other people's needs (that means you can say yes, too), and the result is:

—a renewed interest in your work (you now feel separate from it).

—greater self-esteem (you no longer eliminate the self).

—more fire in your belly (you no longer throw cold water on your desires. And in desires, remember, begin responsibilities).

So the message is *feeling free* to work, play tennis, and make love because we *want to,* not because we *ought to.* Going to work tomorrow because we *must* makes us hate our jobs; playing tennis because we *ought to* could give tennis a bad name; making love because we *should* is simply self-immolation.

Attitude is everything. But it's not an easy thing.

"Can two-paycheck couples 'have it all'?"

The hearts-and-dollars marriage has caught organizations by surprise, and government, business, and academia are just beginning to adjust. The problems are acute for working couples, too.

"Keeping options open" is the expression used by two-paycheck couples who want it all—money, fame, self-fulfillment, and a home in the country—now. The great fear is that younger men, like their fathers, will be caught up living for work rather than working for a living. And working women are frightened by the marriage trap, and marriage (and work) can be traps. But flexibility is itself a trap: Elasticity of choice is so stretched there is no tension or shape to some people's lives. Postponing commitment to another person (or a career) postpones gratification.

With working couples, the dilemma of his job (versus her career), his promotion (her reassignment) seems central. Everyone knows someone who has made twelve relocations in twenty-four years of marriage. Everyone tells tales of broken marriages that seemingly foundered on the inability of two people to compromise.

The heart of the two-paycheck marriage is coping with trade-offs. In plain English, no, we can't have it all at once; yes, we can have it *all,* one thing, maybe two things, at a time.

I can't invest $30,000 in a graduate education and at the same time take two years off in Ibiza *and* write a novel.

My wife can't have another child *and* at the same time run in the Boston Marathon.

Our best married friends can't start a chain of wine and cheese shops *and* at the same time expect to take a year off and see Scandanavia.

That's reality.

Feeling free in love and work means cooperating with a reality that is changing all the time (a promotion for him, a graduate degree for her, a second child for both). Consequently, working couples are often moving from one holding pattern to another, now allies, then adversaries, now temporarily living apart to pursue short-term assignments, now working at building a business together and not working on salary at all, now backing off and returning to traditional jobs once the kids are ready for college.

The good news about working couples is that they make more money. Making money at work we like is certain to increase our self-esteem. It might improve our sex life. But the bad news is that it works in reverse, too: A bad job (or no job) and scut wages (or unearned earnings) often destroy self-esteem. And that might monkey-wrench our sex life.

"Do disparate earnings cause two-paycheck couples to founder?"

It's possible, if you're younger and married, that her earnings might exceed yours. As a matter of fact, if you are middle-aging, it might happen. And for mentally robust people, it can't happen too soon.

Working couples earn two paychecks. If her paycheck is more than mine, combined with mine we both earn more. The threat of my wife taking over and controlling me is *my* problem. For my wife to back off and earn less because she is sensitive to my feelings is bushwa.

Working couples need straightening out on this point. Income is community property—it belongs equally to both parties. So if I make $10,000 per annum as a free-lance writer and my wife earns a cool $90,000 as a corporate lawyer, who's ahead? Both of us, Gaston.

Some working wives back off from success on the job (a *little* success is okay) out of feelings of responsibility for their husbands' feelings with attendant irresponsibility to their own. Worldly success causes many working wives to think their husbands won't love them anymore—indeed no man will ever love them. Crazy. Any working wife who values herself is going to kiss off any man who believes her success is his failure.

Some men are wary of women who make more money than they. "Let my wife make more money than me," he thinks, "and she'll call all the shots."

Attitude is everything. And if working couples think our self-worth is measured by the money we are paid, we value ourselves by the price other people put on our services. And letting other people establish our worth isn't feeling free. If he earns $45,000 as a systems analyst and she earns $18,000 as a schoolteacher, he must be "worth" more than she.

It's reminiscent of Joe Stalin asking how many divisions the Pope could mobilize. It's like weighing the greatness of a nation by its landmass or measuring the value of a person by his height. So long as money is the measure of all things, as Oscar Wilde wrote, we know the price of everything and the value of nothing. The quality of a marriage has more to do with equity than equities.

"Yes, but the wife or husband who makes the most money can call the shots."

For me to think that my wife *controls* me (she makes more money), for me to think I'm controlled by my wife is crazy. Nobody controls anyone else.

Many men have inherited a malignant attitude toward work, which is destructive to happiness. Men are altogether too serious about what they *do:* Every workday, trudging off to work with lunch pail, briefcase, or sample box in tow, men earn the money to protect their families from the wolf at the door. Workingmen of the world are responsible. Even thieves, crooks, and scalawags are often good family men.

Thus, of an evening—after work and especially before dinner— men think, "I've done my job, earned my pay, kept big bad wolf from the door, done what *they* (employers) want. Now it's my turn to do what I want." Working wives don't necessarily feel this acute sense of responsibility.

Working wives simply don't take work as seriously as men do. Oh sure, single workingwomen (especially the single working mother) might show the same symptoms. But in the main, men are so caught up in work—even those in alternative work—that *what* they do is *who* they are.

A comparable state of mind for most workingwomen is the seriousness with which they approach the home. Try as they will, women feel the home is their responsibility. Workingwomen anguish about matters at home, the grocery shopping, the flaking bathroom wallpaper, the children's tattered wardrobes—responsibilities their husbands never see. A man doesn't see these things because he doesn't feel responsible. And a woman often doesn't see how important the world of work is to her husband.

So, men, don't take work so seriously. Women, don't start taking work too seriously. In fact, quit taking life seriously. This is a really serious proposition!

Learning how to love and work takes a lifetime. Happy people leave the office at the office. Good insurance-sales types don't discuss new rate schedules over morning coffee with their spouses; lawyers don't make their briefs after making love; cops don't talk about robbers after their tour is up.

Imagine yourself to be a circle; imagine your mate to be a circle. Now overlap both circles. If there is a perfect overlap, yours is a one-person marriage; if there is far more overlap than not, yours is a traditional marriage; if there is less overlap than not, yours is a hearts-and-dollars marriage.

At the point where you intersect with each other (for those of you into long geometry) a third *torpedo*-shaped circle develops. To the extent each partner feels separate from the other, each is free to expand the circumference of the third circle. To the extent neither partner feels free, the circumference of their common circle contracts or one circle absorbs the other.

In the hearts-and-dollars marriages that *work,* the points on his circular compass that touch hers mean a cooperative venture; each partner knows how to operate (and cooperate). The marriage is a confederation of equals, not a federation of unequals. Confederates are both allies and adversaries, an alliance that either can break at any time. The federated are neither allies nor adversaries; they are in an indissoluble union.

"Yes, but if we both put the marriage before ourselves won't we burn out?"
Inevitable.

Forgetting the ends of marriage and focusing entirely on the means is a definition of fanaticism, said Santayana. We are invested in the marriage and no longer vested in ourselves.

Burned out.

Small wonder we burn out. "I'm not getting anything out of this marriage," this guy complains. "I'm not charged up on the job anymore," that woman moans. And it's usually our attitude; we don't feel free.

At work, we feel power; at home, we feel powerless. On the job, we feel in control; at home, we feel controlled. At our desk, we feel in charge of our environment; in our living room, we feel our surroundings surround us.

But attitude is everything.

To work evenings and weekends in order to avoid unhappy home situations isn't cooperating with reality. And if we perceive we are in someone else's control at home, the trouble is not in our stars but in ourselves. Changing our attitudes and learning some new moves is the way to fight burnout.

Reconciling love/work issues means putting the Worth Ethic ahead of the work ethic. Marriage is a career. But if his job and her career are more important than their lives together, if both want the pleasure of marriage but won't pay its price, neither is cooperating with reality.

Pound for pound and square inch for square inch, people in hearts-and-dollars marriages are the most responsible class in the country. Producers. Taxpayers. Parents. Working couples are the glue that holds the nation together. They repair the social fabric ripped by irresponsible people. And like concerned and responsible people everywhere, they fret about the cost of pork loin.

Working couples take pride in being caring citizens, responsible parents, and producers of products and services other people need. Working couples "work" at their marriage.

But working couples who work at marriage often don't take pleasure in it. Oppressed. Burned out. The harried married. But the whole point of love and work is the pleasure of each other's company and the pleasure we take in exercising our skills on the job.

Taking pleasure in love and work is risking pleasure every day. On the job, it's a great pleasure exercising your skills; at home it's a pleasure taking pleasure in the company you keep. Having people in for dinner is a pleasure if we invite them for the pleasure they bring us; having people in for dinner is a burden if we invite them because we "owe" them.

"Is fighting important in the two-paycheck marriage?"
The romantic definition of marriage is the complete absorption of each partner in the other; an apathetic definition of marriage is two parallel lines that never meet; the traditional view of marriage is an overlap between the two circles, but where the wife's circle is increasingly swallowed up by her husband's or vice versa. The definition of a hearts-and-dollars marriage is the creation of a *third* circle of involvement. But the trick is for both partners to feel free.

Neither partner can be involved with the other so long as each feels trapped. Solution? Repeated quarrels. But problems can't be solved without confrontations.

Fighting clears the air: It's the best antipollution device available. The husband reveals what he wants (a vacation home, a trip to the Far East, a business of his own, a chance to be with the kids). This frees up the wife to reveal what she wants (a shot at another job, a remodeled kitchen, a chance to work at home, a fancy private-school education for the kids). Working couples can't solve problems, can't have a *worthwhile* marriage, unless they fight about what each wants: the Worth Ethic. If, of course, he blows a case in court and she botches the inventory at work, neither is going to take pleasure in the other. Each person's self-esteem has taken a licking. If neither party blows up at the other, it's a miracle. If *both* parties blow up at the other, it's a marriage. But if they can't stand the heat in the kitchen, then neither is qualified for marriage. The marriage of strong wills means playing with the pain. If we stub our toe, we say "ouch!" If we suffer from a bad blow at work, we say "ouch!" And our partners hear us howl.

Taking responsibility for other people's feelings and being irresponsible to our own is being concerned. Concerned folk often don't know what they are feeling.

The result is burnout both on the job and in marriage. You botch love and work. Unseparate from work; uninvolved in marriage.

Parallel lines don't meet. Real talk is minimal, sex is grabbed on the run, and time together, much less with yourself, is "wasted."

In time-rich marriages, partners say no to work and yes to themselves. They are *willing* to love and work. A free will is the key to time management. People who don't know what they want never have enough time. They are suckers to fill other people's needs. People who know what they want find time.

In two-paycheck marriages, time management causes as many conflicts as sexual misfires, money matters, and house management. Many working couples are scheduled like airliners, with specific destinations on airtight schedules. Time becomes a commodity, like money, that must be spent and conserved wisely.

In marriage, both of you might think of working *part-time*. That adds up to one full-time career. The price paid is reduced income; the pleasure consumed is more time with yourself and yourselves. Start saying no to success. If our jobs consume us, life together won't work. "There will be no marriage today because of a lack of interest," the announcement in the paper reads.

"So a hearts-and-dollars marriage is a question of time management?"
Time for the self; time with your family; time with your work. It's commonplace that time is money; what's not so clear is that money is time. Small wonder working couples fight for free time. It's a crock.

Anthropologists tell us that we are a time-bound culture. Everybody is using time constructively. But is anyone having any fun? We dress up to go to a party, throw a banquet, and plan a vacation. But we vaccinate ourselves against the *pleasure*. The working vacation is an example; entertaining people we work with is another; planning a trip for its educational value still another.

Other people have turned the Puritan ethic inside out and abandon the ceremony of party giving entirely, eat on the run, and drift rather than travel. If an activity is constructive, these people think, it must be bad.

What's missing is an appreciation of how to savor time. Learning how to savor time in America is an acquired characteristic. It should be a required course in schools of business administration. Often our best ideas in work come to us off the job when we play.

Some people can't wait to get back to work. Playtime is wasting time. Wasting time tickles the conscience. So it's back to work with a heigh and a ho. The point is to leave your conscience at home along with your watch. Happiness is the unimportance of being earnest, and a cheerful attitude toward both work and play means taking a vacation from time, obligation, and conscience. Money management and time management are indissolubly linked. If our time here on earth is like the days of the week, for plenty of us it's Friday afternoon.

"What's the difference between a caring person and a concerned one?"

A truly caring person challenges his staff, his wife, and his children. A caring person is not so interested in being supportive as in helping people support themselves. On the job, a caring person is neither nasty nor nice and twice as effective. At home, a caring person is never dominant or submissive and therefore twice as intimate.

CARING	CONCERN
"I care about what I do."	"I worry how I'm doing."
"I care about myself."	"I worry about how well others think I'm doing."
"I care about my boss knowing what I think."	"I worry about what the boss is thinking."
"I care about what's right."	"I worry about who's right."
"I care about my staff making decisions."	"I worry my staff will make mistakes."
"I care about success."	"I worry whether I'm successful."

Attitude is everything. Caring is not to worry. A truly caring person feels free with those she cares about: her husband, her children, her job, her boss. A worrywart feels trapped by what he cares about: his wife, his children, his job, and his boss.

"What about when there's a clear conflict between her career and his job?"

The "her career, his job" factor causes conflict; but *conflict causes problems to be solved.* Some working couples avoid confrontation, conflict, and cooperation, and thus feel oppressed. They no longer take pleasure in each other. The parallel or apathetic marriage is the outcome. And both parties wrongly blame it on conflicting careers.

Part of reality is what we think of it. True responsibility is being responsive to our own feelings. If two working people love each other, each partner's career is secondary to their career (the marriage).

Each partner in a two-paycheck marriage has his or her career. But *their* career is each other. Tough.

Tough on employers who are finding out they don't come first.

Tough on working wives who work every day but still worry about the home.

Tough on men who no longer call all the shots.

"What about working couples employed by the same organization?"

Some considerations to think through:

(1) In interviewing for similar or different jobs in the same organization, inevitably one is going to be considered the stronger candidate. It takes an unusually strong ego to handle being number two or the guilt of being number one.

(2) It's unrealistic to think both partners will advance in the organization at the same rate of speed. If you jog while your partner dashes, you'll need a heroic ego.

(3) Both partners might be overlooked for significant reassignments and enviable relocations because the organization refuses to separate married couples.

(4) If both partners work in different departments that are adversarial (the business versus the editorial department, the marketing versus the production department), tensions on the job might overflow into the home, and conflict-of-interest issues raise their ugly heads.

Moreover, working couples must avoid not only a real conflict of interest but must conduct themselves so as to avoid the *appearance* of a conflict. The way to protect interests and not be in conflict with your partner's is to master the art of anticipatory problem solving: Working couples anticipate potential problems between organizational interests and self-interests and lance the boil before it does its mischief; it is individuals (not organizations) that must take the initiative.

(5) Working wives, increasingly sensitive to discrimination on the job, must cultivate tough egos to cope with male preferment. Men with working wives must do the same; they might be victims of affirmative-action discrimination.

Changing organizational employment patterns through flex-time hours, job sharing, and part-time jobs is tough. Don't expect organizations to change without you and your allies helping it happen. Personal change, we have seen, is hard work. If you have trouble changing, think about organizations. And remember, it's easier changing organizations when you are on a payroll; coming in from the outside and pushing for a corporate day-care center is much, much tougher.

"How successful are commuter marriages?"

Many marriages, both traditional and two-paycheck, often involve temporary separations. But commuter marriages don't work over the long haul; a sleep-alone arrangement must be a sometime thing. That's because two people need each other's ego to sharpen their own. That can't be done if he works in Tulsa and she punches a time clock in Chicago. Think twice (three times) about a sleep-alone arrangement. Not thinking about it could be a signal neither partner loves the other. A commuter arrangement makes sense only because neither is together in any sense. What makes more sense is a divorce.

"Do two-paycheck marriages work if both partners are in a similar field?"

Desirable but not essential. Opposites attract. A working wife who is an investment banker finds refreshment in a husband who is a ceramics dealer.

Believing so doesn't take into account that a hearts-and-dollars marriage is a career, that many men and women are making two and three career changes in their lives, that younger and middle-aging people are dropping into alternative occupations, that the Worth Ethic is more important than the work ethic.

"How does a woman handle sexual harassment?"

Sexual involvement of any sort on the job, volitional or otherwise, is mistaking the boardroom for the boudoir. It undermines organizational effectiveness and morale. It's also inevitable.

An aspect of judgment jobs is how emotionally involved we become in doing the job. Often on the job we invest ourselves, while at home we hold back. The consequence is that at work we are open, vulnerable, and effective, and at home we are closed, defensive, and passive. Accordingly, our defenses being down at work, a colleague easily captures the castle: He falls in love with his secretary; she falls in love with her special assistant.

So yes, working people are more susceptible in some ways to romance on the job. All the more reason to remember the incest taboo.

"The incest taboo?"

The late Margaret Mead observed that the destructive politics of on-the-job sex makes the incest taboo in the workplace all the more important. "Thou shalt not play around with thy working brethren" is good advice.

Organizations can't regulate sexual activity; but working people can regulate themselves. The sexual integration of the work force makes the incest taboo all the more important. Sex rears its head wherever men and women meet, but working people are often confused about the consequences of sexual expression associated with the job and the steep price people pay who romance on the company payroll.

Working people perform a task; they are a task force. Task forces are like families. Brother and sister go outside the family to find sex; working couples leave the organizational perimeter and go home to do the same.

Ignoring the incest taboo accounts for the outcry among workingwomen (sexual harassment), the workingman's lament (sexual entrapment), and general grumbling from working stiffs on the line (sexual politics). So it's high time to take into account the price of double-crossing Mother Nature.

ITEM: His company wants him to represent it at the annual conference in San Juan. He invites his attractive special assistant to accompany him at the organization's expense. It's made clear her nominal function (conference delegate) disguises her real role (prostitute). And if she doesn't take a dive—good jobs are hard to find—her last duty working for him is finding her replacement.

Such a proposition is an intolerable violation of her freedom and the incest taboo. It's simple coercion. And her options: (a) going to *his* boss and charging sexual harassment, (b) refusing his proposal, and (c) reasoning with the dummy—which could lead in the end to her exiting from the organization and scouting up another job. A fourth option, a lawsuit, is expensive and time-consuming and requires proof.

Oh yes, there is another possibility: She genuinely digs the guy and considers a Puerto Rican trip and the pleasure of his company another company perk.

So there might be more at stake here than coercion and play-for-pay. But even if she's his *willing* tool, it's still prostitution. And even platonic relationships give the appearance of sexual complicity. No working person can forget that appearances are everything; smart politicians don't travel *alone* with opposite-sex assistants; smart managers sexually recreate off the company turf.

ITEM: His attractive special assistant makes a down payment on an oceanfront condominium and is having difficulty making the mortgage. He hand-carries her new position description (executive special assistant) through Personnel, establishing a substantial raise in pay. It's understood her boss is the only overnight guest at the upcoming housewarming.

Sexual entrapment.

A much more common (very common) violation of the incest taboo is the mindless mashing working women suffer at the hands of macho associates. Every woman needs to cultivate one doggone, knockout obscenity to upgrade her second-strike capability. The instant after a clumsy forward pass, a verbal karate chop delivered in the company of other males powerfully concentrates a man's focus on his work rather than his workmate.

Observing the incest taboo is avoiding Big Trouble. Making others aware of it, too, is every working person's responsibility. The trick is avoiding not only the act of sexual complicity but its appearance.

"Don't dip your quill in the company ink" is excellent advice for all working people. But since the workplace is the most likely place (more so than single bars, Club Med, church socials) for meeting available men and women, small wonder that working people are confused.

The solution is to cultivate the art of anticipatory problem solving. Are you attracted to someone on the job and that person to you? Well, recognize it and act on it. That means one or the other of you needs to hustle up a job elsewhere. That's a painful price. But the price two people gladly pay when they know they want each other. Otherwise there is going to be grumbling and gossip in the ranks, your on-the-job effectiveness will decline, and one or both of you might find yourself unwillingly out on the sidewalk.

The way to lance problems before they become unmanageable is to anticipate conflict-of-interest factors whenever love raises her beautiful head. Make tracks and exit from the job and find work elsewhere. That will stop the talk and keep the romance alive, too.

EPILOGUE

An Afterword from the Author

Teaching people how to find jobs is a cinch; finding *any* job, relatively easy; finding a judgment job, quite difficult. But hardest of all is learning and making a habit of taking responsibility for our lives, involving our own deepest feelings, and focusing continually on what we want to do with our life next.

There's a difference between writers and readers: Writers always have the last word. But evidently there is no last word on the job search. Each reader will have questions unaddressed in this book. If so, write and I'll give the questions my best shot and probably include your query and my reply in the fourth edition.

The intent has been to repeat a few general themes in a different context, using various octaves. So the message has been repeated in cunning disguise throughout the book. Nobody remembers anything read only once. That's why in the Navy every order is repeated three times. My point has been made when you feel *impaled* on it.

If my tone has been insufferably breezy and occasionally prickly, no apology. Cross my heart and hope to die, it's a defense mechanism. I laugh about the business of the job search; otherwise I couldn't write about it. The unimportance of being earnest, remember, is important.

Finally, it's clear, the effective job searcher makes his or her own luck. So if you don't like your circumstances, stand up and change them. And then get on your knees and thank God you're on your feet (an old Irish blessing).

Write when you find work!

INDEX